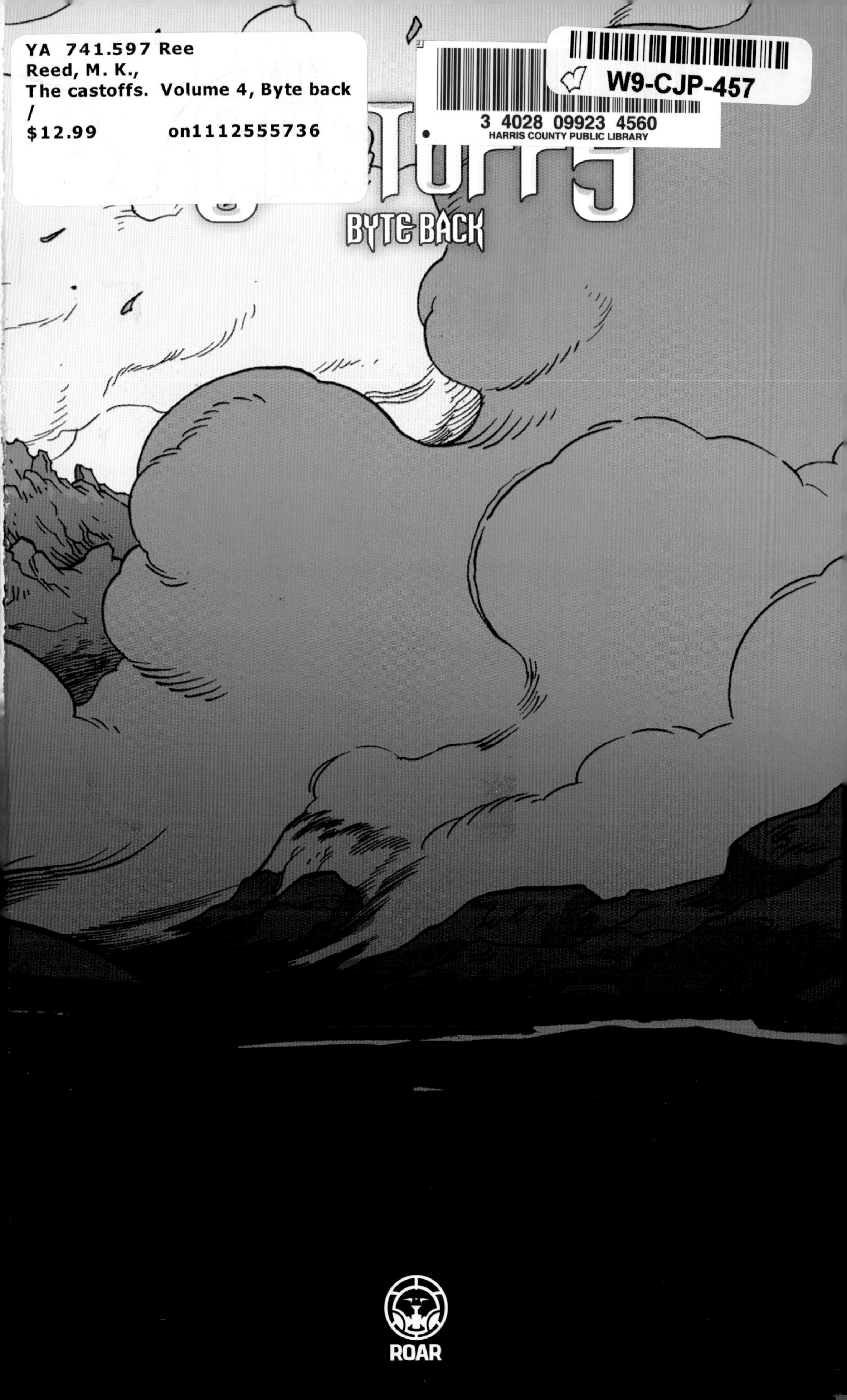
BYTE BACK
ROAR

THE CASTOFFS

VOLUME 4

BYTE BACK

MK REED & WYETH YATES *WRITERS*

WYETH YATES *ARTIST*

MARISSA LOUISE *COLORIST*

HAZEL NEWLEVANT & STEENZ
EDITOR

AW'S DC HOPKINS
LETTERER

AMANDA VERNON
ASSISTANT EDITOR

ANDWORLD DESIGN
DESIGNER

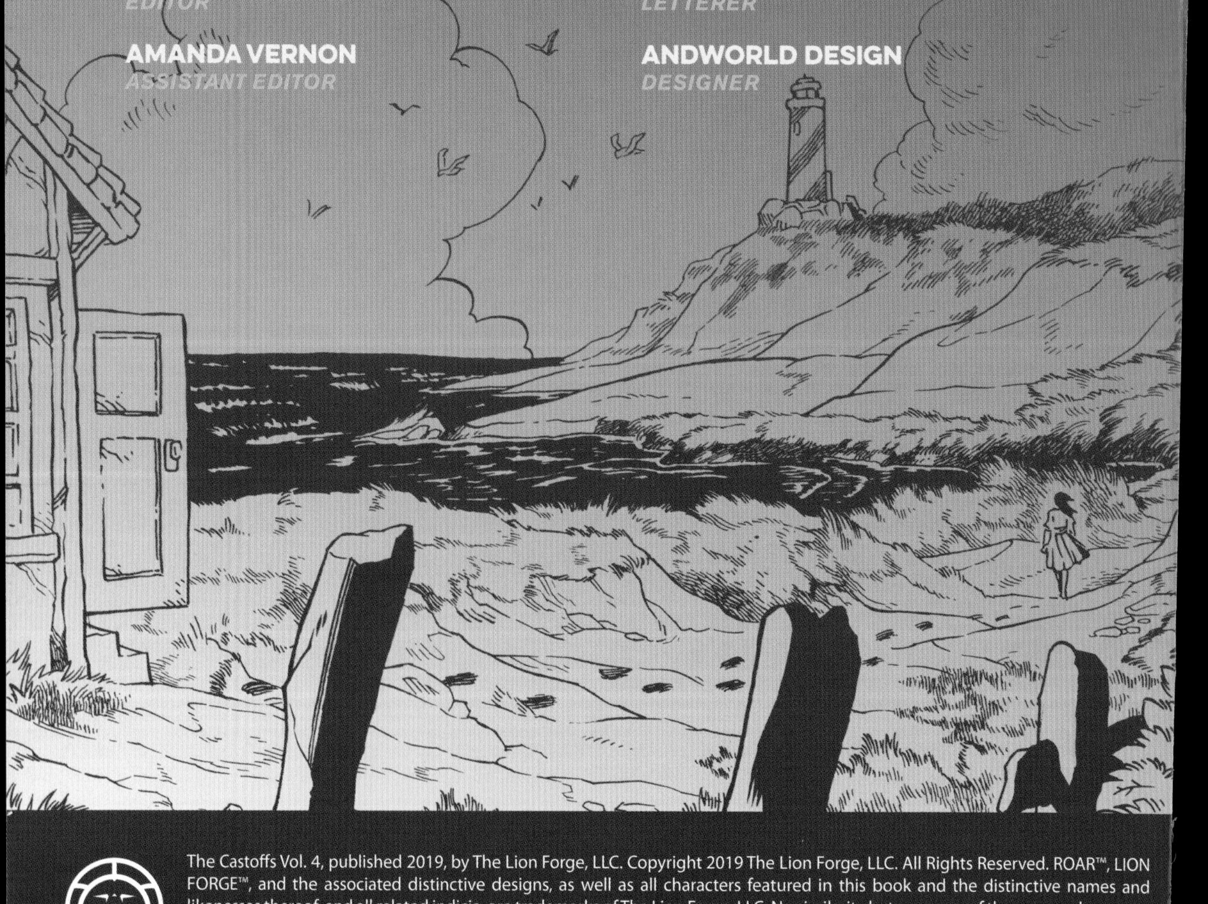

ROAR

LCCN: 2017953492
ISBN: 978-1-941302-81-1

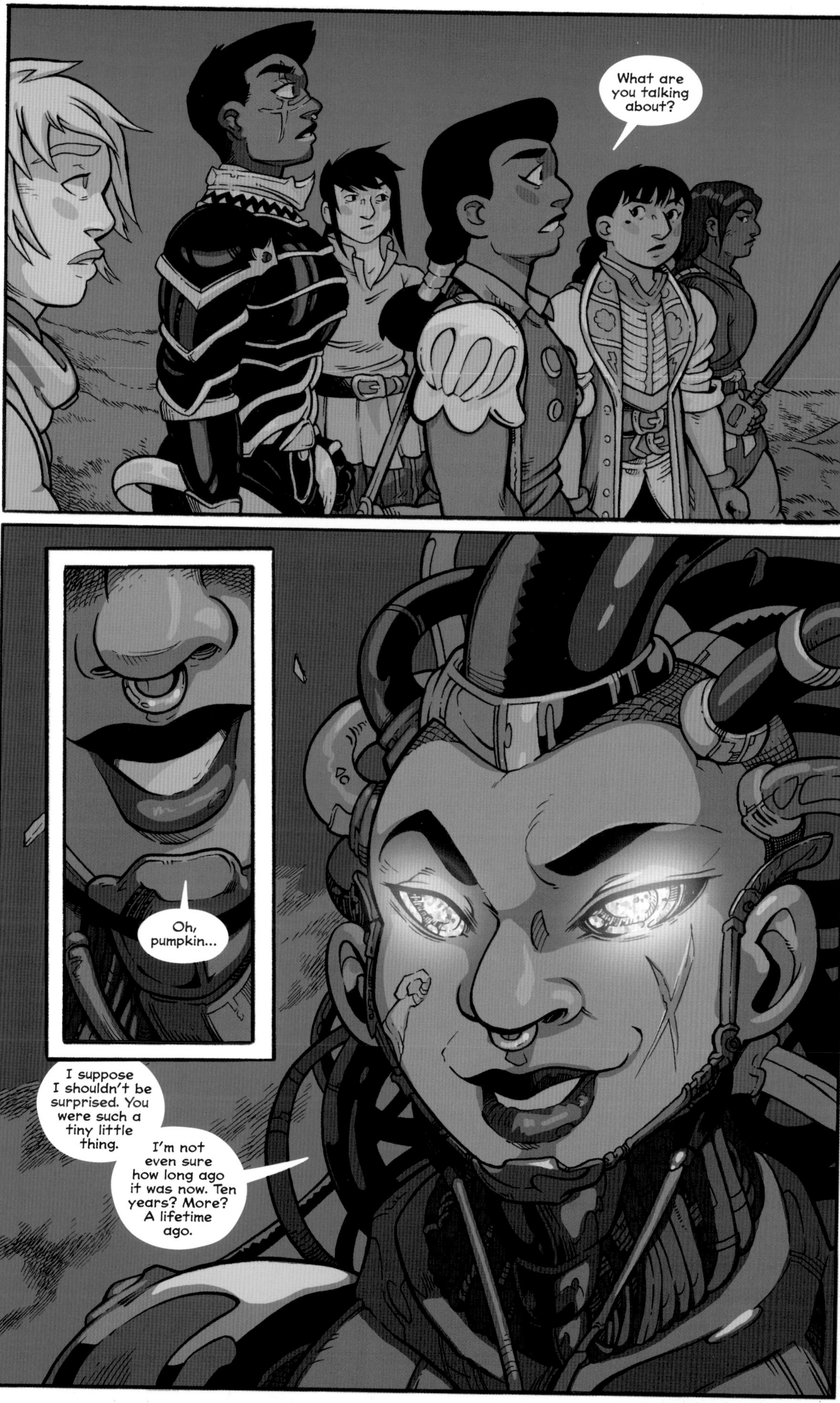
What are you talking about?
Oh, pumpkin...
I suppose I shouldn't be surprised. You were such a tiny little thing.
I'm not even sure how long ago it was now. Ten years? More? A lifetime ago.

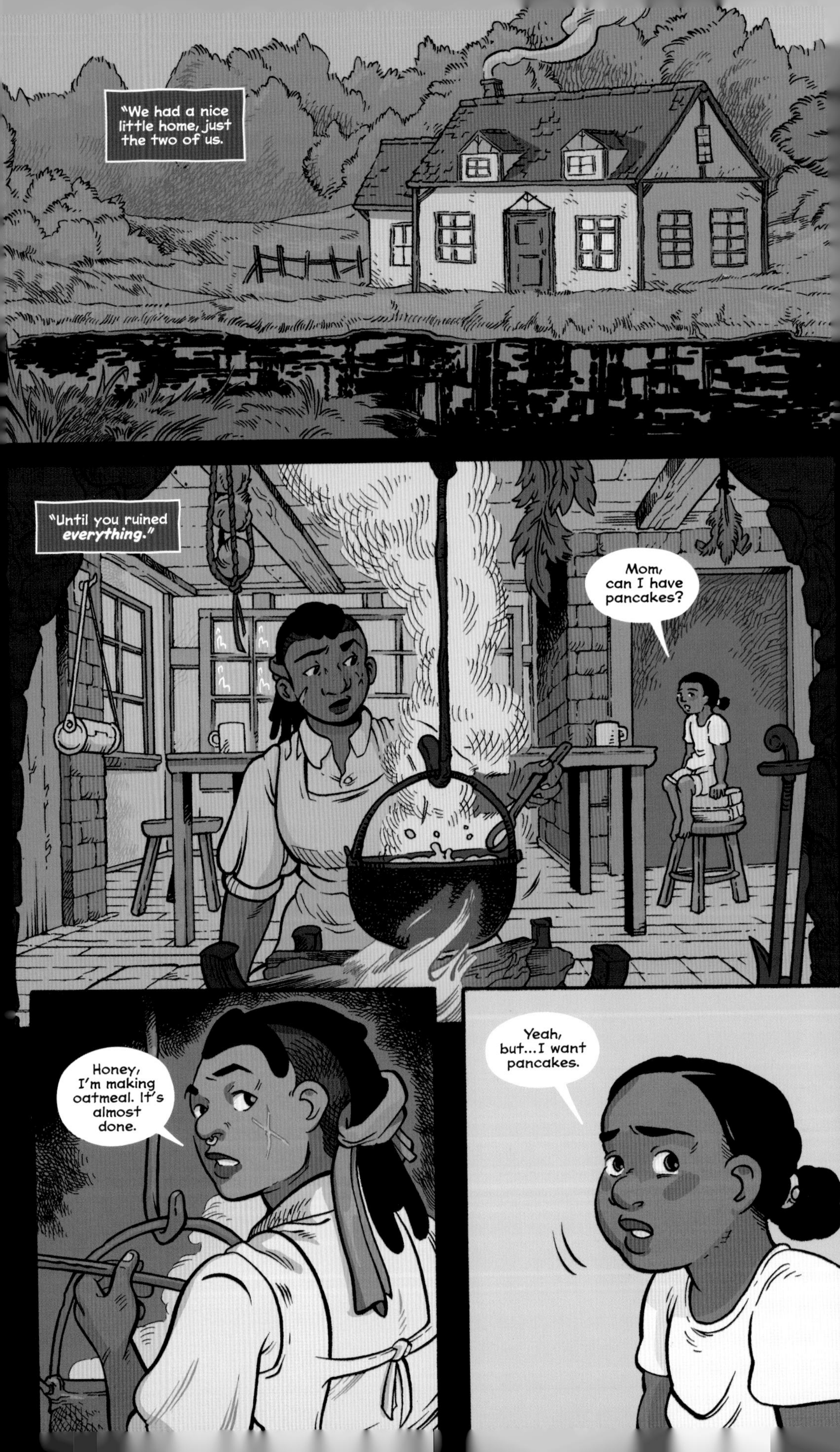
"We had a nice little home, just the two of us.
"Until you ruined *everything*."
Mom, can I have pancakes?
Honey, I'm making oatmeal. It's almost done.
Yeah, but...I want pancakes.

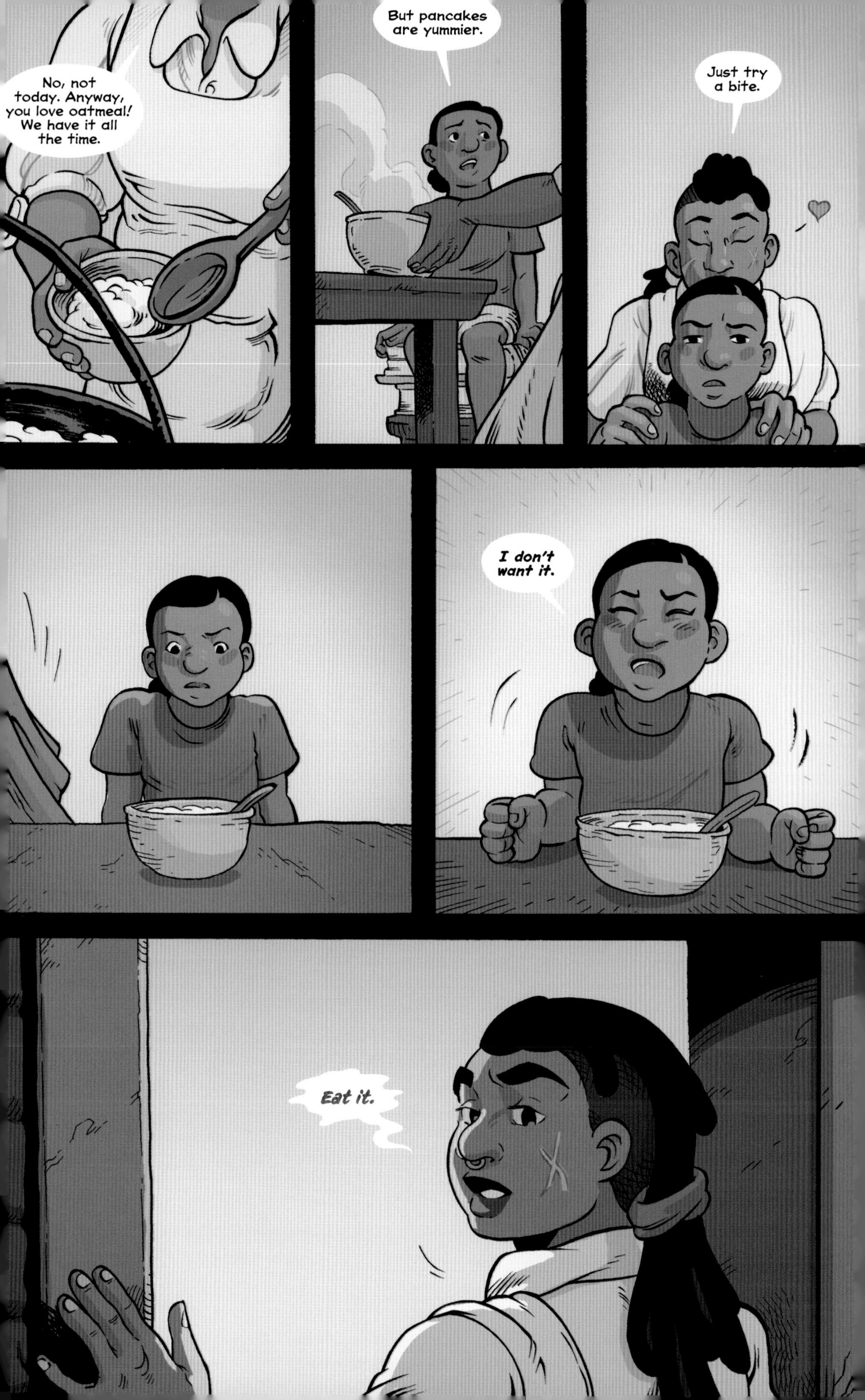
No, not today. Anyway, you love oatmeal! We have it all the time.
But pancakes are yummier.
Just try a bite.
I don't want it.
Eat it.

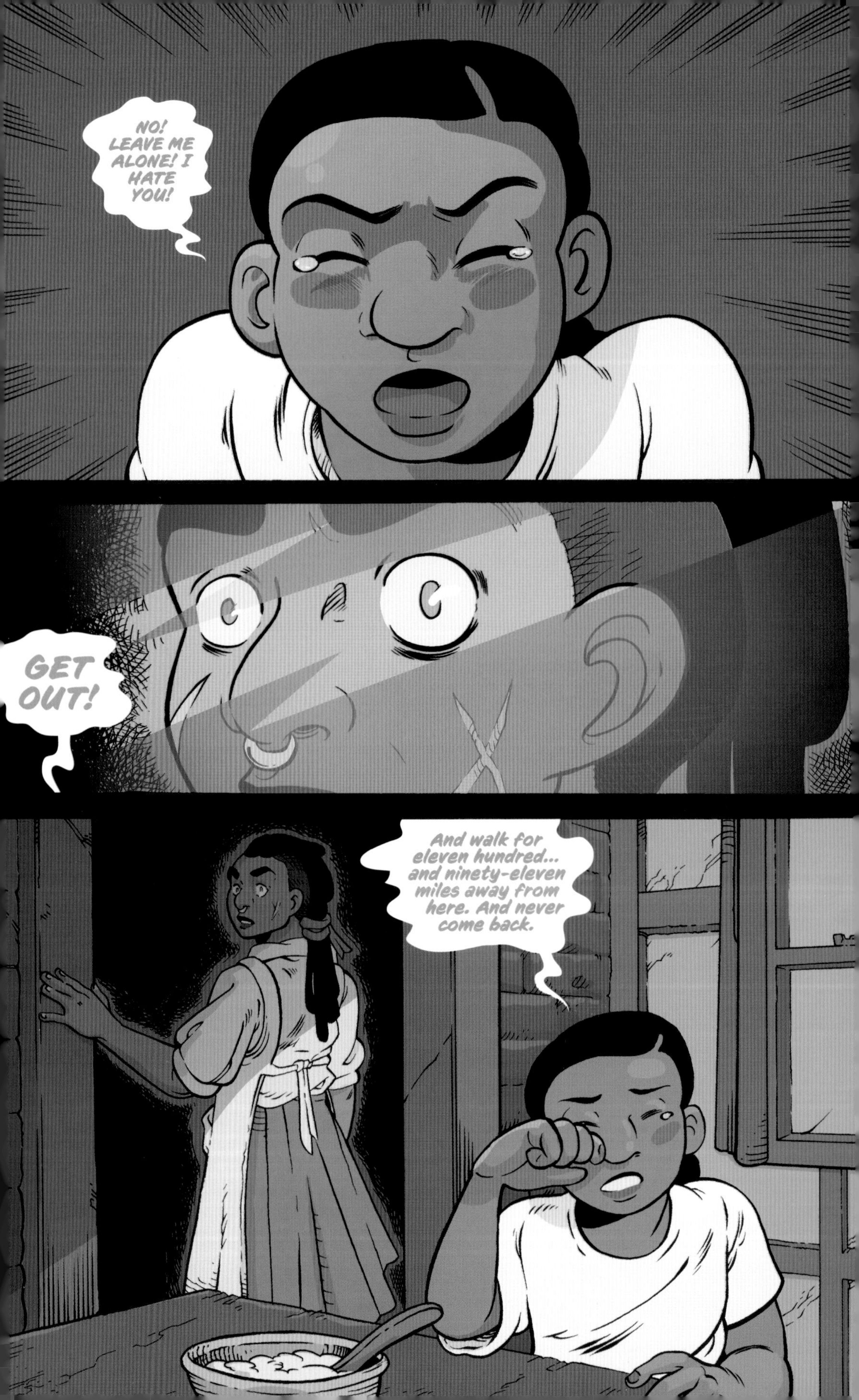
NO! LEAVE ME ALONE! I HATE YOU!
GET OUT!
And walk for eleven hundred... and ninety-eleven miles away from here. And never come back.

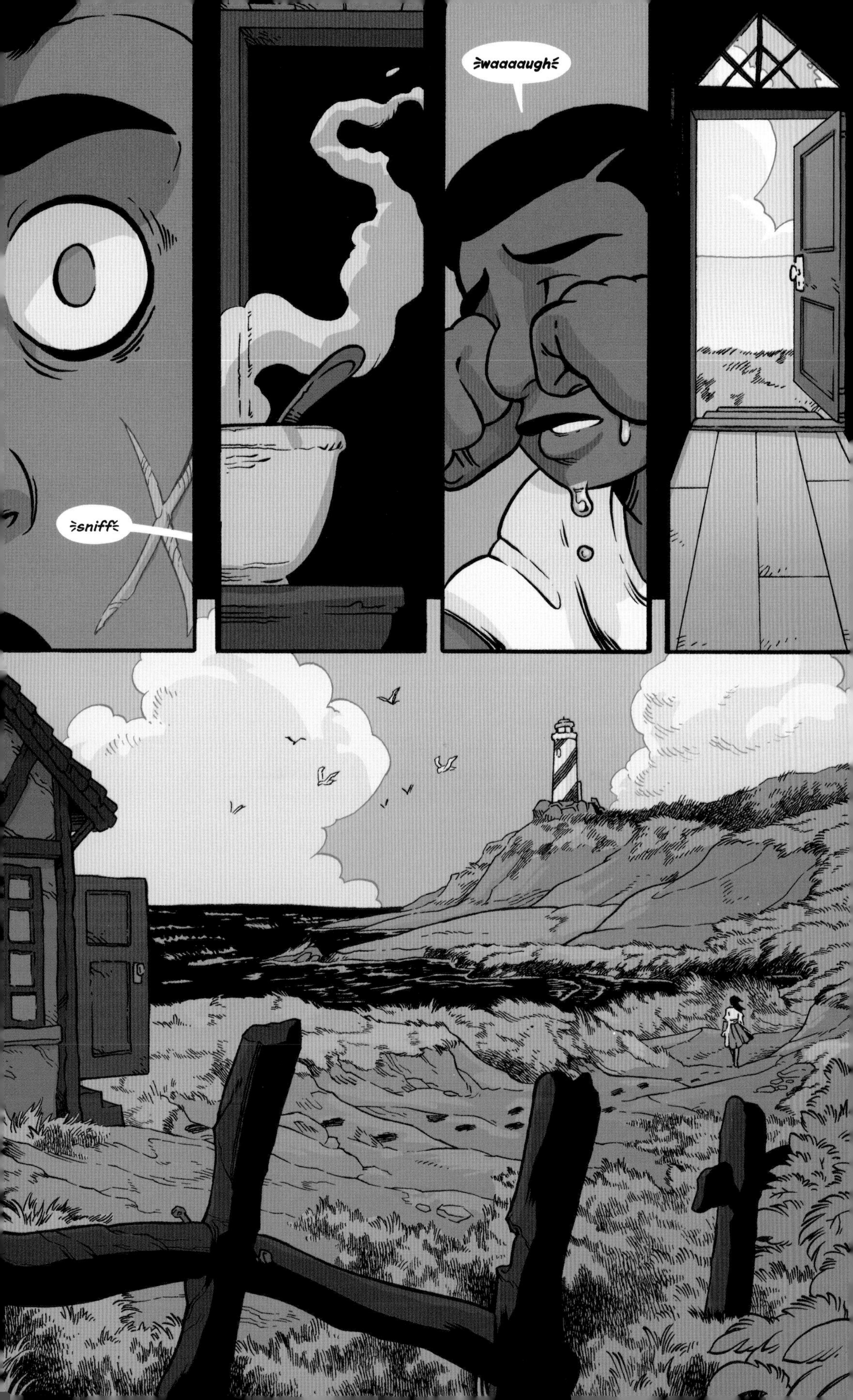

sniff
waaaaugh

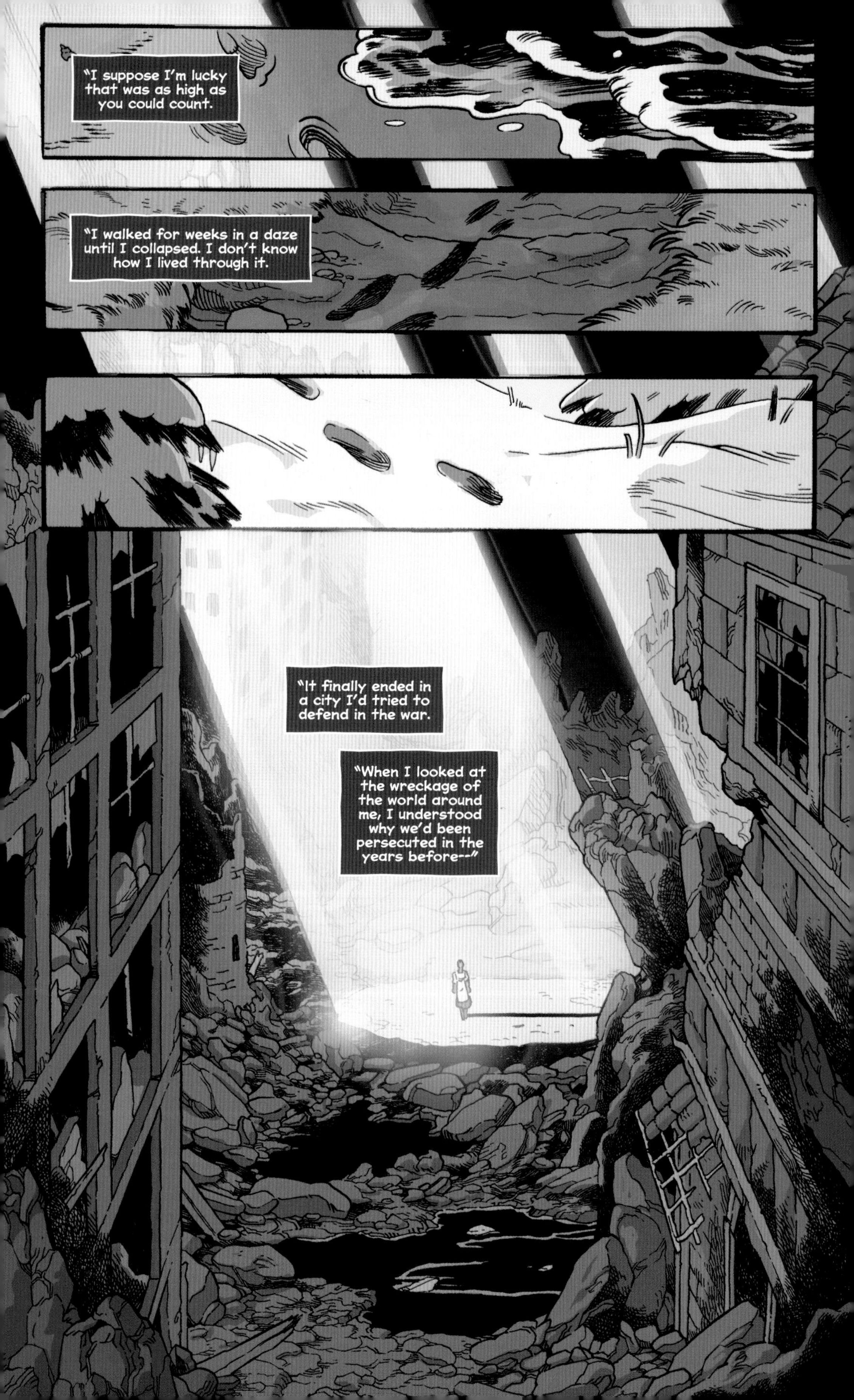
"I suppose I'm lucky that was as high as you could count.
"I walked for weeks in a daze until I collapsed. I don't know how I lived through it.
"It finally ended in a city I'd tried to defend in the war.
"When I looked at the wreckage of the world around me, I understood why we'd been persecuted in the years before--"

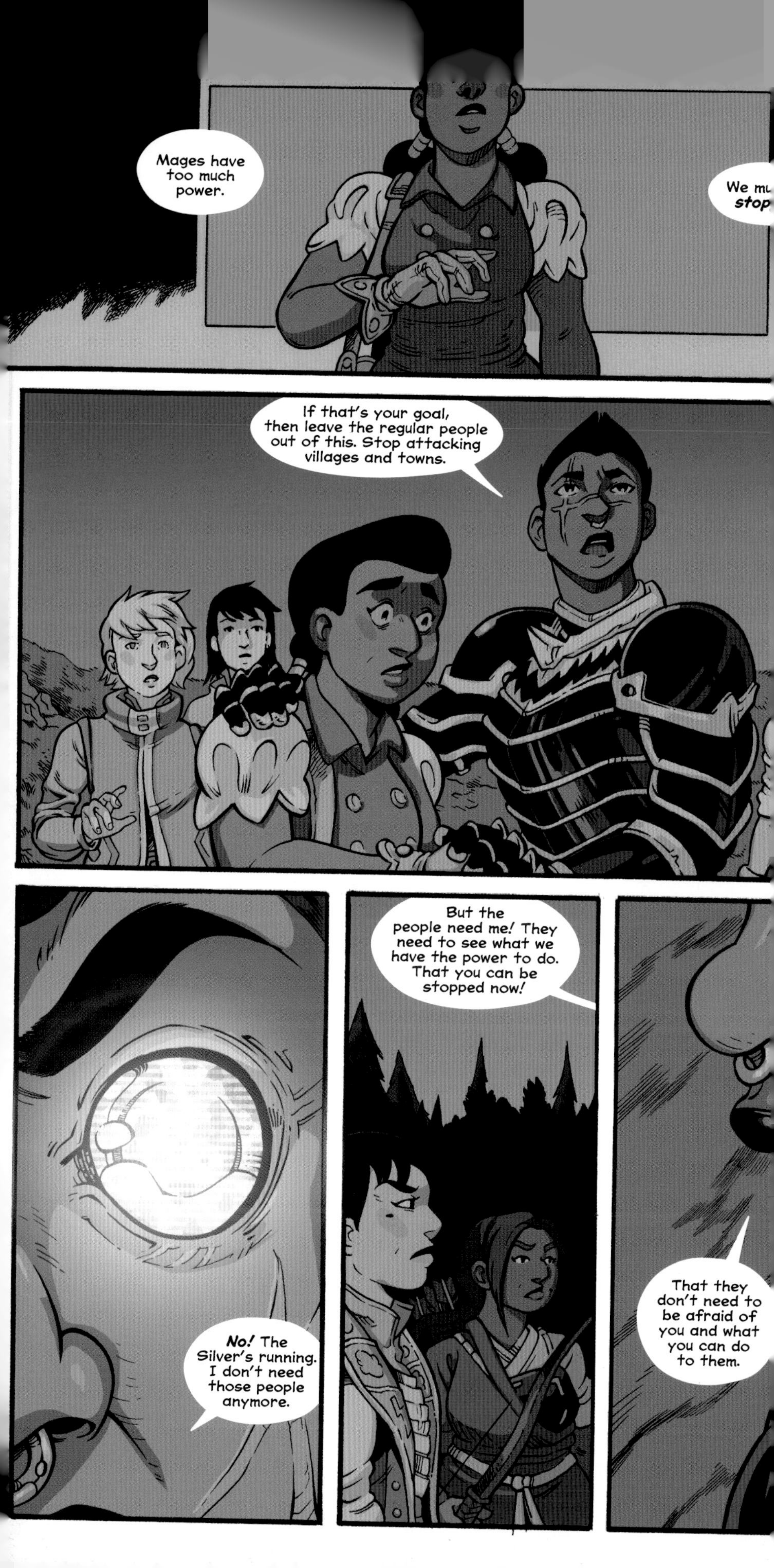
Mages have too much power.
We mu
stop
If that's your goal, then leave the regular people out of this. Stop attacking villages and towns.
No! The Silver's running. I don't need those people anymore.
But the people need me! They need to see what we have the power to do. That you can be stopped now!
That they don't need to be afraid of you and what you can do to them.

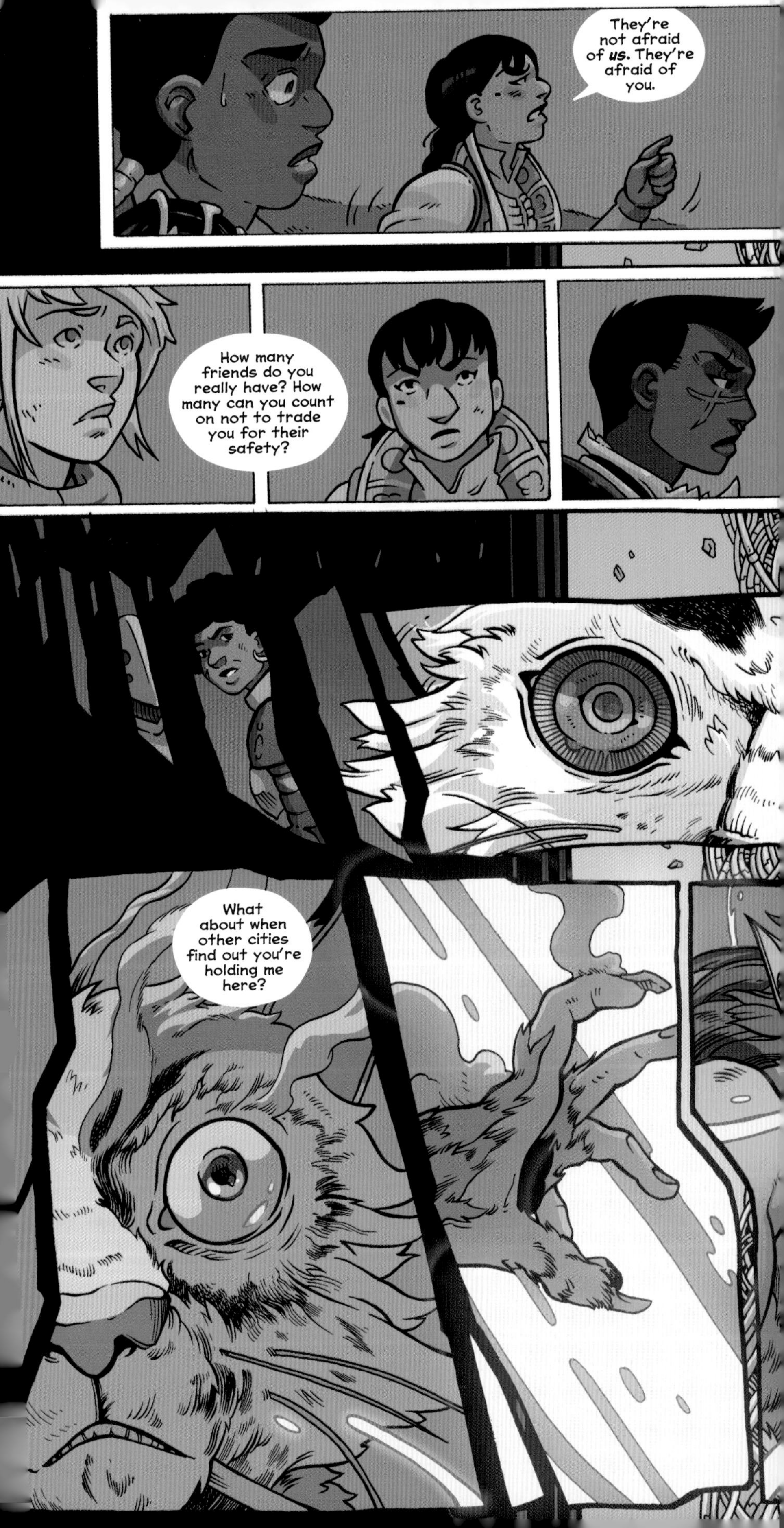
They're not afraid of *us.* They're afraid of you.
How many friends do you really have? How many can you count on not to trade you for their safety?
What about when other cities find out you're holding me here?

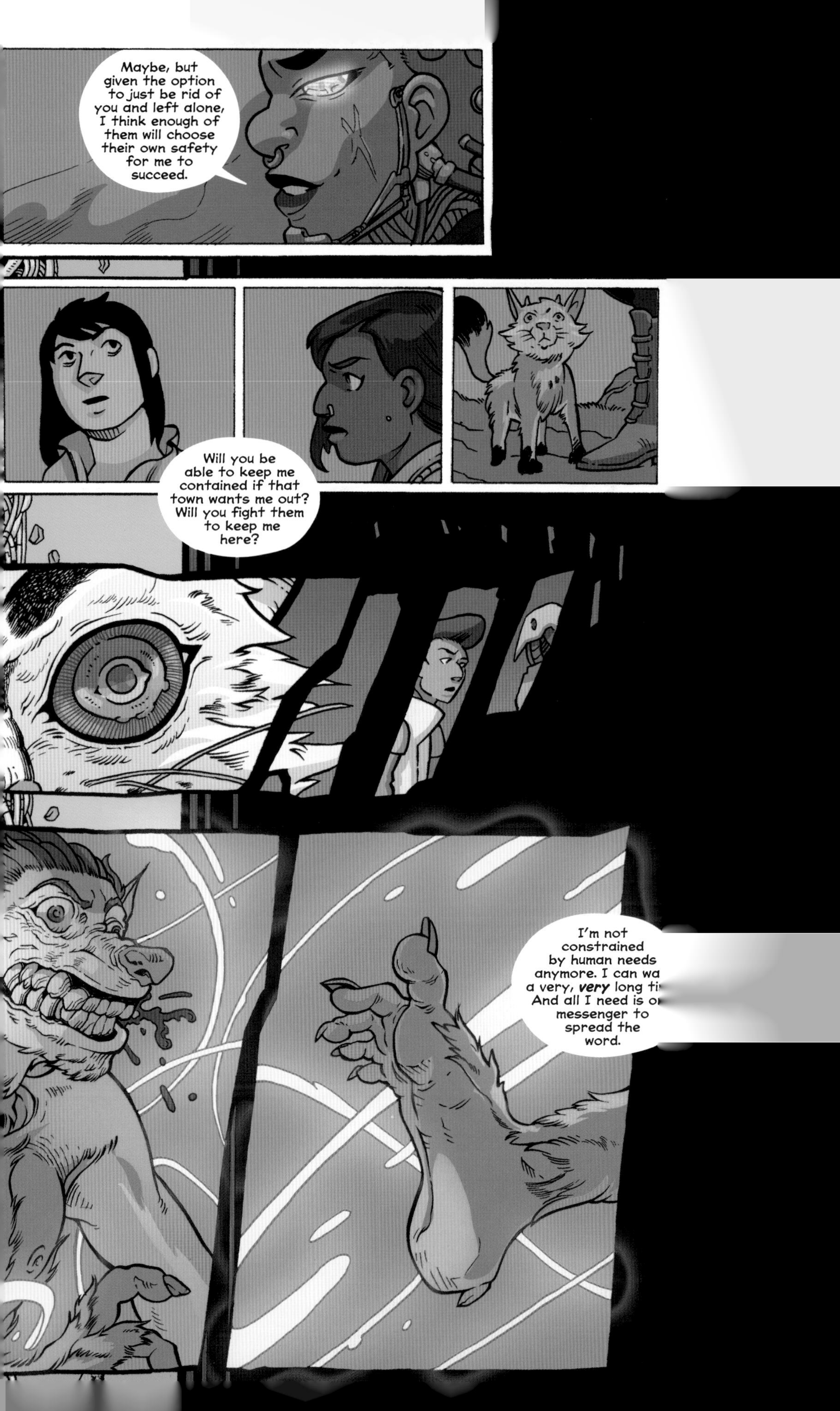
Maybe, but given the option to just be rid of you and left alone, I think enough of them will choose their own safety for me to succeed.
Will you be able to keep me contained if that town wants me out? Will you fight them to keep me here?
I'm not constrained by human needs anymore. I can wa
a very, *very* long ti
And all I need is o
messenger to spread the word.

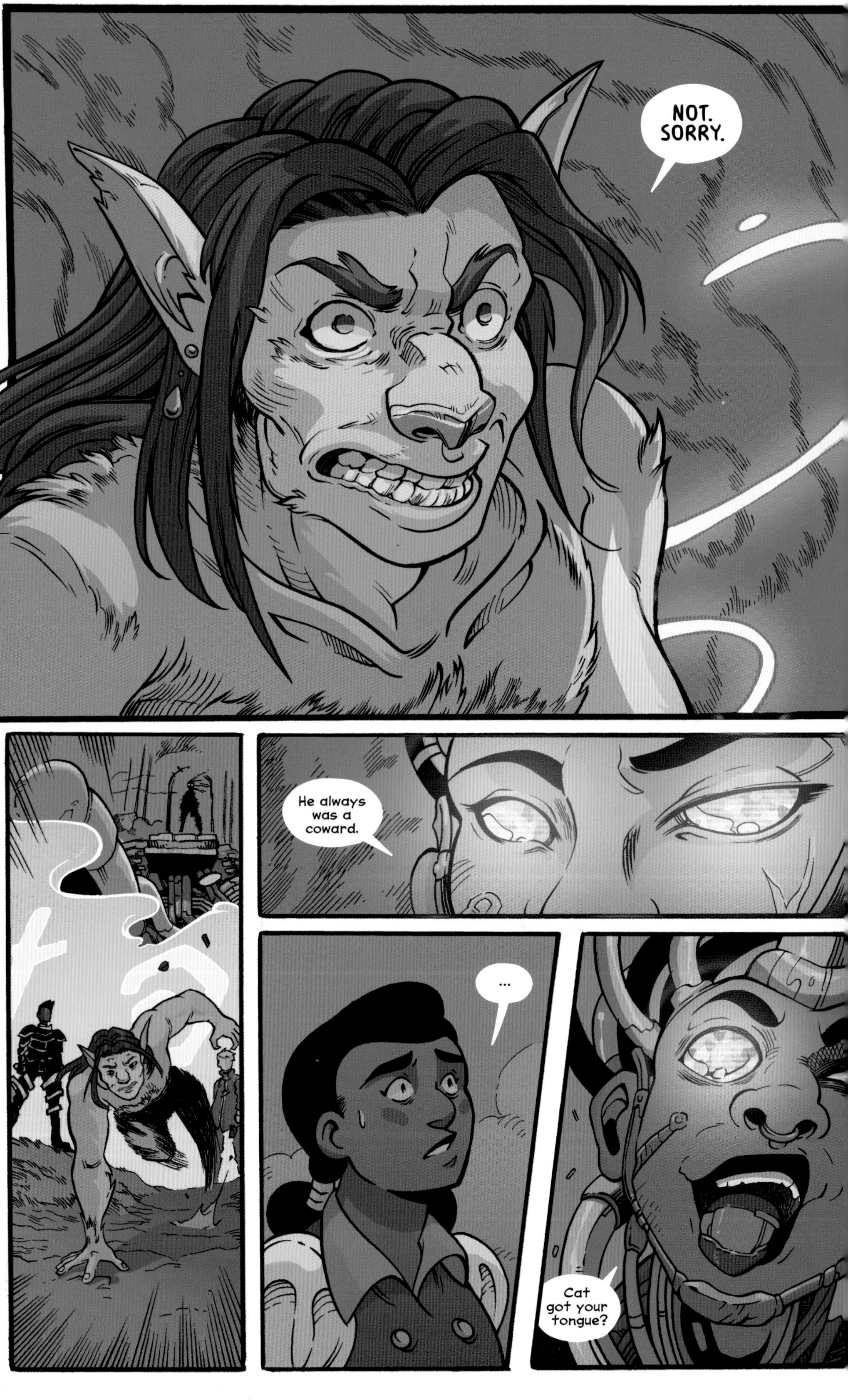
NOT.
SORRY.
He always was a coward.
...
Cat got your tongue?

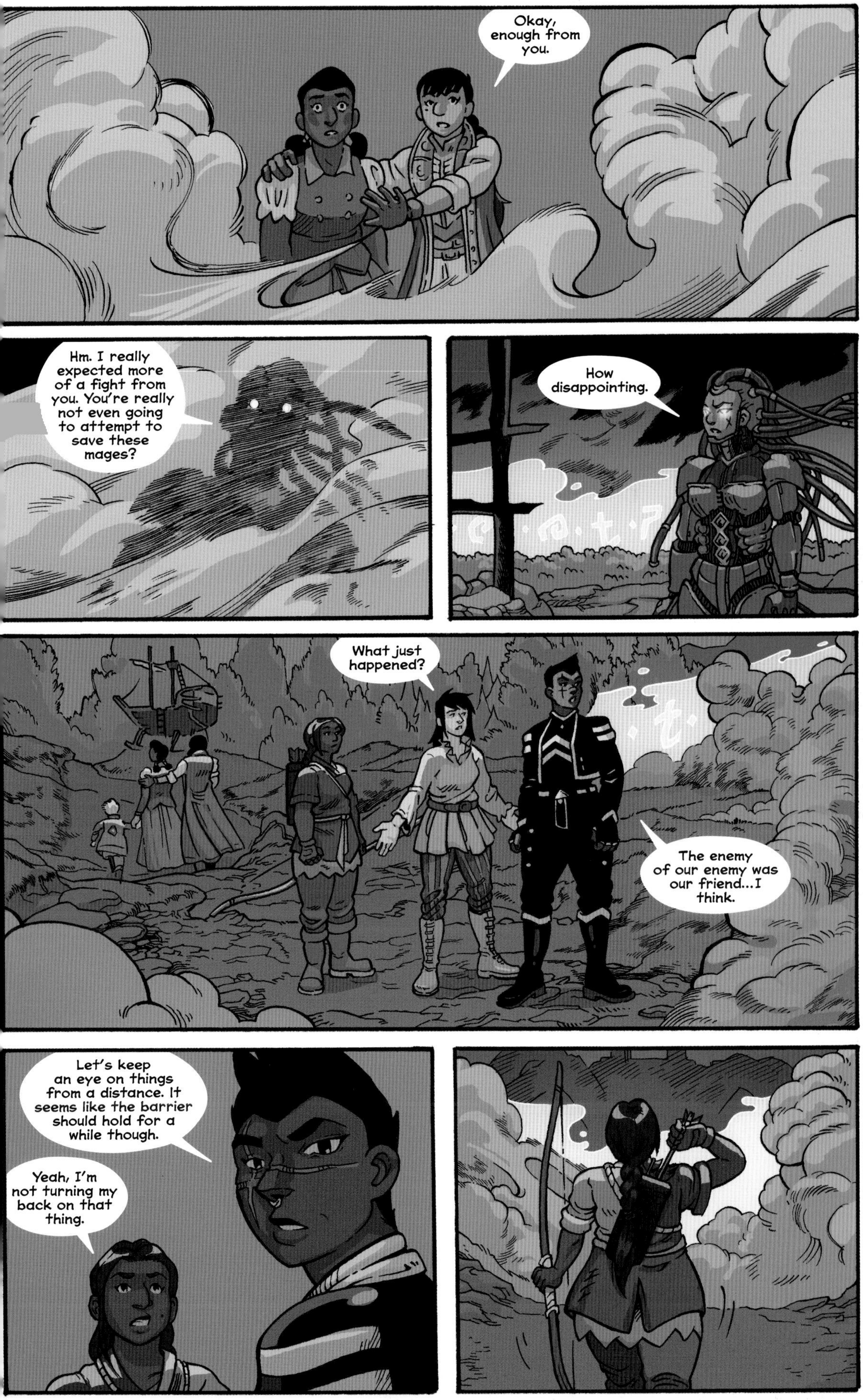
Okay, enough from you.
Hm. I really expected more of a fight from you. You're really not even going to attempt to save these mages?
How disappointing.
What just happened?
The enemy of our enemy was our friend... I think.
Let's keep an eye on things from a distance. It seems like the barrier should hold for a while though.
Yeah, I'm not turning my back on that thing.

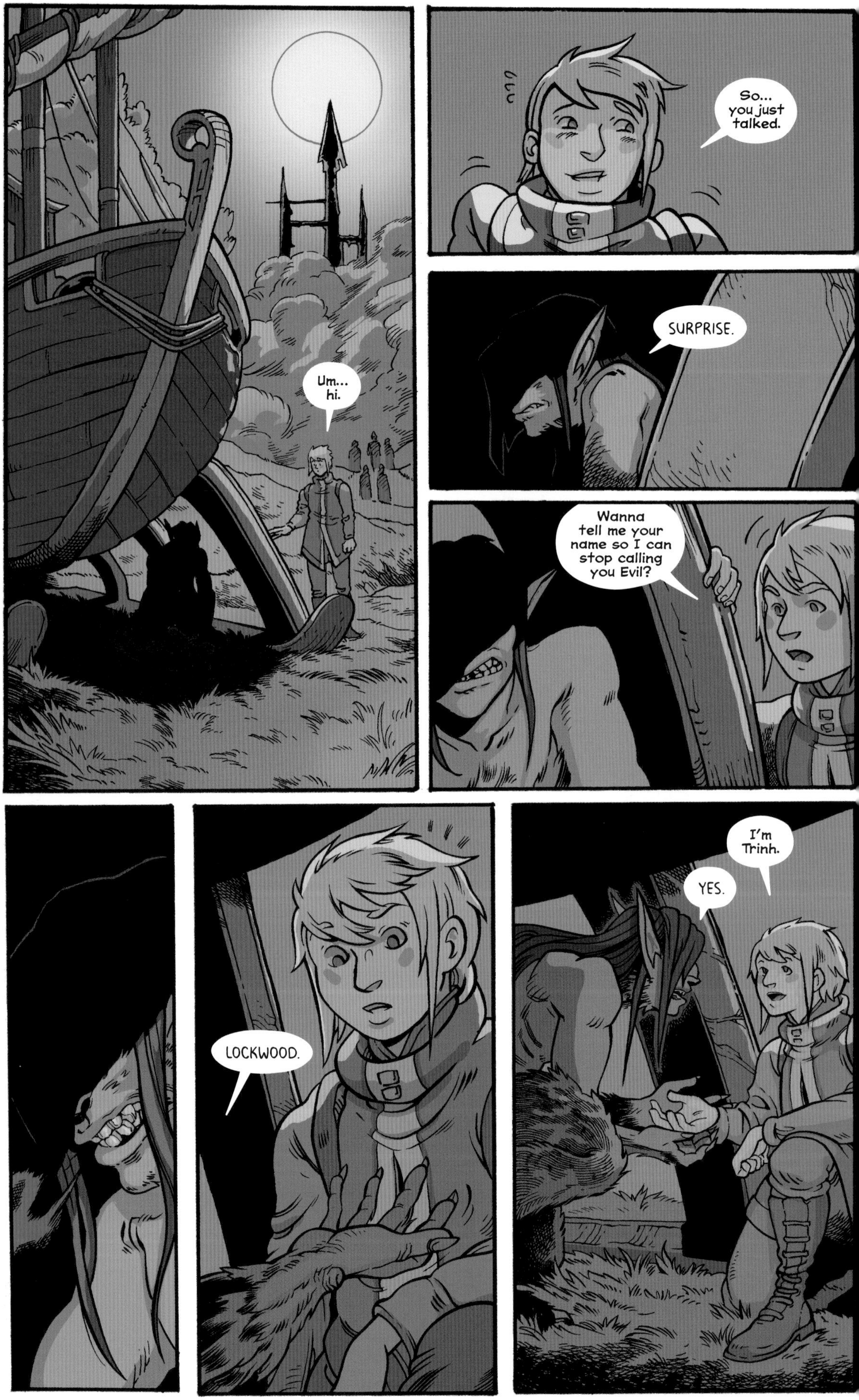
Um... hi.
So... you just talked.
SURPRISE.
Wanna tell me your name so I can stop calling you Evil?
LOCKWOOD.
I'm Trinh.
YES.

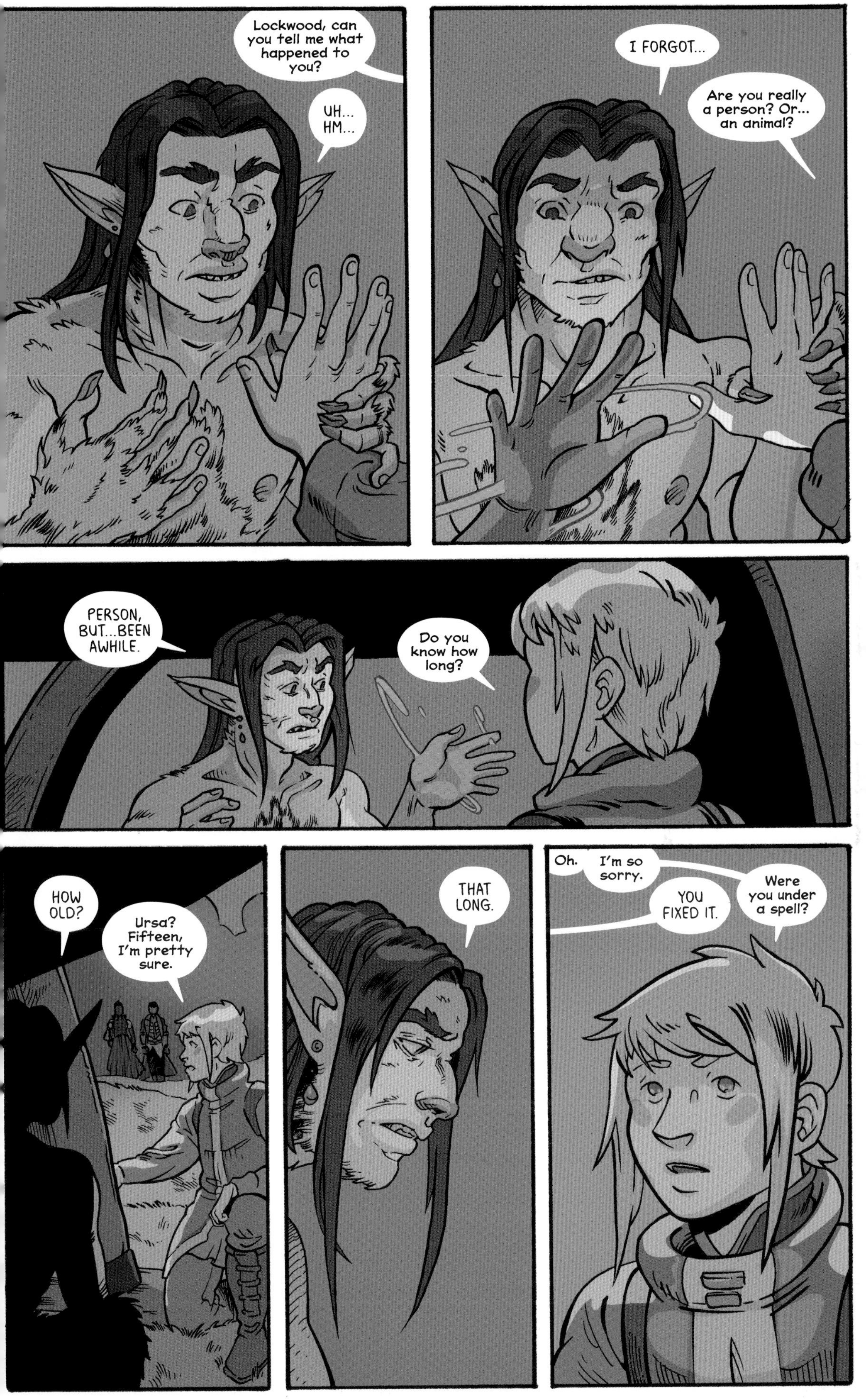
Lockwood, can you tell me what happened to you?
UH... HM...
I FORGOT...
Are you really a person? Or... an animal?
PERSON, BUT...BEEN AWHILE.
Do you know how long?
HOW OLD?
Ursa? Fifteen, I'm pretty sure.
THAT LONG.
Oh.
I'm so sorry.
Were you under a spell?
YOU FIXED IT.

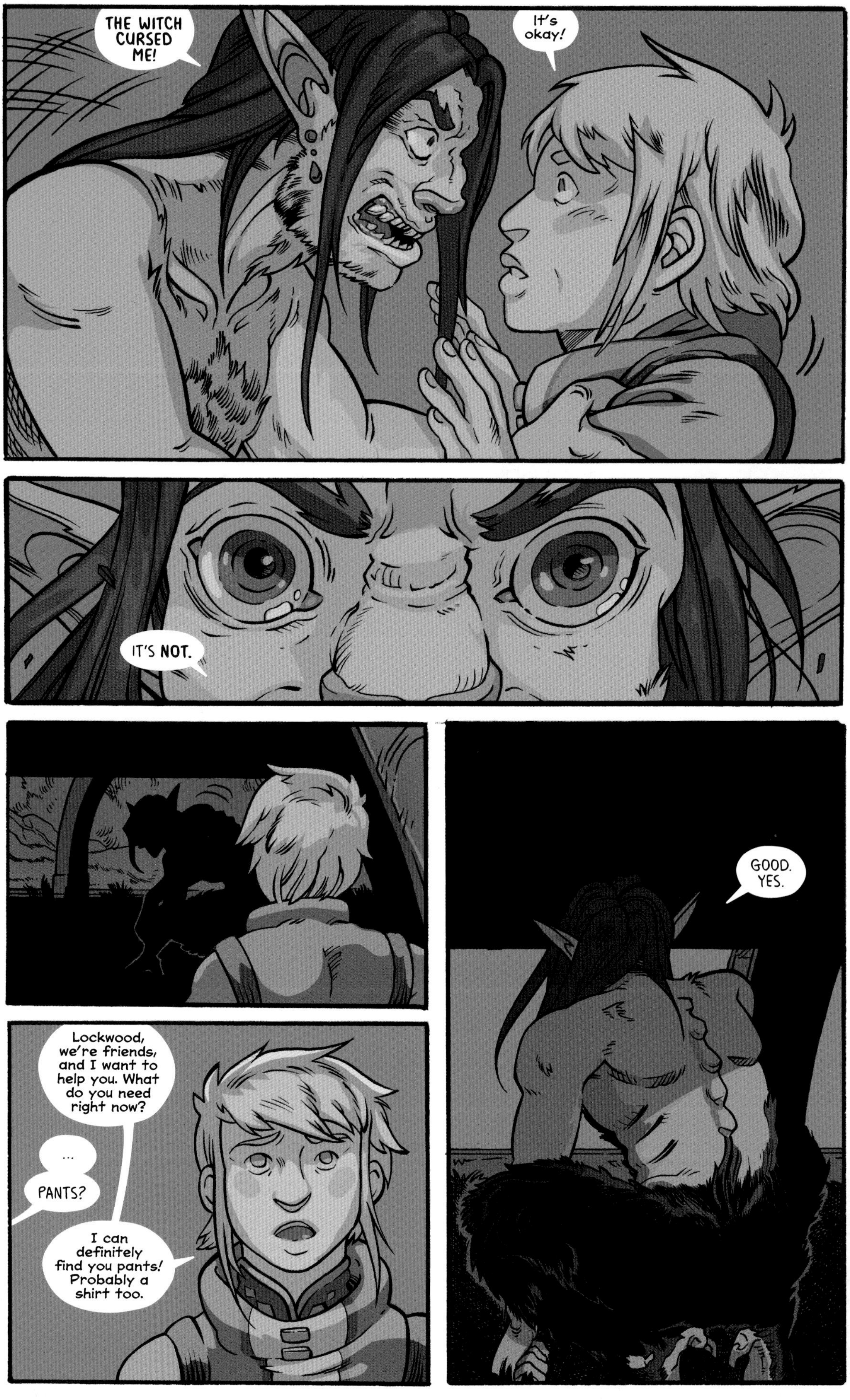
THE WITCH CURSED ME!
It's okay!
IT'S **NOT.**
GOOD. YES.
Lockwood, we're friends, and I want to help you. What do you need right now?
...
PANTS?
I can definitely find you pants! Probably a shirt too.

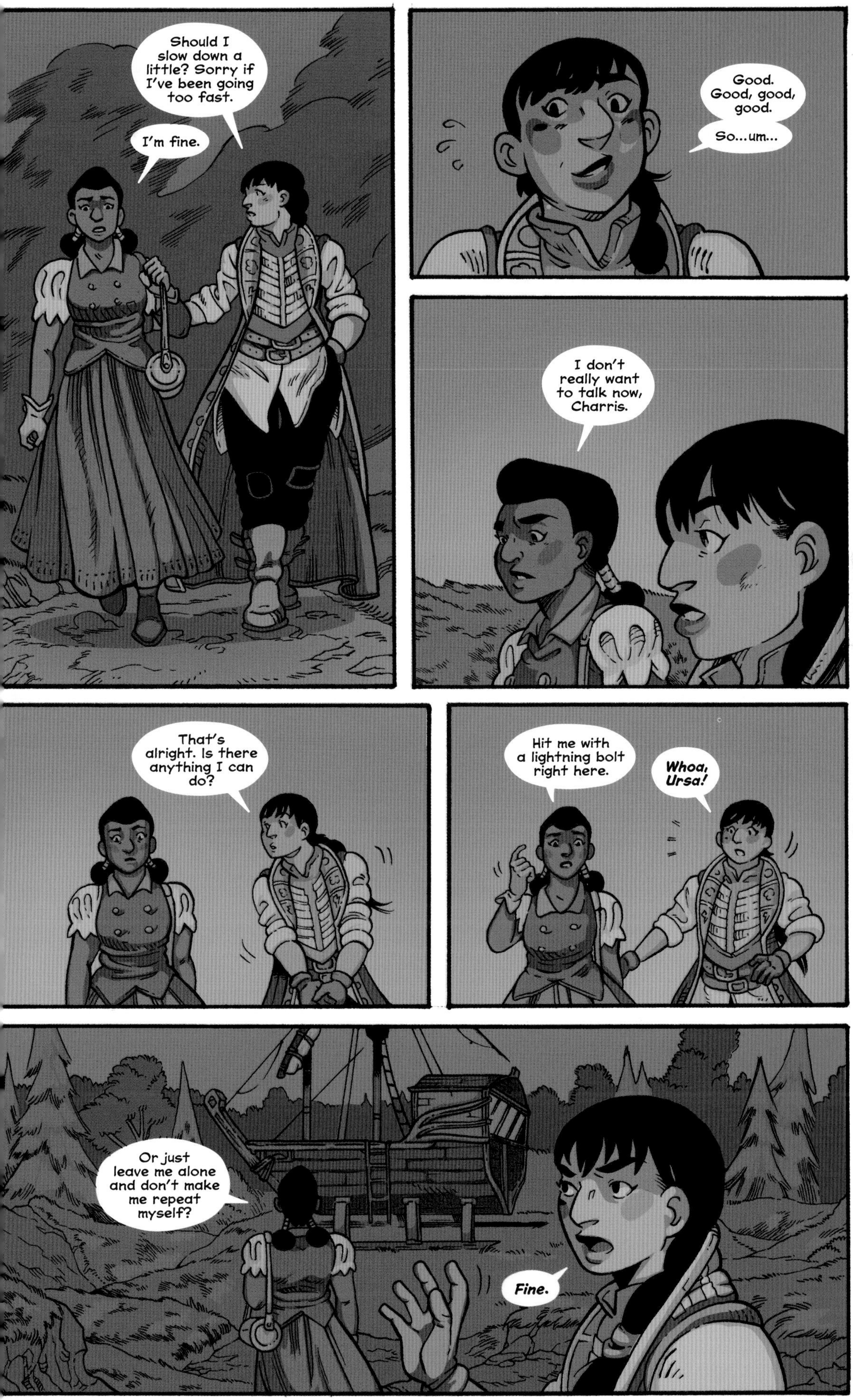
Should I slow down a little? Sorry if I've been going too fast.
I'm fine.
Good. Good, good, good.
So...um...
I don't really want to talk now, Charris.
That's alright. Is there anything I can do?
Hit me with a lightning bolt right here.
Whoa, Ursa!
Or just leave me alone and don't make me repeat myself?
Fine.

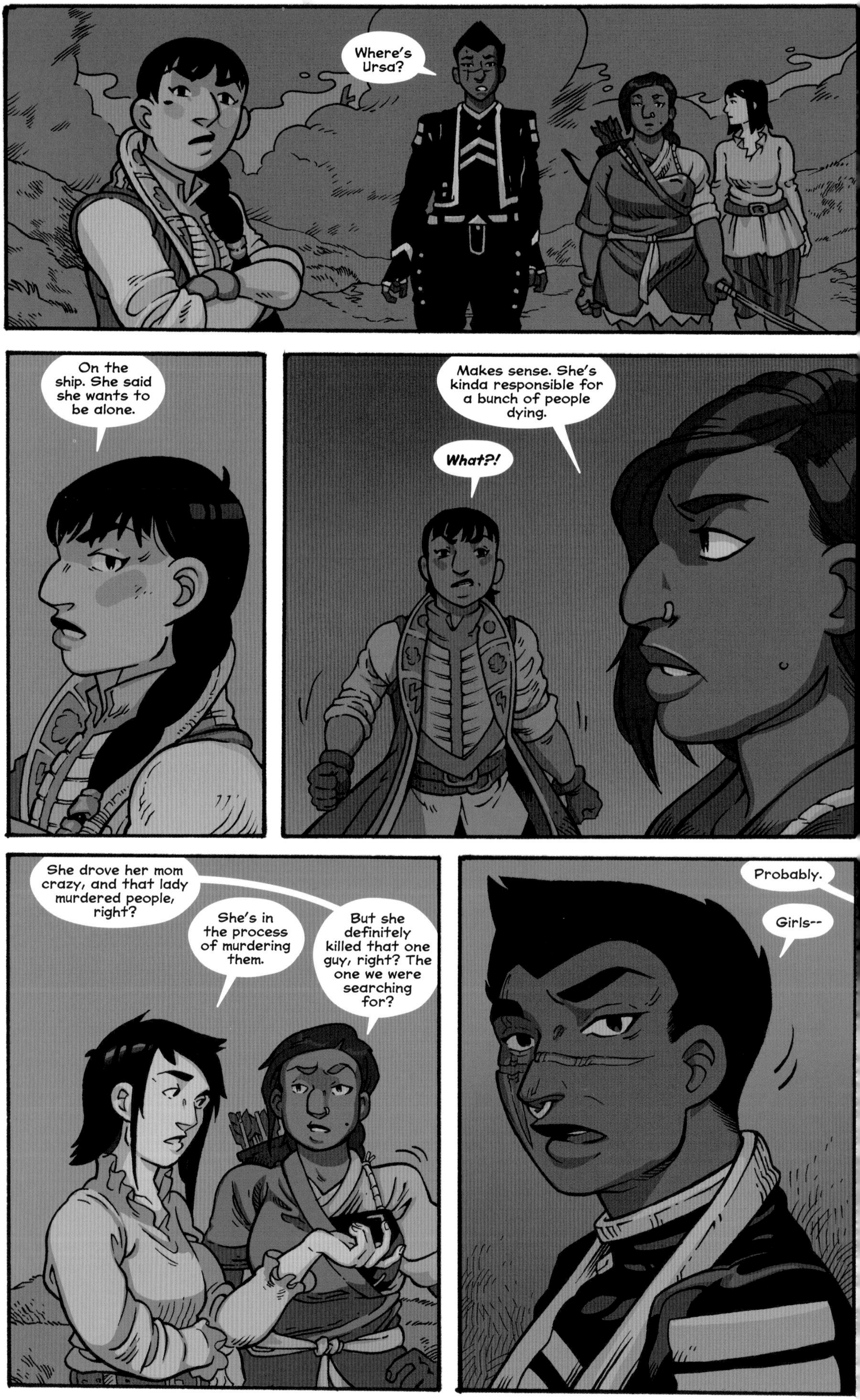
Where's Ursa?
On the ship. She said she wants to be alone.
Makes sense. She's kinda responsible for a bunch of people dying.
What?!
She drove her mom crazy, and that lady murdered people, right?
She's in the process of murdering them.
But she definitely killed that one guy, right? The one we were searching for?
Probably.
Girls--

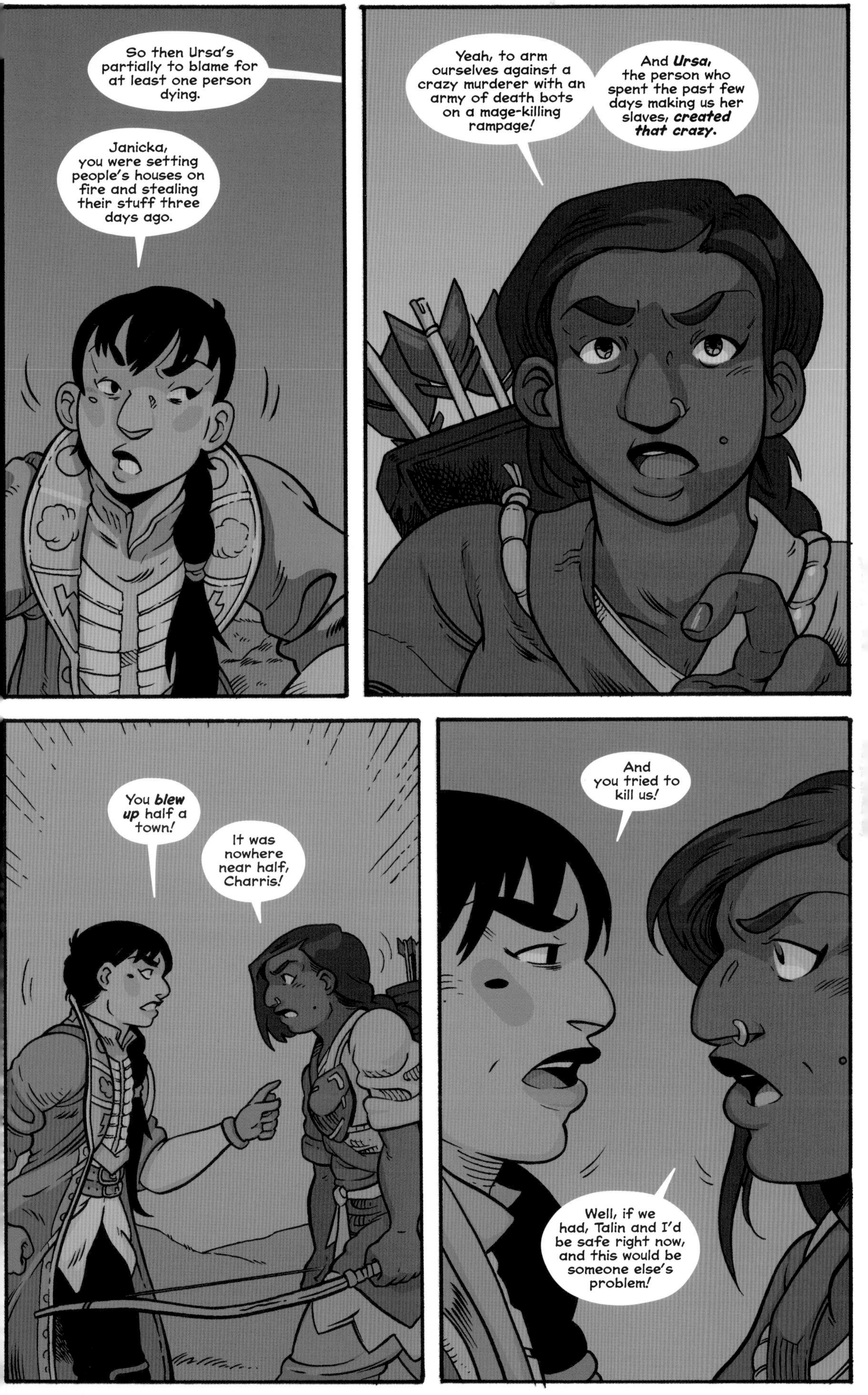
So then Ursa's partially to blame for at least one person dying.
Janicka, you were setting people's houses on fire and stealing their stuff three days ago.
Yeah, to arm ourselves against a crazy murderer with an army of death bots on a mage-killing rampage!
And *Ursa,* the person who spent the past few days making us her slaves, ***created that crazy.***
You ***blew up*** half a town!
It was nowhere near half, Charris!
And you tried to kill us!
Well, if we had, Talin and I'd be safe right now, and this would be someone else's problem!

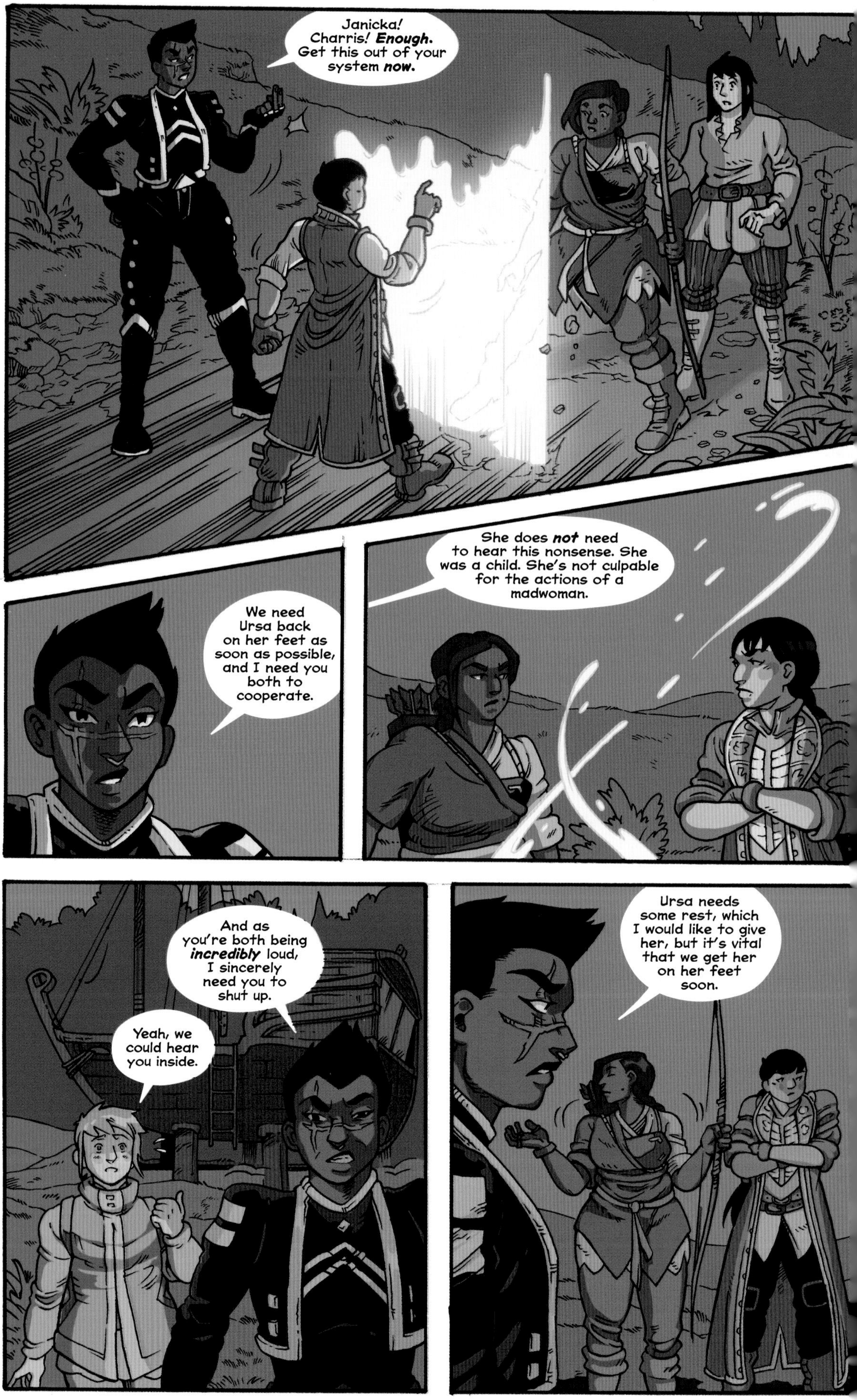
Janicka! Charris! **Enough.** Get this out of your system **now.**
We need Ursa back on her feet as soon as possible, and I need you both to cooperate.
She does **not** need to hear this nonsense. She was a child. She's not culpable for the actions of a madwoman.
And as you're both being ***incredibly*** loud, I sincerely need you to shut up.
Yeah, we could hear you inside.
Ursa needs some rest, which I would like to give her, but it's vital that we get her on her feet soon.

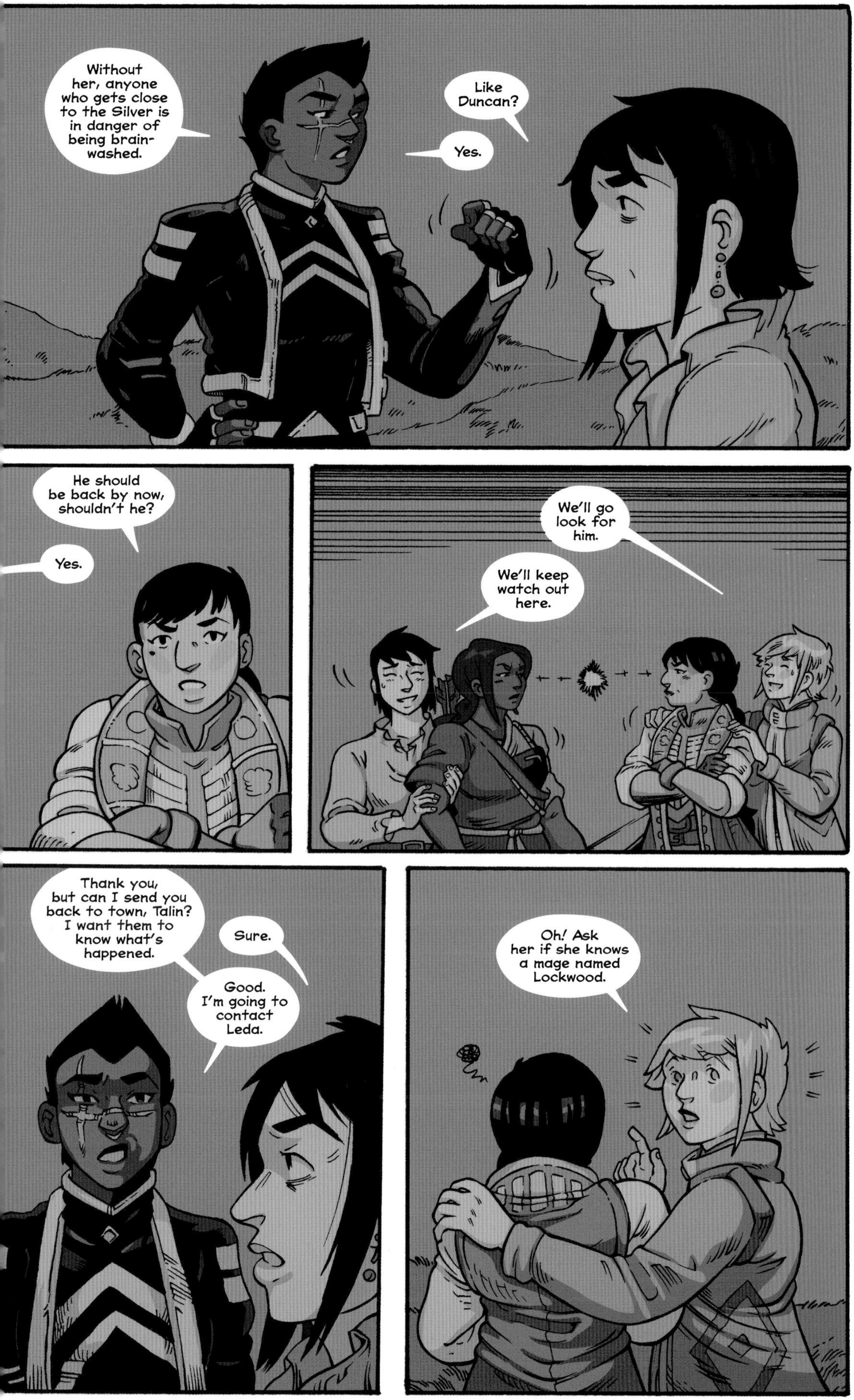
Without her, anyone who gets close to the Silver is in danger of being brain-washed.
Like Duncan?
Yes.
He should be back by now, shouldn't he?
Yes.
We'll go look for him.
We'll keep watch out here.
Thank you, but can I send you back to town, Talin? I want them to know what's happened.
Sure.
Good. I'm going to contact Leda.
Oh! Ask her if she knows a mage named Lockwood.

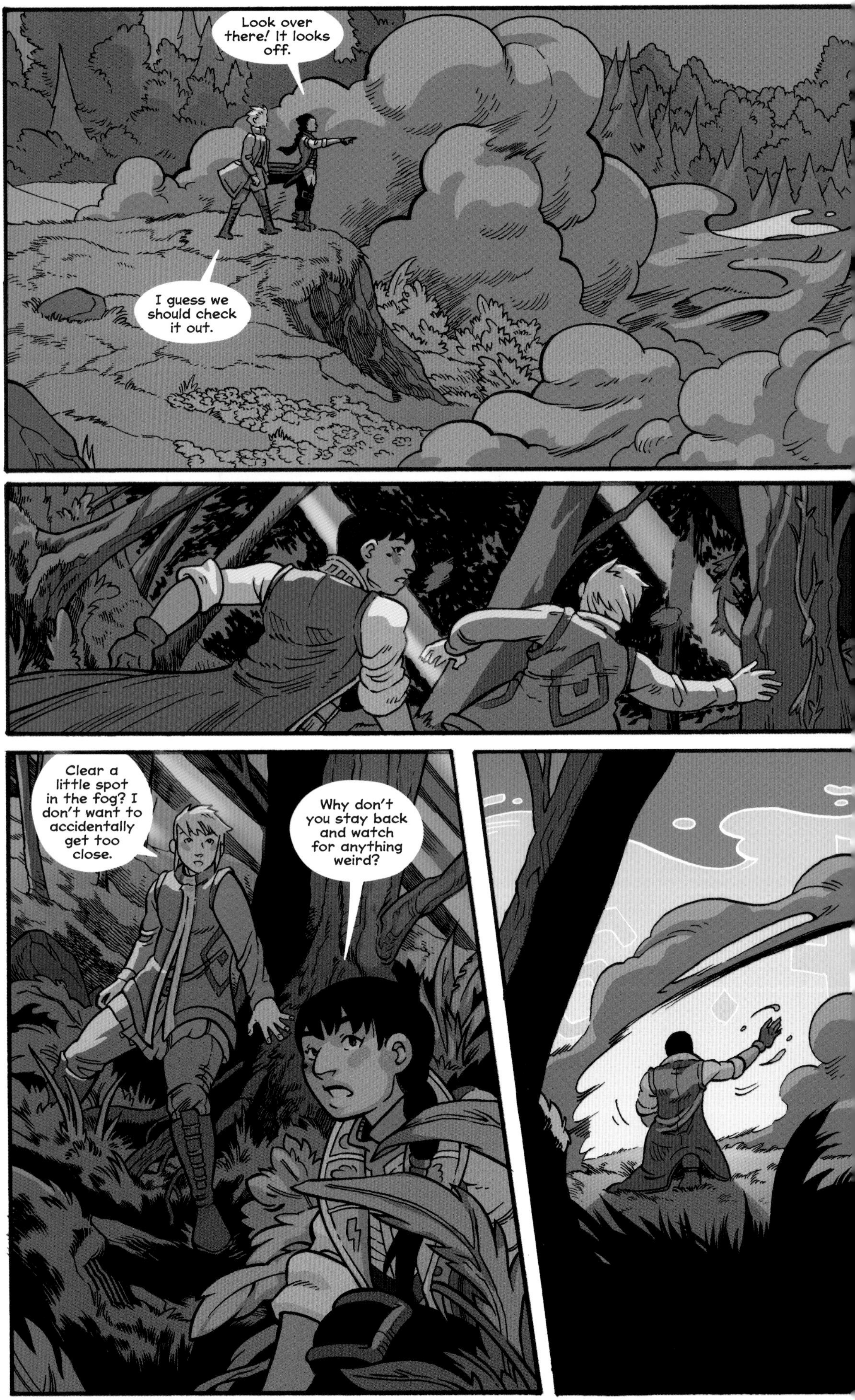
Look over there! It looks off.
I guess we should check it out.
Clear a little spot in the fog? I don't want to accidentally get too close.
Why don't you stay back and watch for anything weird?

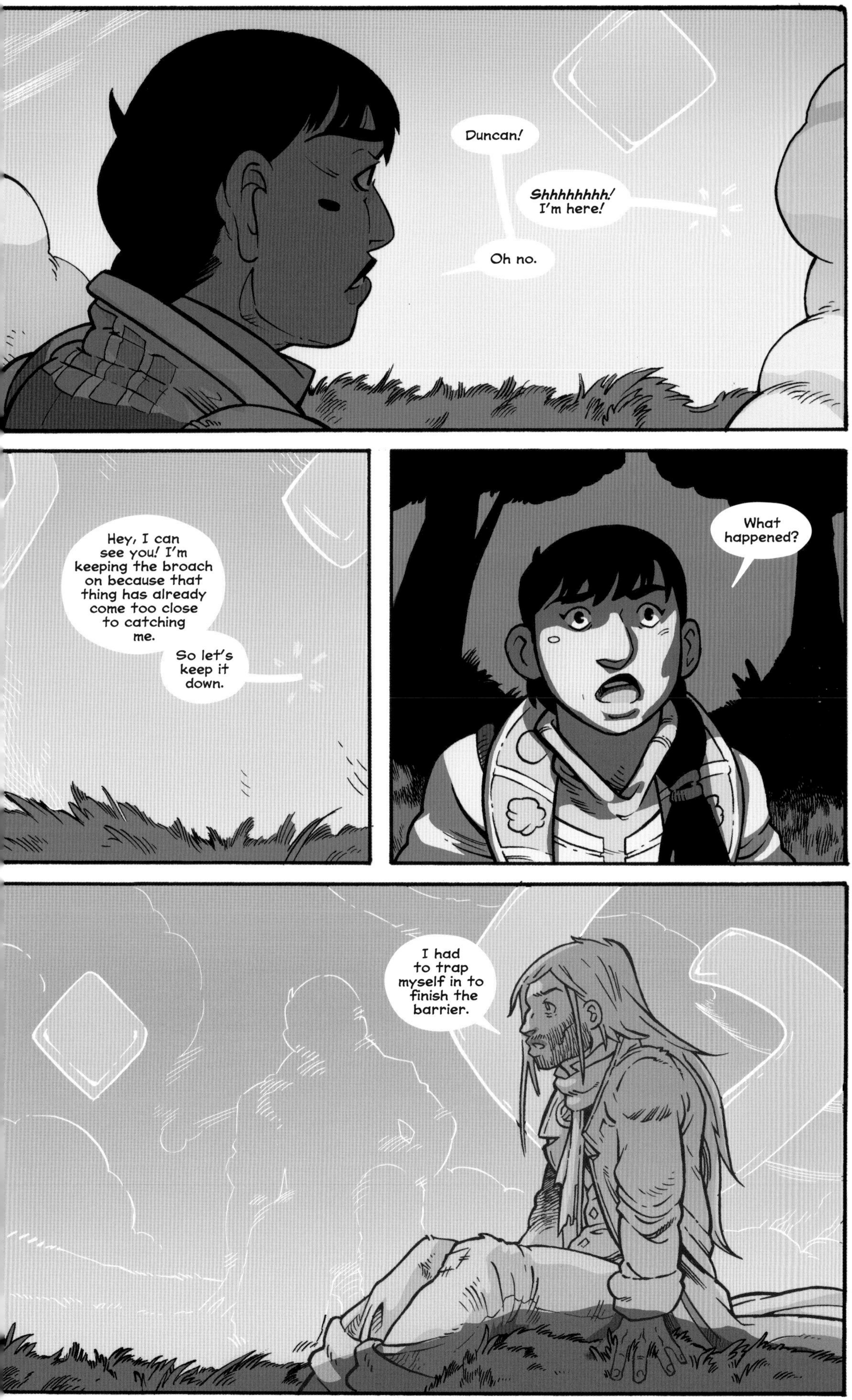
Duncan!
Shhhhhhhh! I'm here!
Oh no.
Hey, I can see you! I'm keeping the broach on because that thing has already come too close to catching me.
So let's keep it down.
What happened?
I had to trap myself in to finish the barrier.

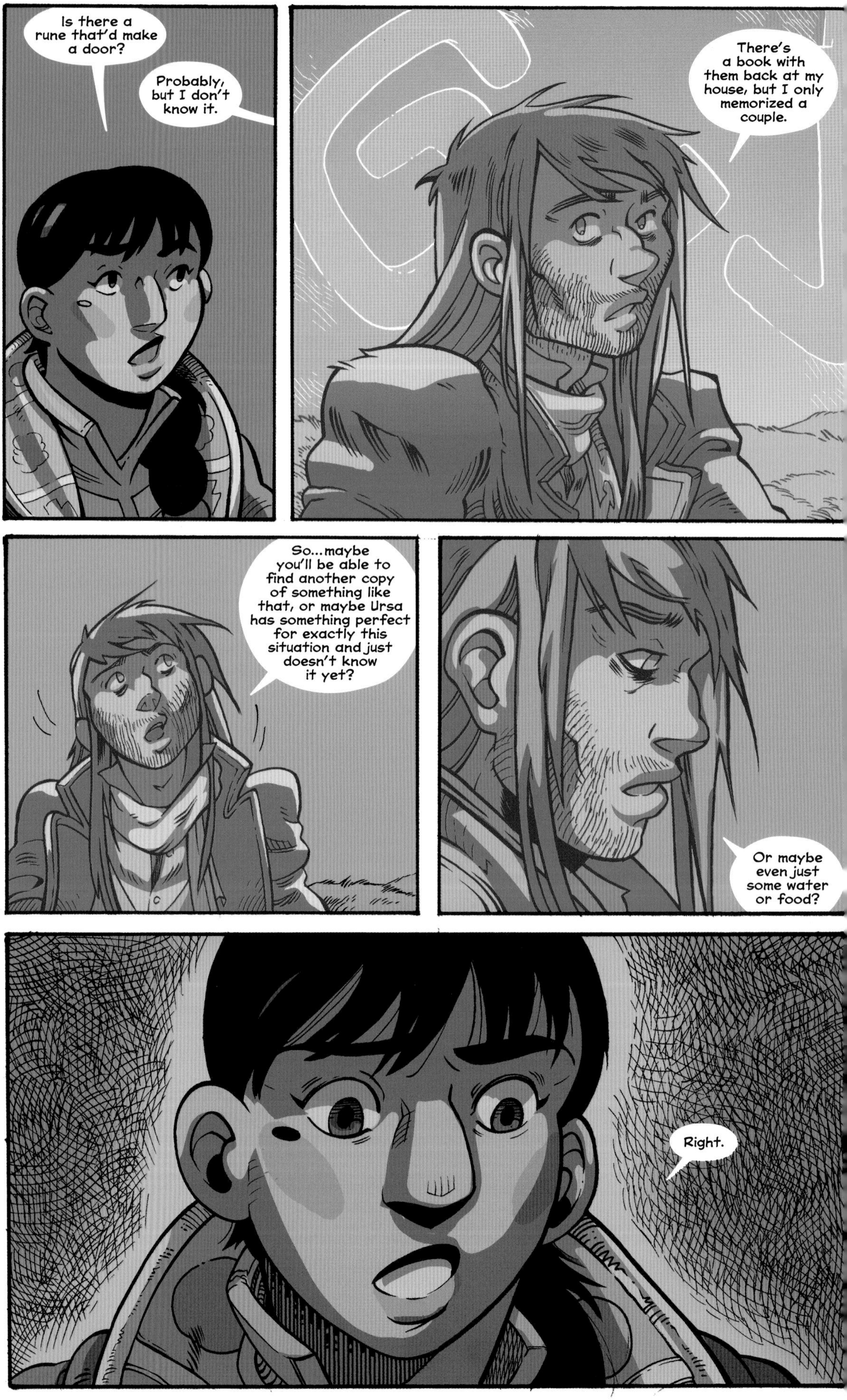
Is there a rune that'd make a door?
Probably, but I don't know it.
There's a book with them back at my house, but I only memorized a couple.
So...maybe you'll be able to find another copy of something like that, or maybe Ursa has something perfect for exactly this situation and just doesn't know it yet?
Or maybe even just some water or food?
Right.

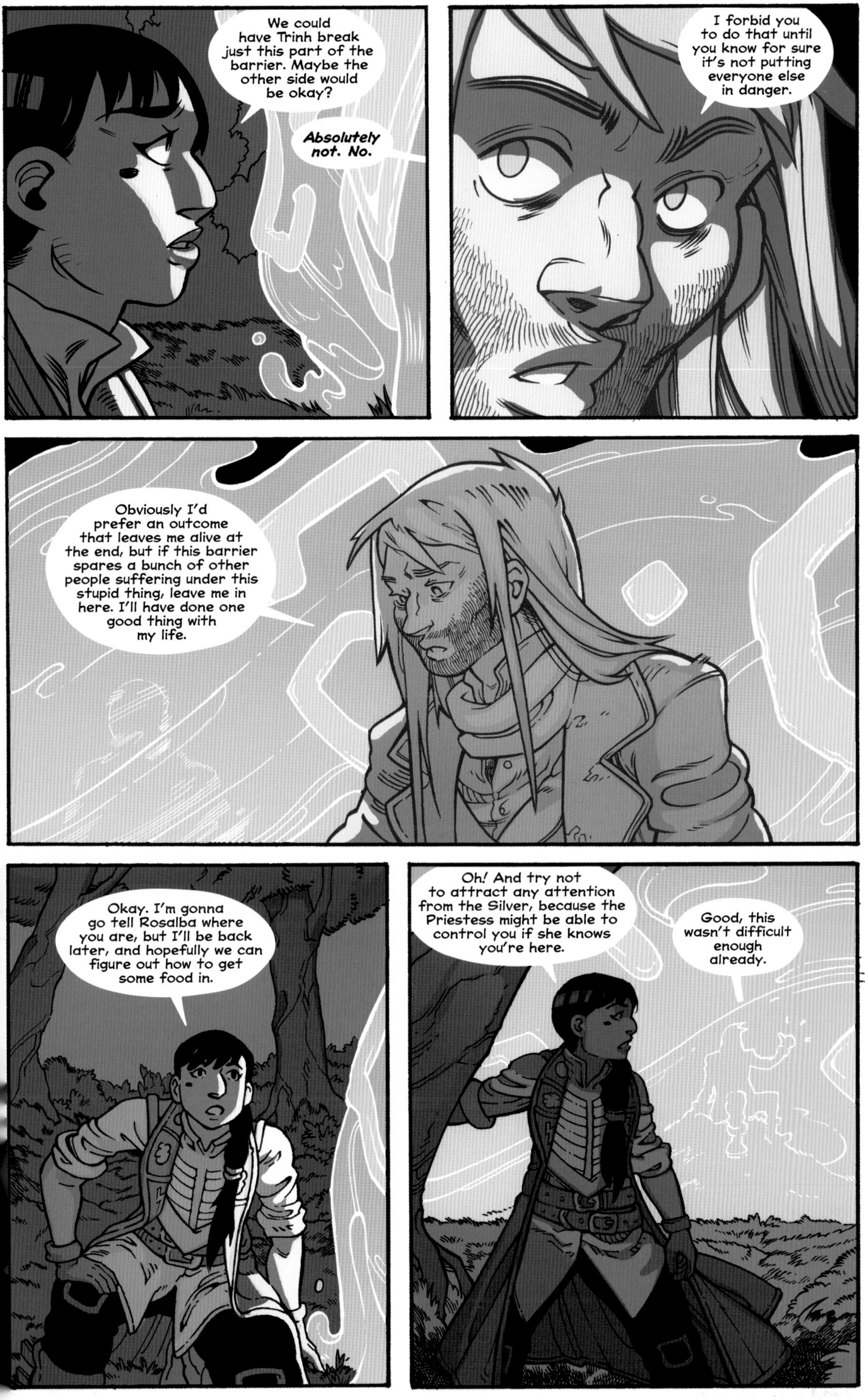

We could have Trinh break just this part of the barrier. Maybe the other side would be okay?
Absolutely not. No.
I forbid you to do that until you know for sure it's not putting everyone else in danger.
Obviously I'd prefer an outcome that leaves me alive at the end, but if this barrier spares a bunch of other people suffering under this stupid thing, leave me in here. I'll have done one good thing with my life.
Okay. I'm gonna go tell Rosalba where you are, but I'll be back later, and hopefully we can figure out how to get some food in.
Oh! And try not to attract any attention from the Silver, because the Priestess might be able to control you if she knows you're here.
Good, this wasn't difficult enough already.

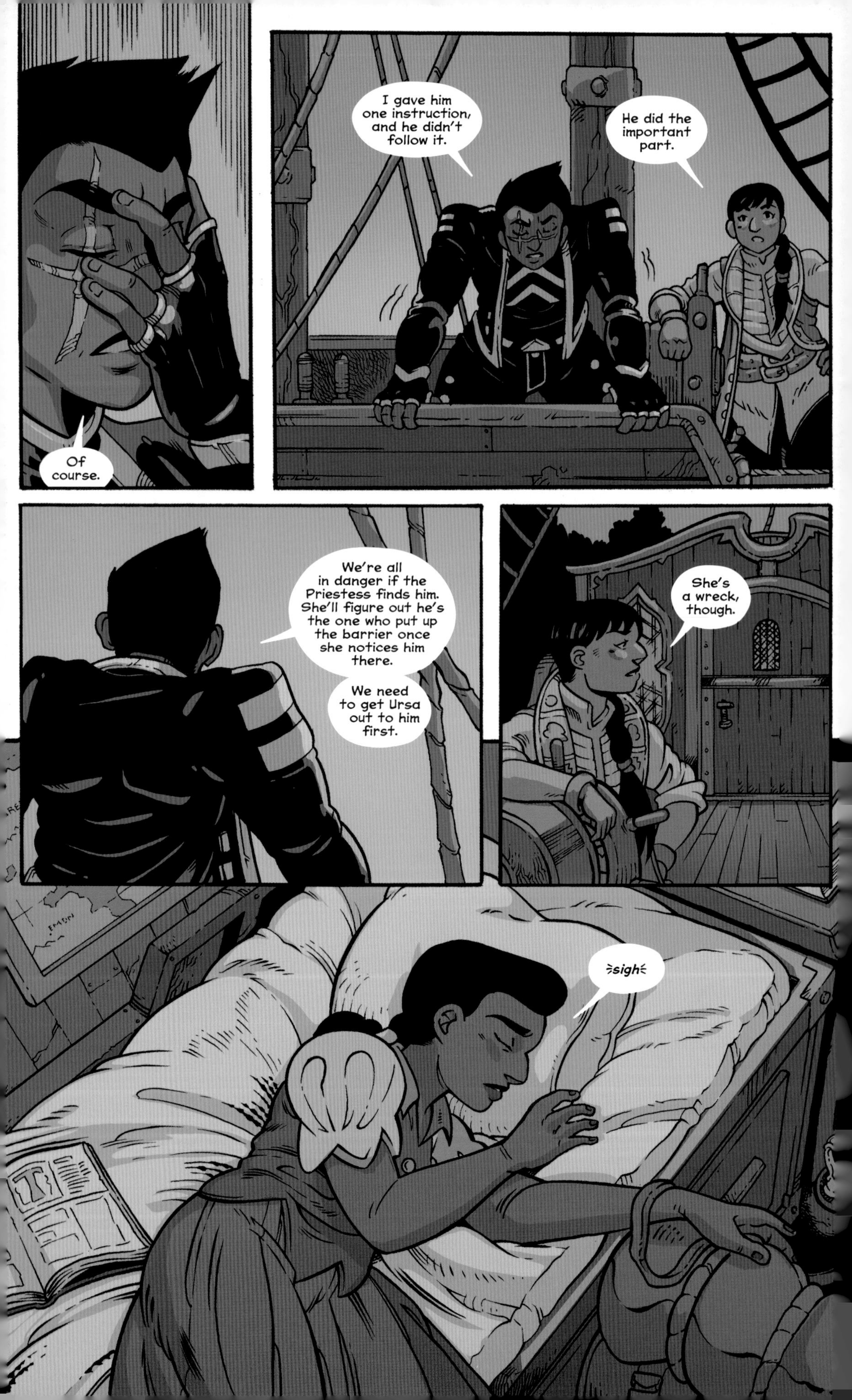
Of course.
I gave him one instruction, and he didn't follow it.
He did the important part.
We're all in danger if the Priestess finds him. She'll figure out he's the one who put up the barrier once she notices him there.
We need to get Ursa out to him first.
She's a wreck, though.
sigh

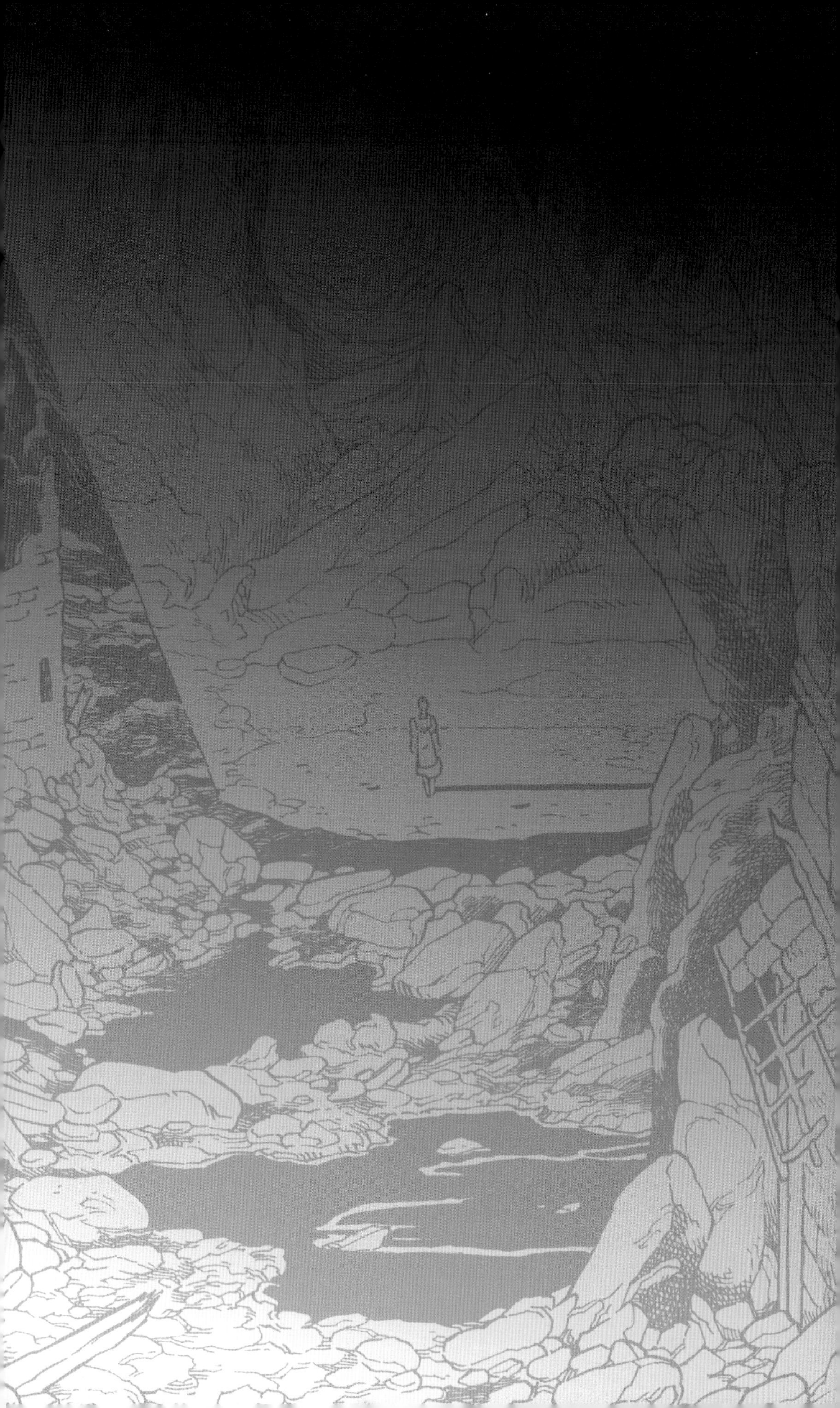

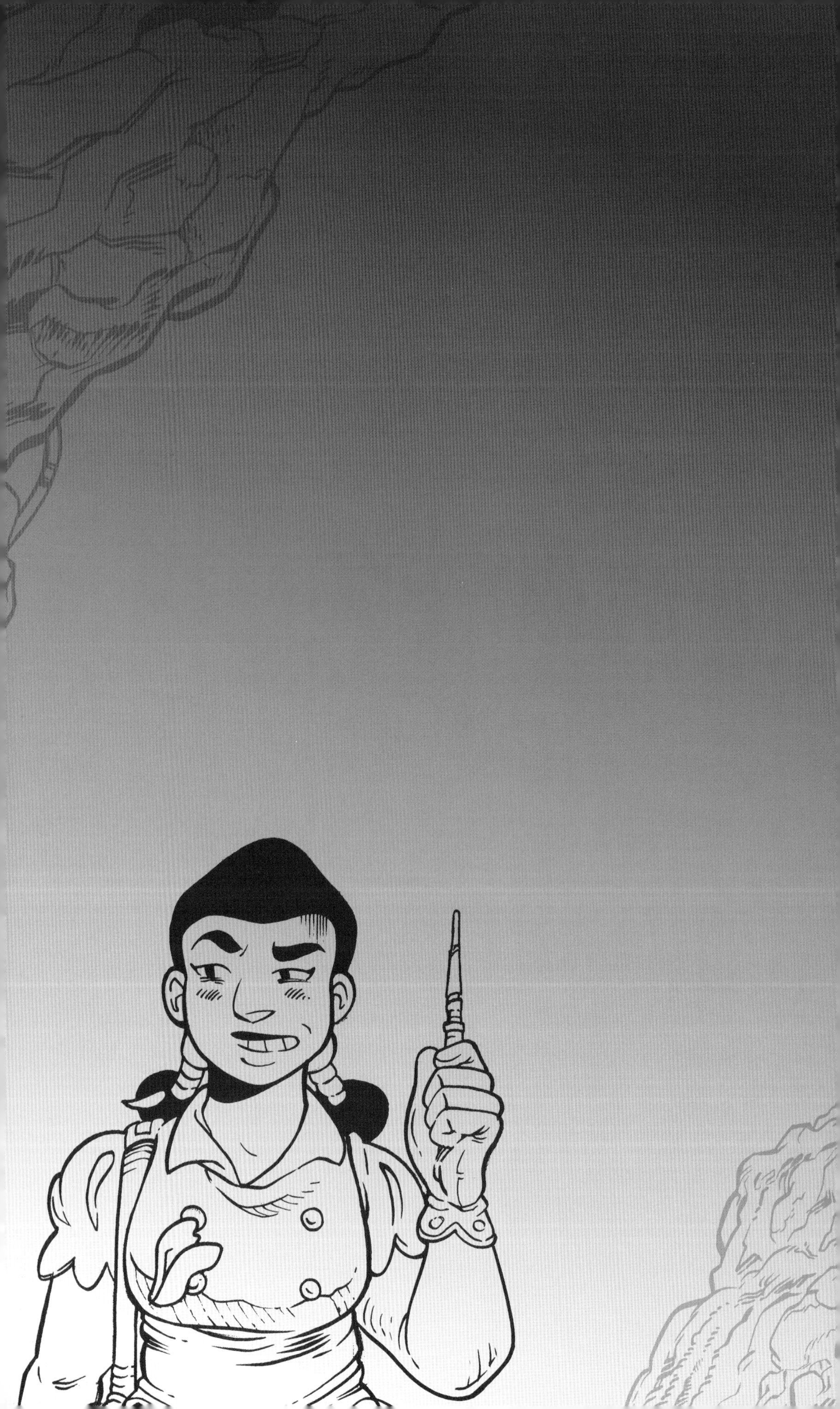

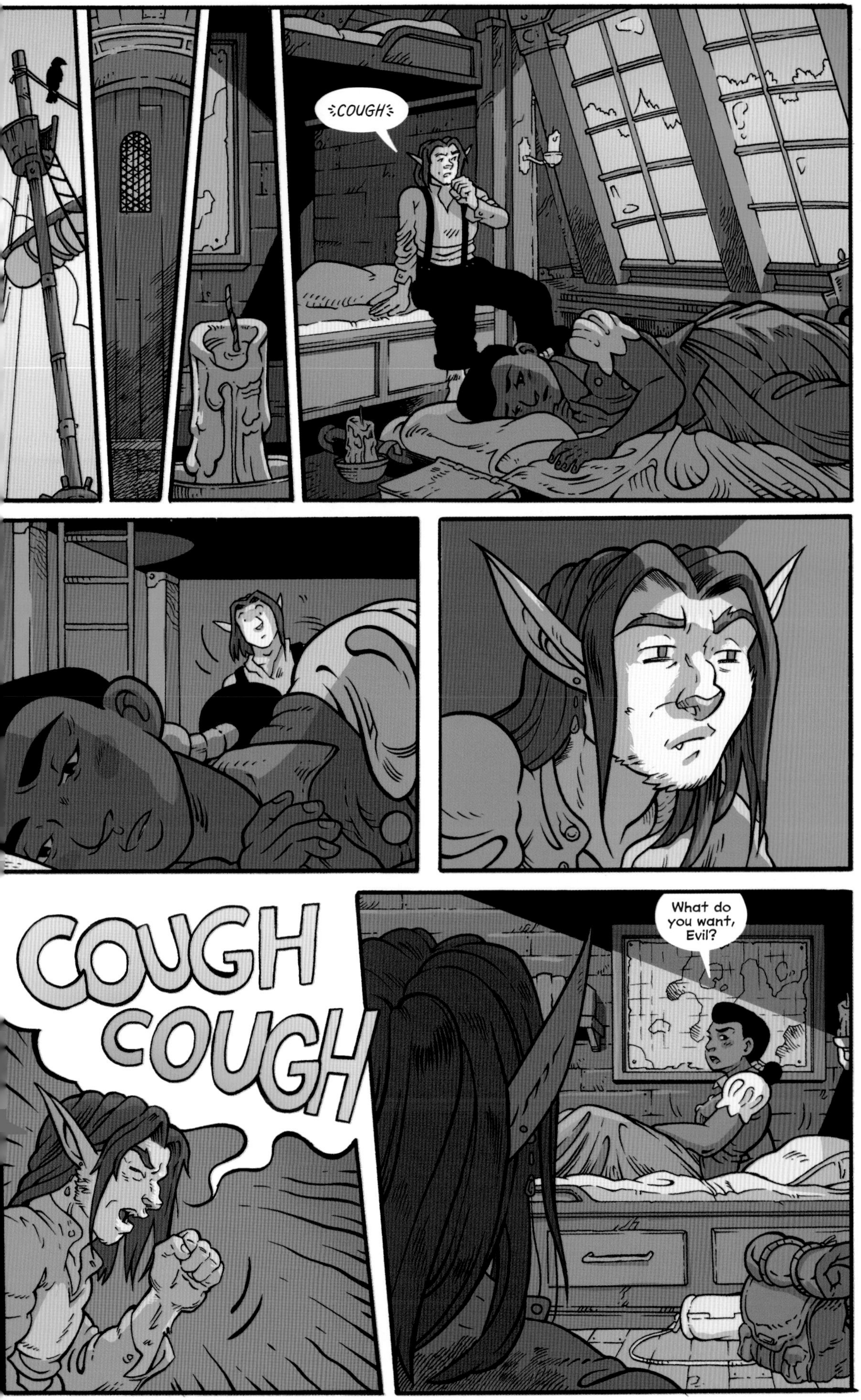
COUGH
COUGH COUGH
What do you want, Evil?

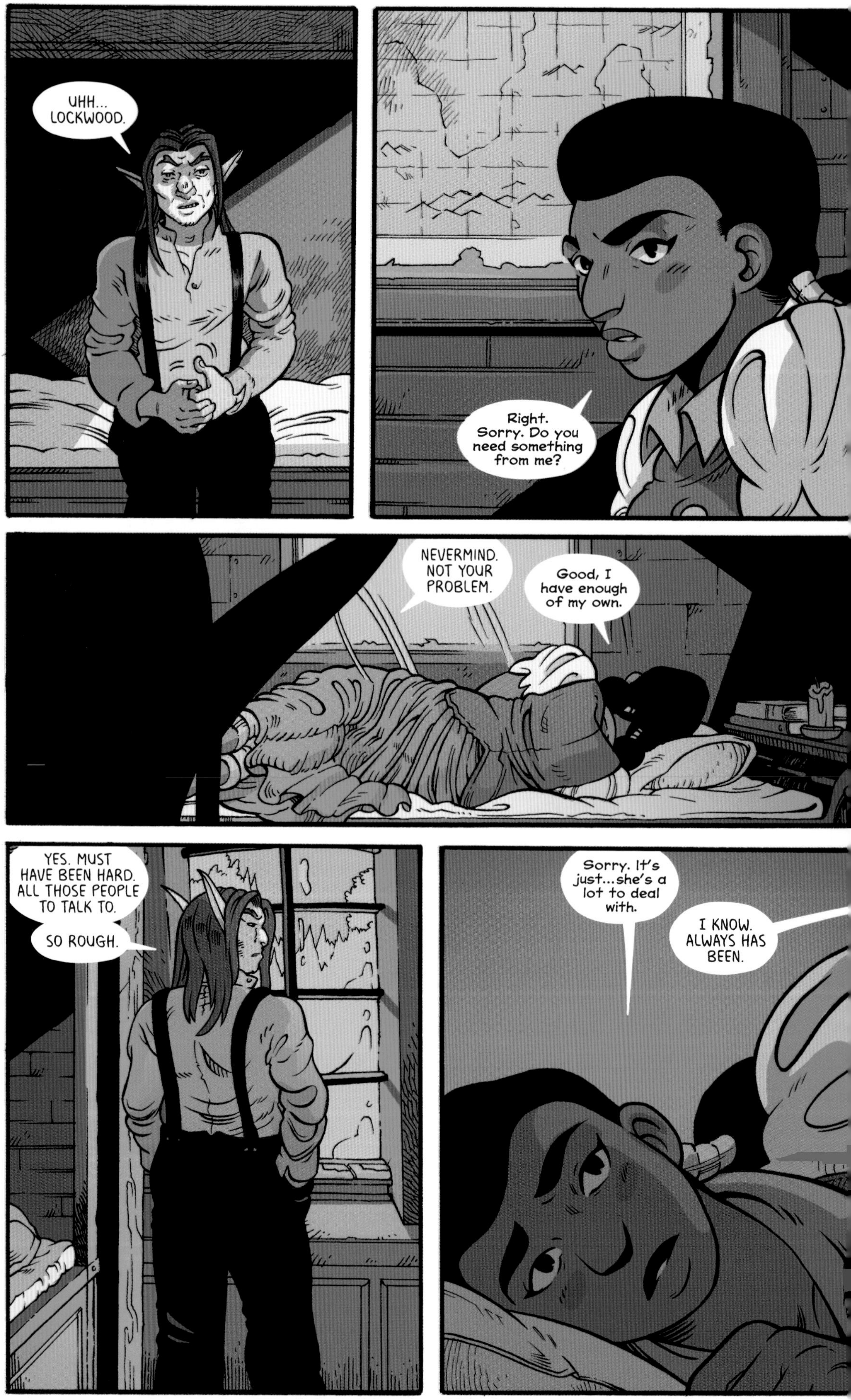
UHH... LOCKWOOD.
Right. Sorry. Do you need something from me?
NEVERMIND. NOT YOUR PROBLEM.
Good, I have enough of my own.
YES. MUST HAVE BEEN HARD. ALL THOSE PEOPLE TO TALK TO.
SO ROUGH.
Sorry. It's just...she's a lot to deal with.
I KNOW. ALWAYS HAS BEEN.

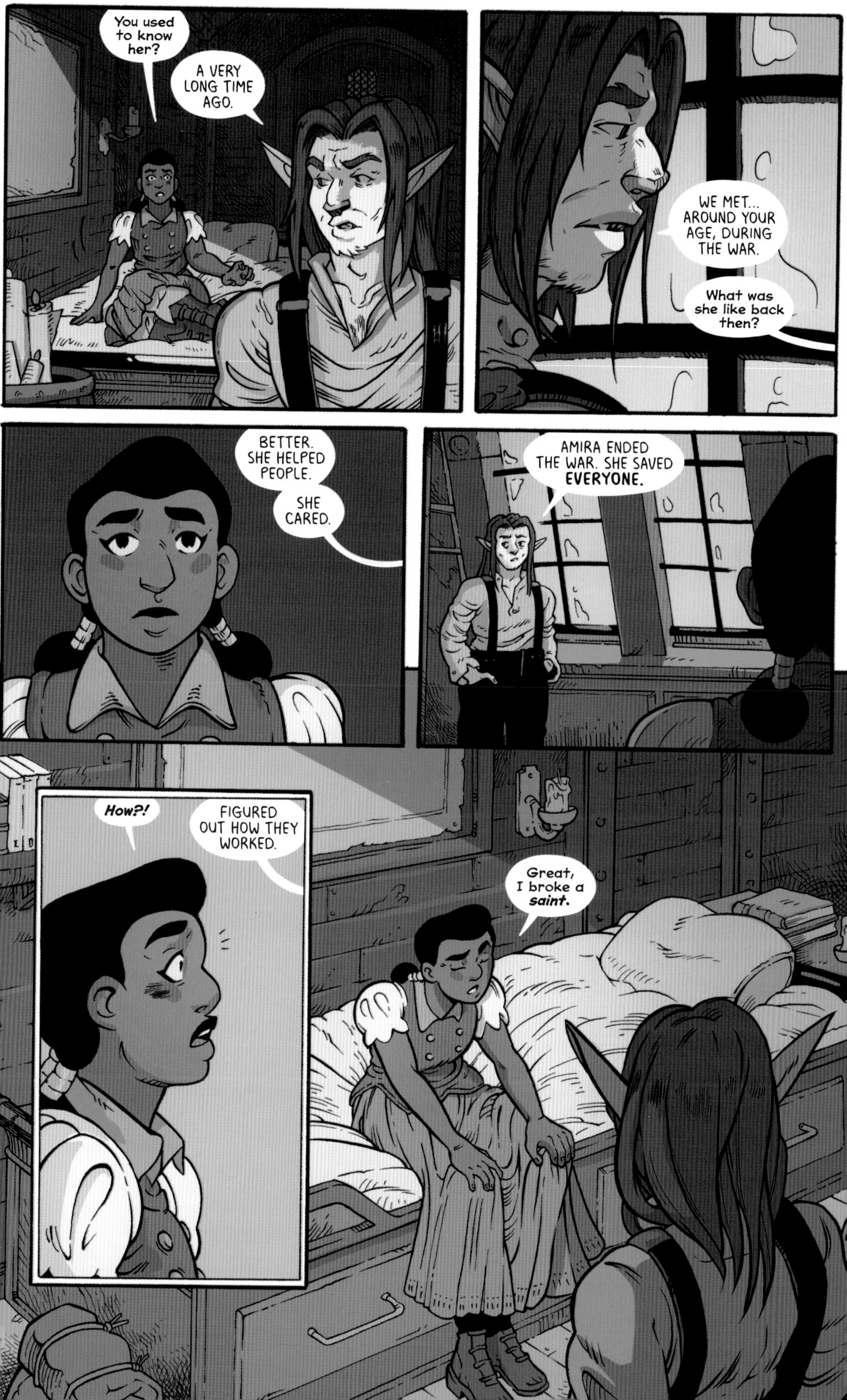
You used to know her?
A VERY LONG TIME AGO.
WE MET... AROUND YOUR AGE, DURING THE WAR.
What was she like back then?
BETTER. SHE HELPED PEOPLE.
SHE CARED.
AMIRA ENDED THE WAR. SHE SAVED **EVERYONE.**
How?!
FIGURED OUT HOW THEY WORKED.
Great, I broke a *saint*.

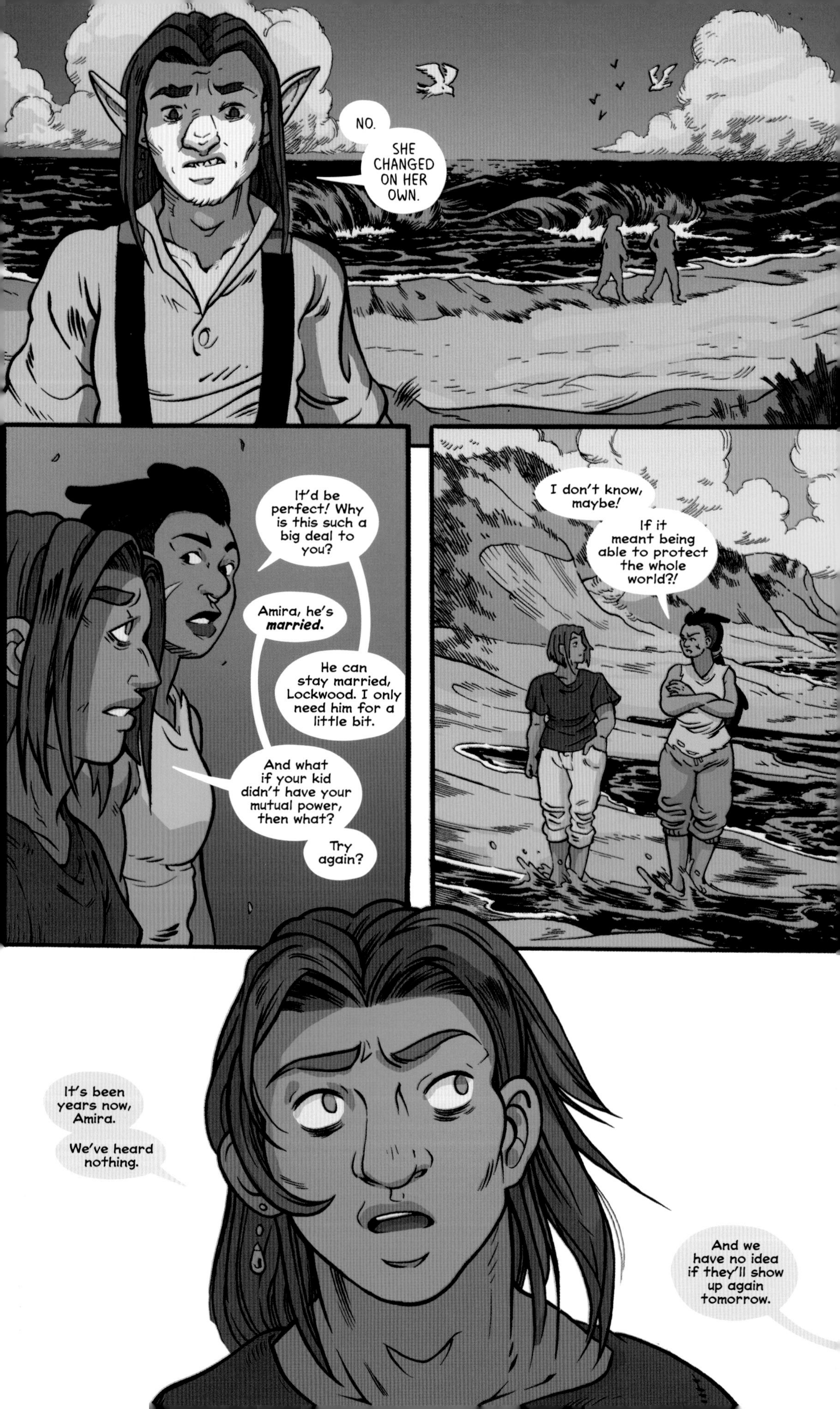

NO.
SHE CHANGED ON HER OWN.
It'd be perfect! Why is this such a big deal to you?
Amira, he's ***married.***
He can stay married, Lockwood. I only need him for a little bit.
And what if your kid didn't have your mutual power, then what?
Try again?
I don't know, maybe!
If it meant being able to protect the whole world?!
It's been years now, Amira.
We've heard nothing.
And we have no idea if they'll show up again tomorrow.

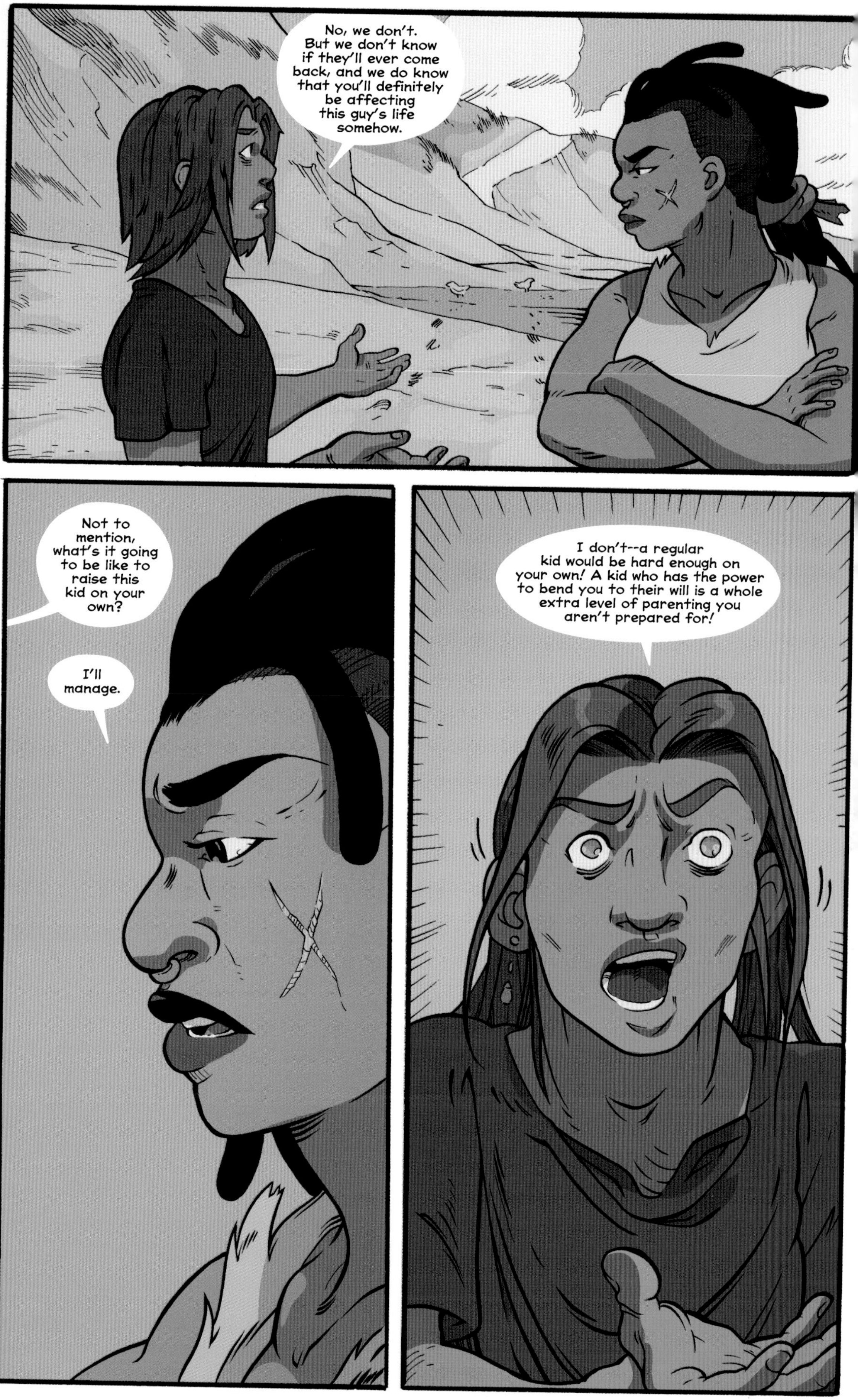

No, we don't. But we don't know if they'll ever come back, and we do know that you'll definitely be affecting this guy's life somehow.
Not to mention, what's it going to be like to raise this kid on your own?
I'll manage.
I don't--a regular kid would be hard enough on your own! A kid who has the power to bend you to their will is a whole extra level of parenting you aren't prepared for!

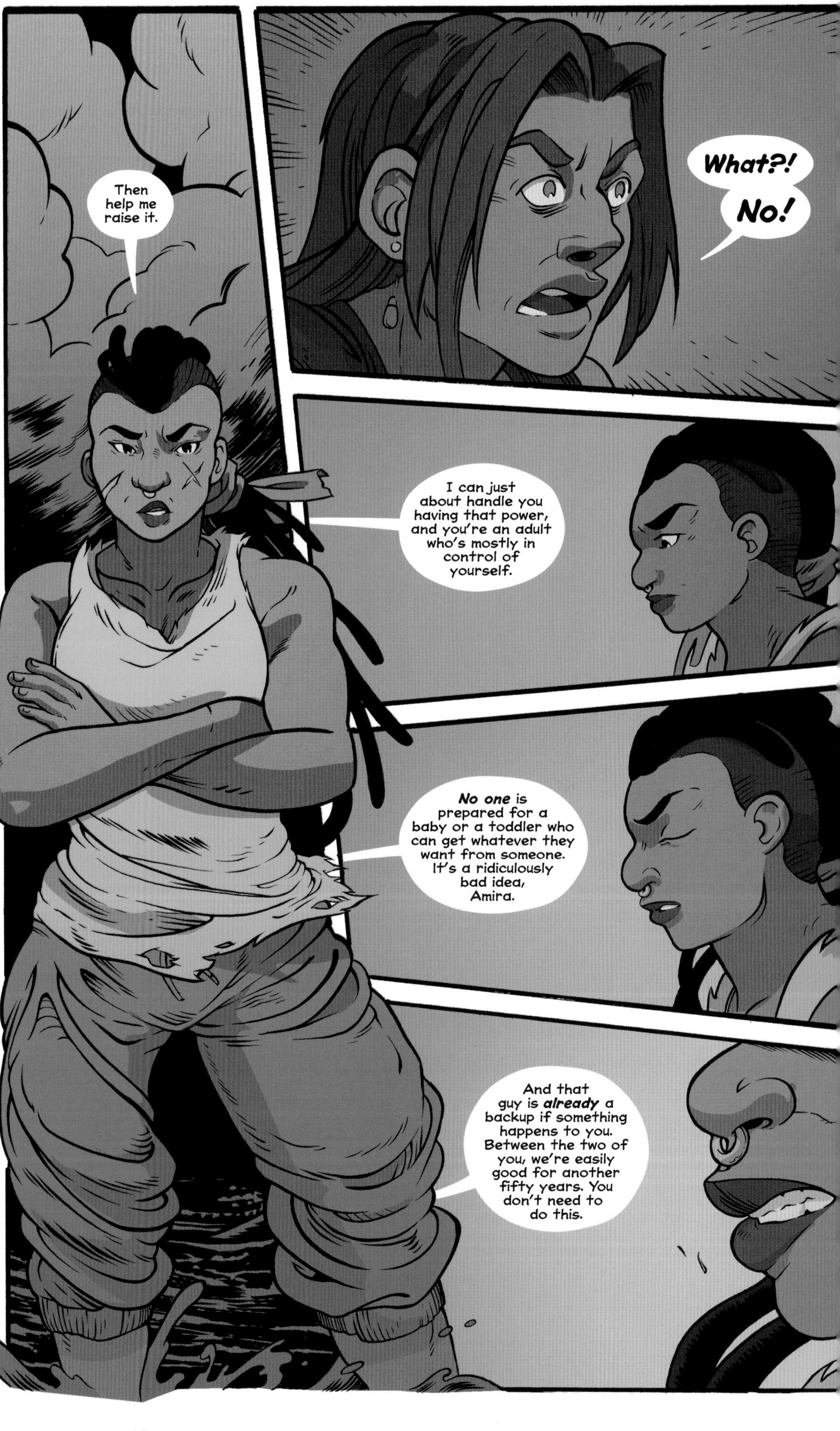
Then help me raise it.
What?! No!
I can just about handle you having that power, and you're an adult who's mostly in control of yourself.
No one is prepared for a baby or a toddler who can get whatever they want from someone. It's a ridiculously bad idea, Amira.
And that guy is *already* a backup if something happens to you. Between the two of you, we're easily good for another fifty years. You don't need to do this.

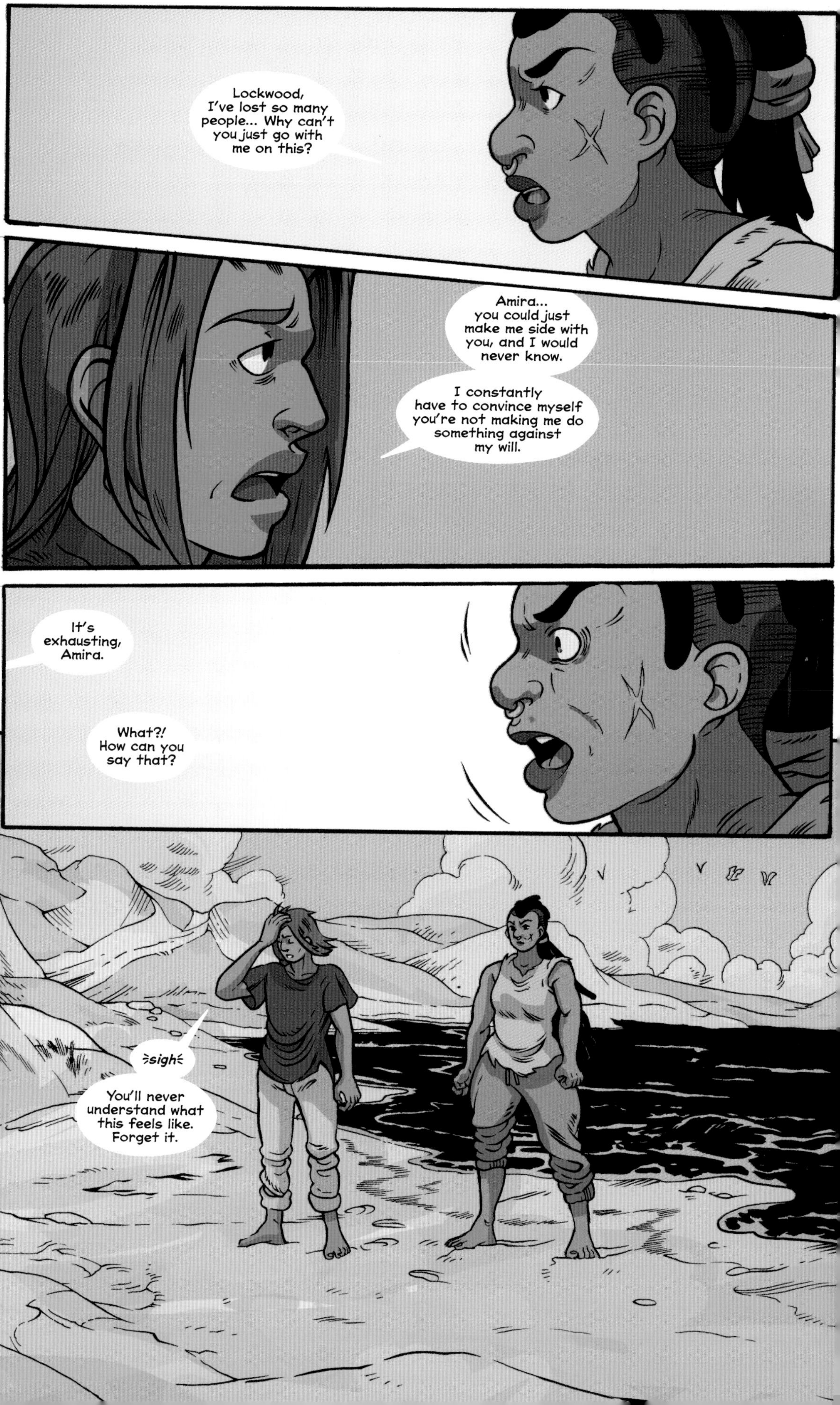
Lockwood, I've lost so many people... Why can't you just go with me on this?
Amira... you could just make me side with you, and I would never know.
I constantly have to convince myself you're not making me do something against my will.
It's exhausting, Amira.
What?! How can you say that?
⇒sigh⇐
You'll never understand what this feels like. Forget it.

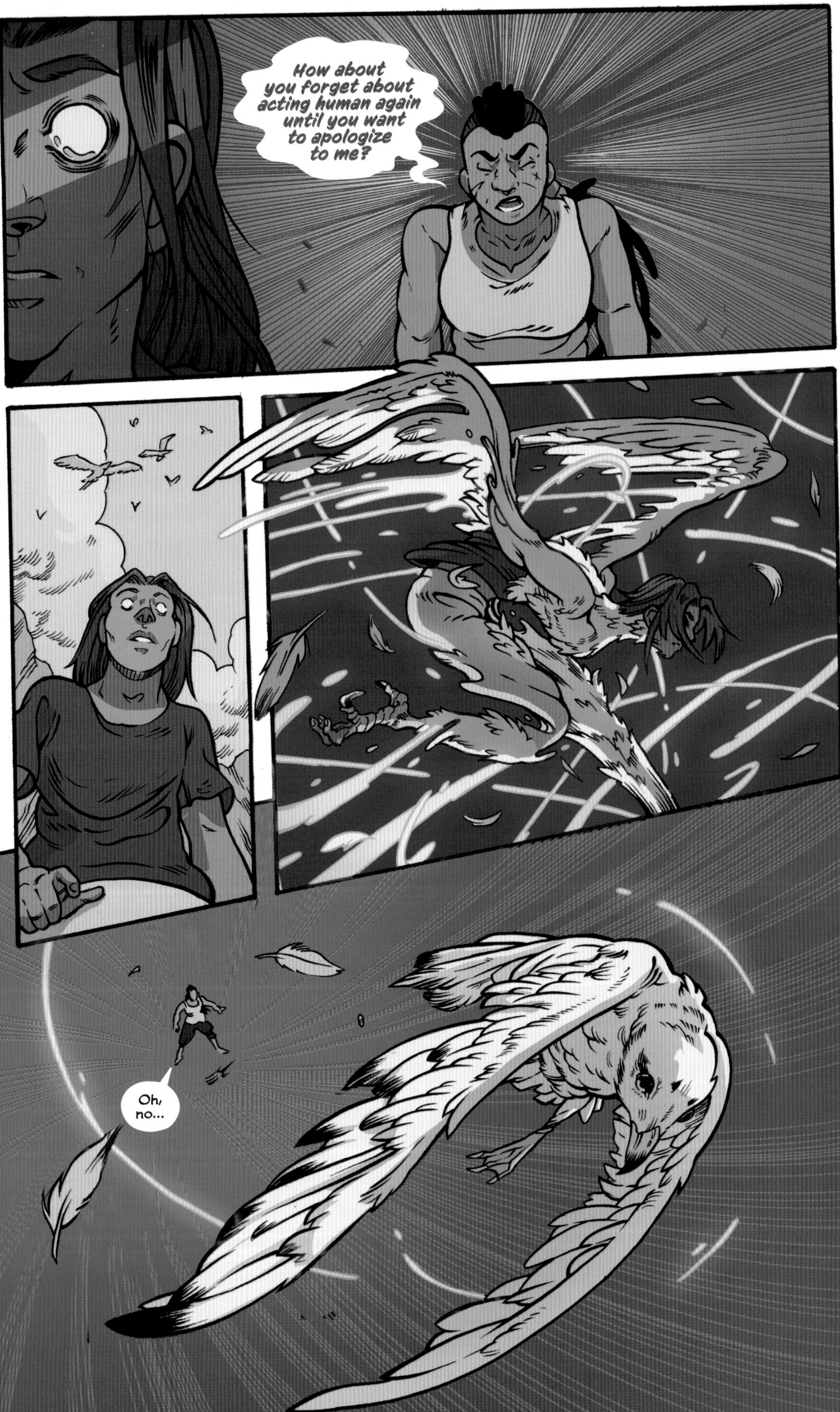
How about you forget about acting human again until you want to apologize to me?
Oh, no...

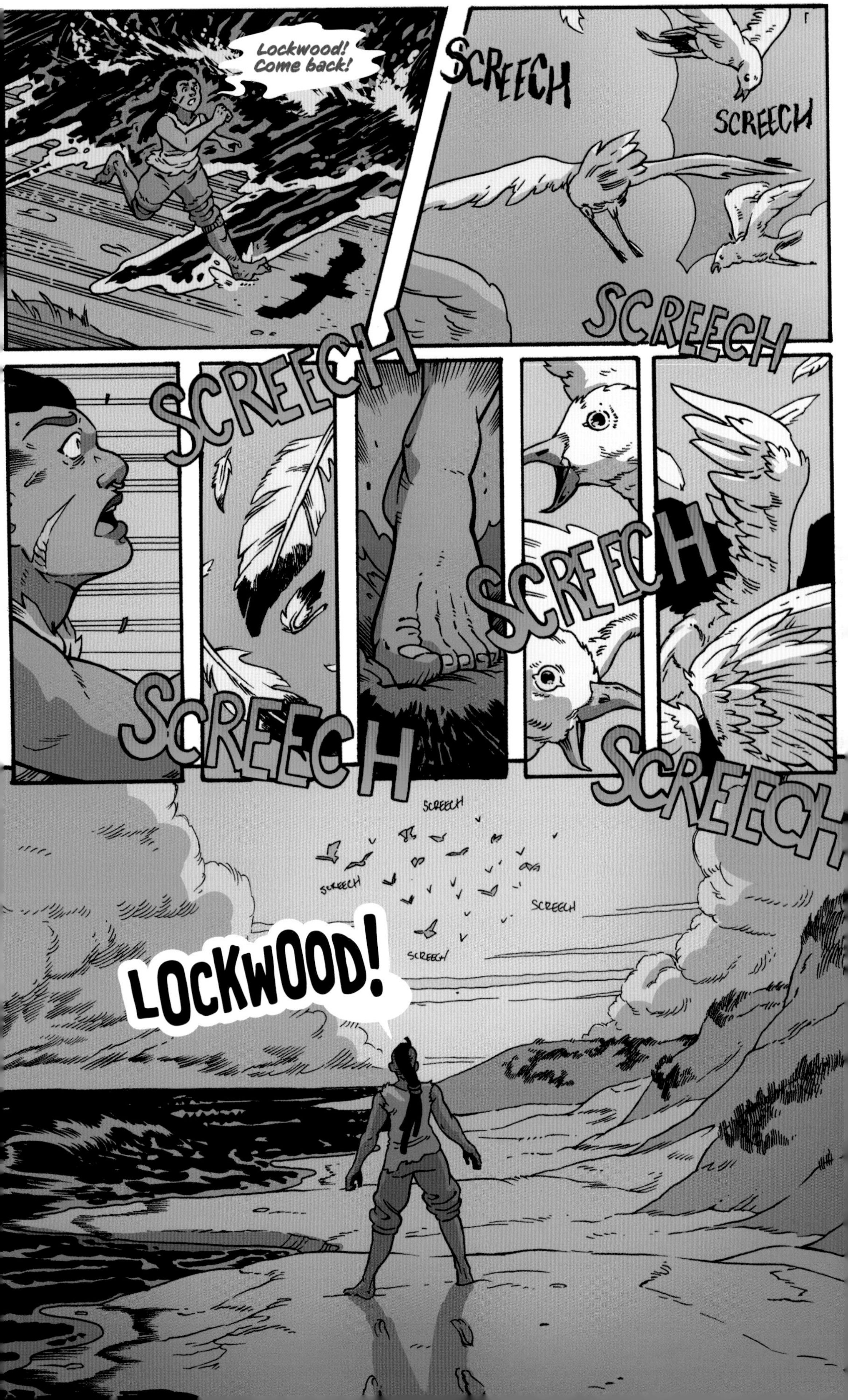
Lockwood! Come back!
SCREECH
SCREECH
SCREECH
SCREECH
SCREECH
SCREECH
SCREECH
SCREECH
SCREECH
SCREECH
SCREECH
SCREECH
LOCKWOOD!

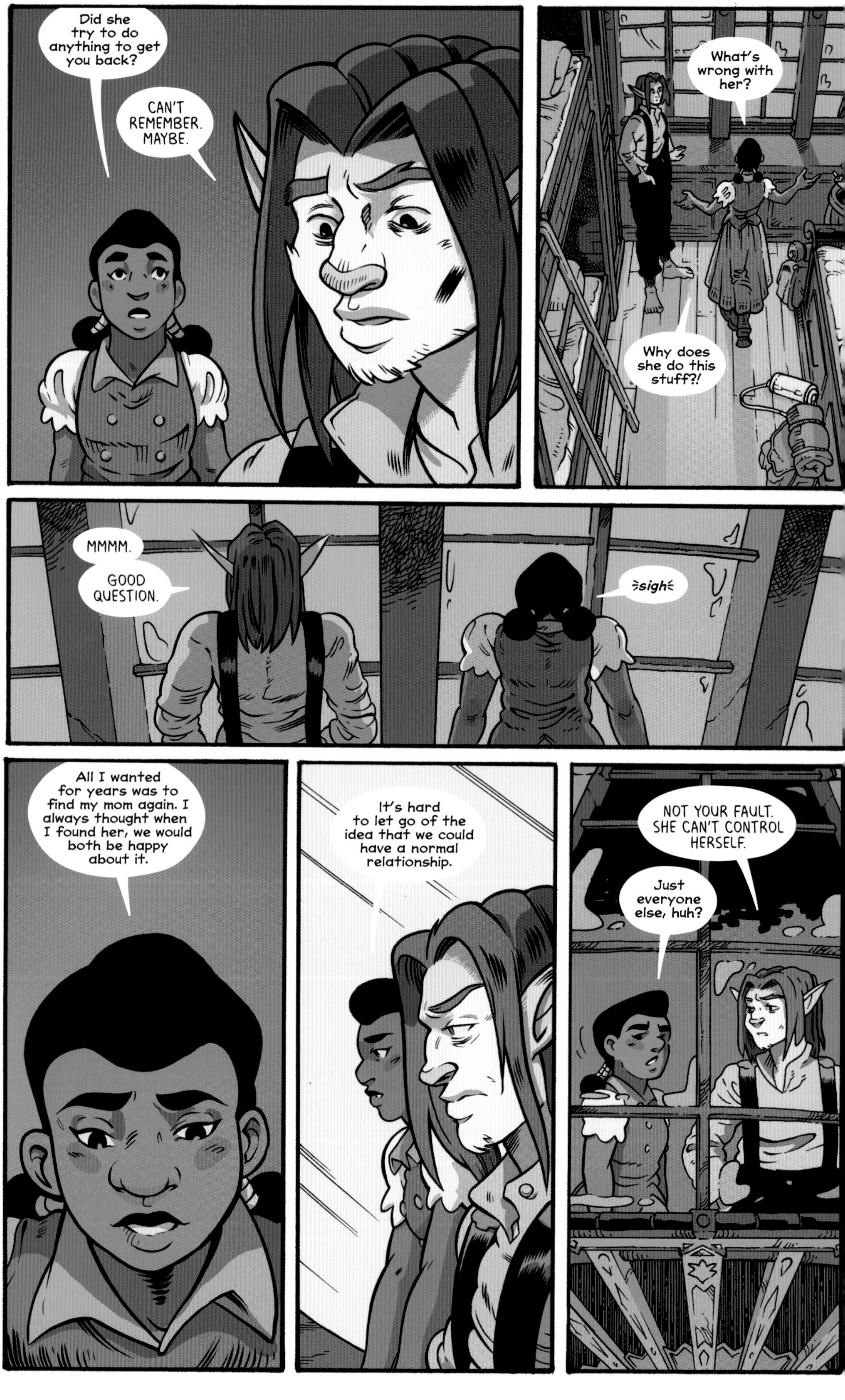
Did she try to do anything to get you back?
CAN'T REMEMBER. MAYBE.
What's wrong with her?
Why does she do this stuff?!
MMMM.
GOOD QUESTION.
≈sigh≈
All I wanted for years was to find my mom again. I always thought when I found her, we would both be happy about it.
It's hard to let go of the idea that we could have a normal relationship.
NOT YOUR FAULT. SHE CAN'T CONTROL HERSELF.
Just everyone else, huh?

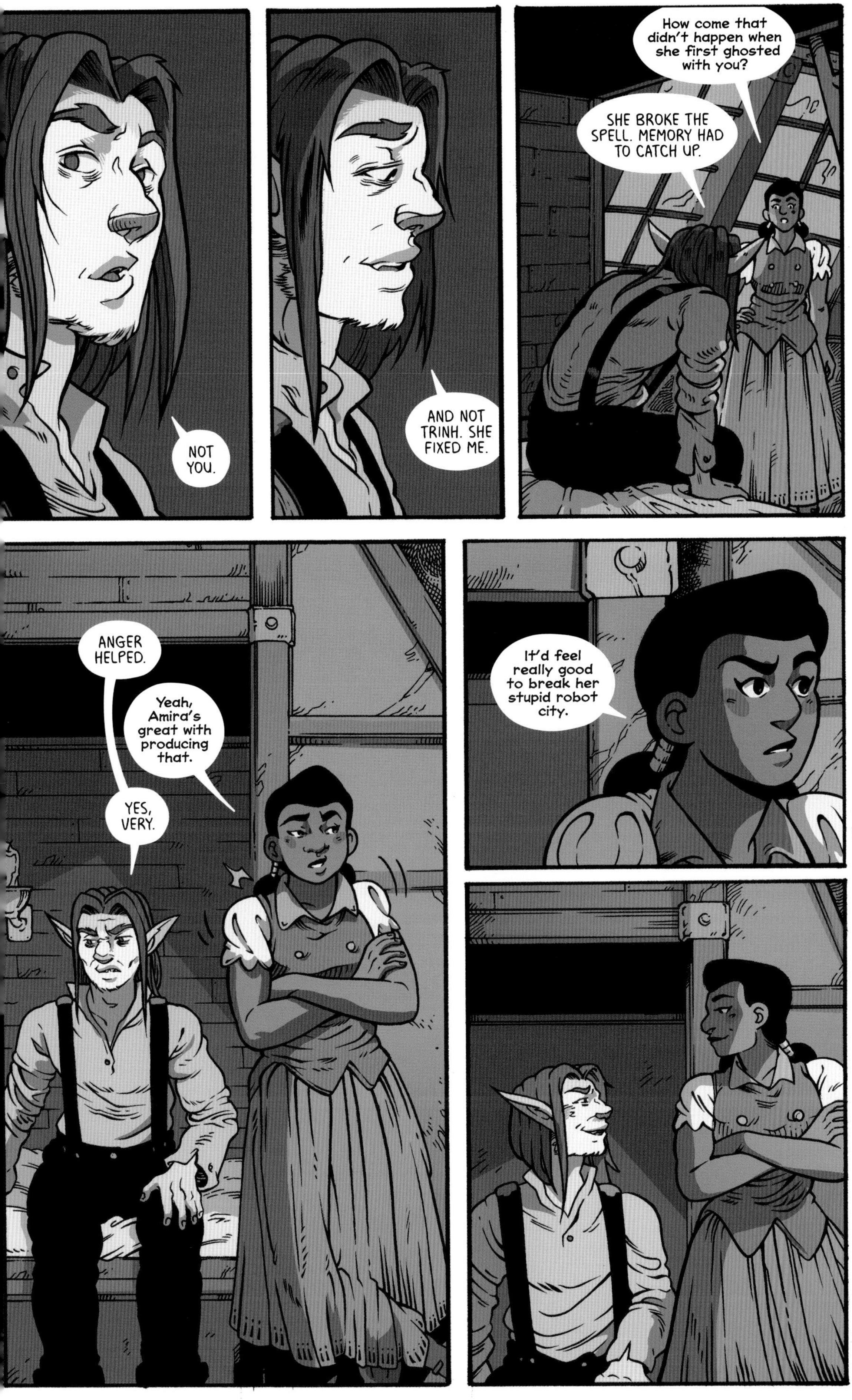

NOT YOU.
AND NOT TRINH. SHE FIXED ME.
How come that didn't happen when she first ghosted with you?
SHE BROKE THE SPELL. MEMORY HAD TO CATCH UP.
ANGER HELPED.
Yeah, Amira's great with producing that.
YES, VERY.
It'd feel really good to break her stupid robot city.

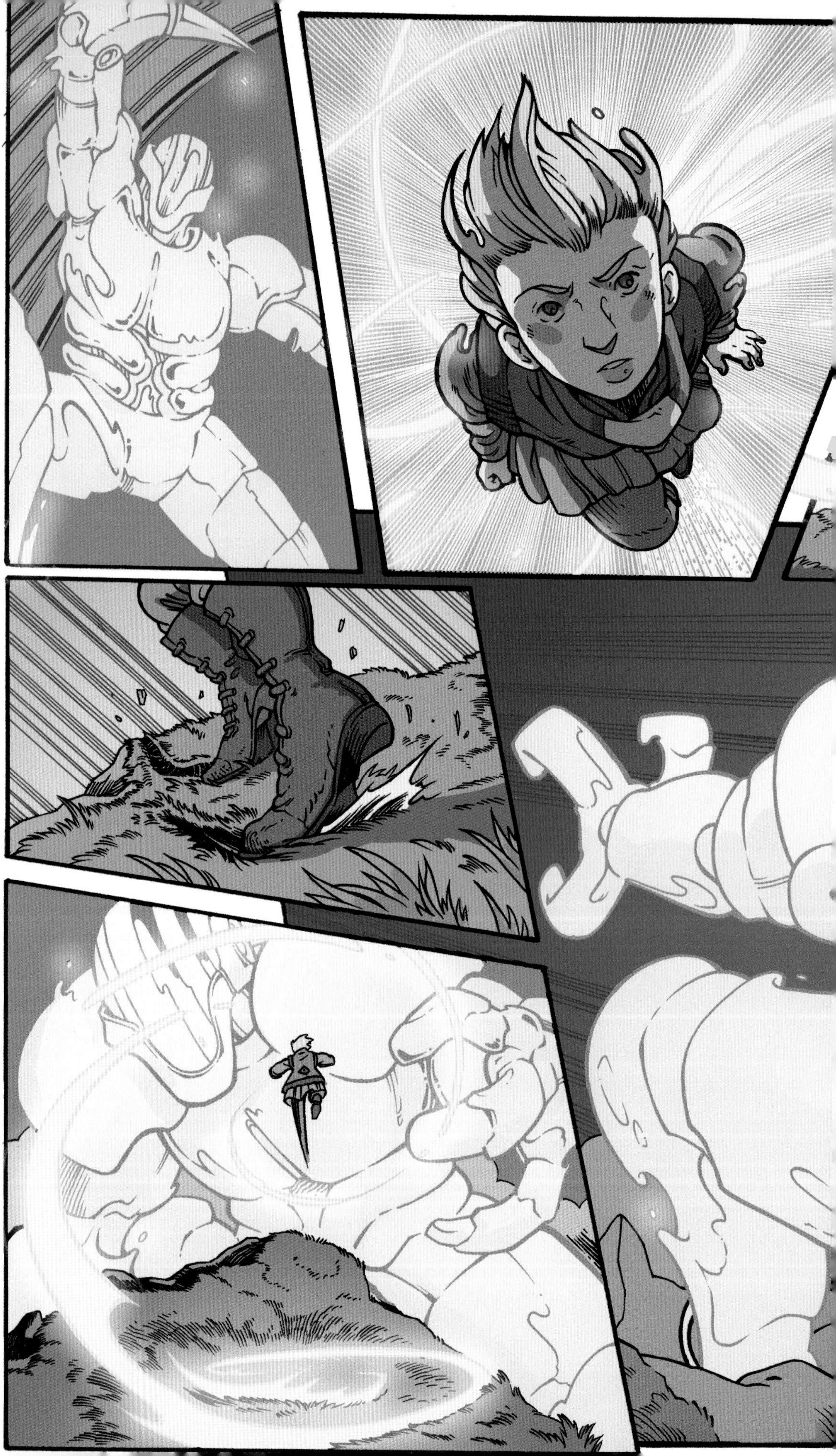

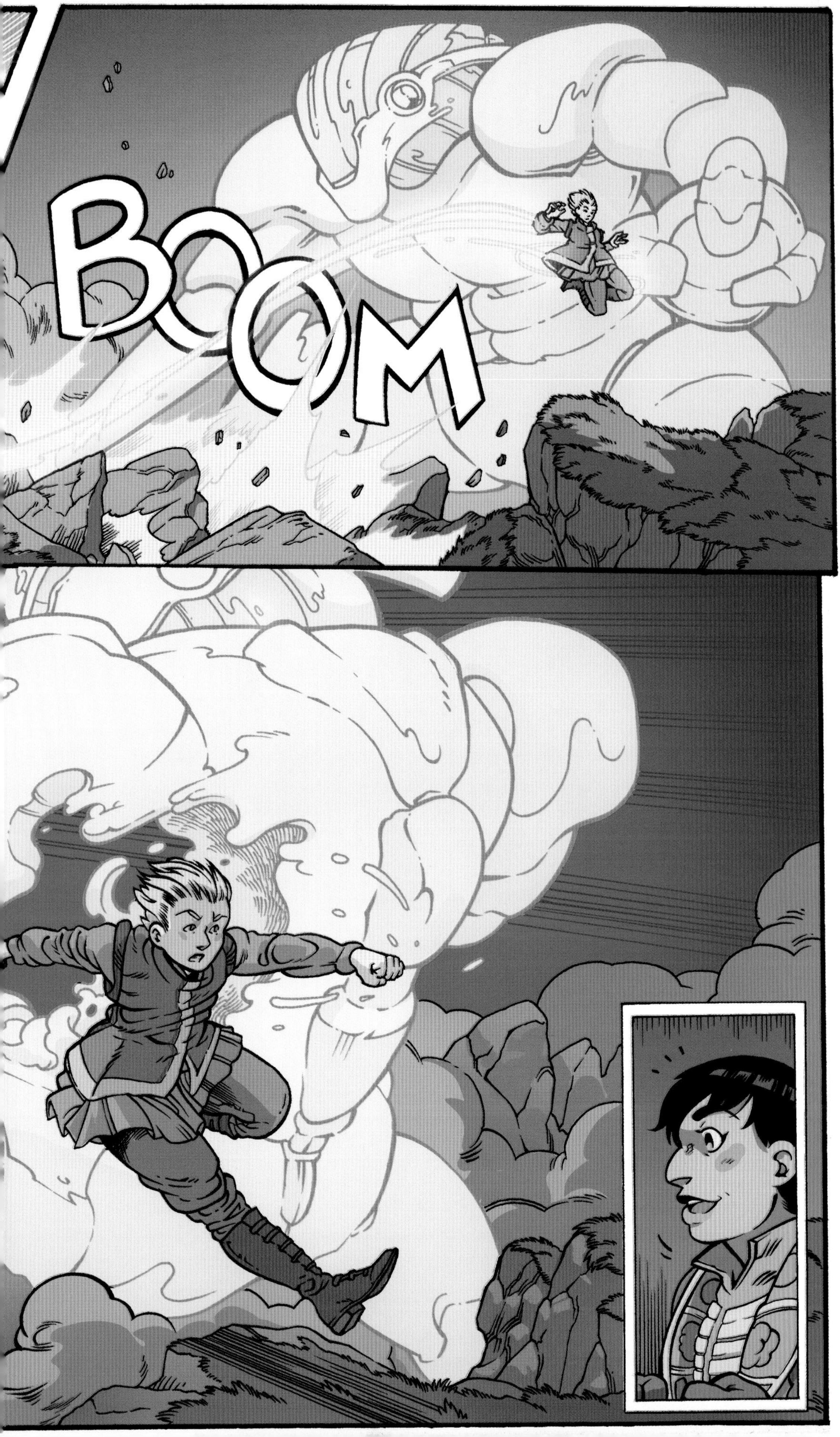
BOOM

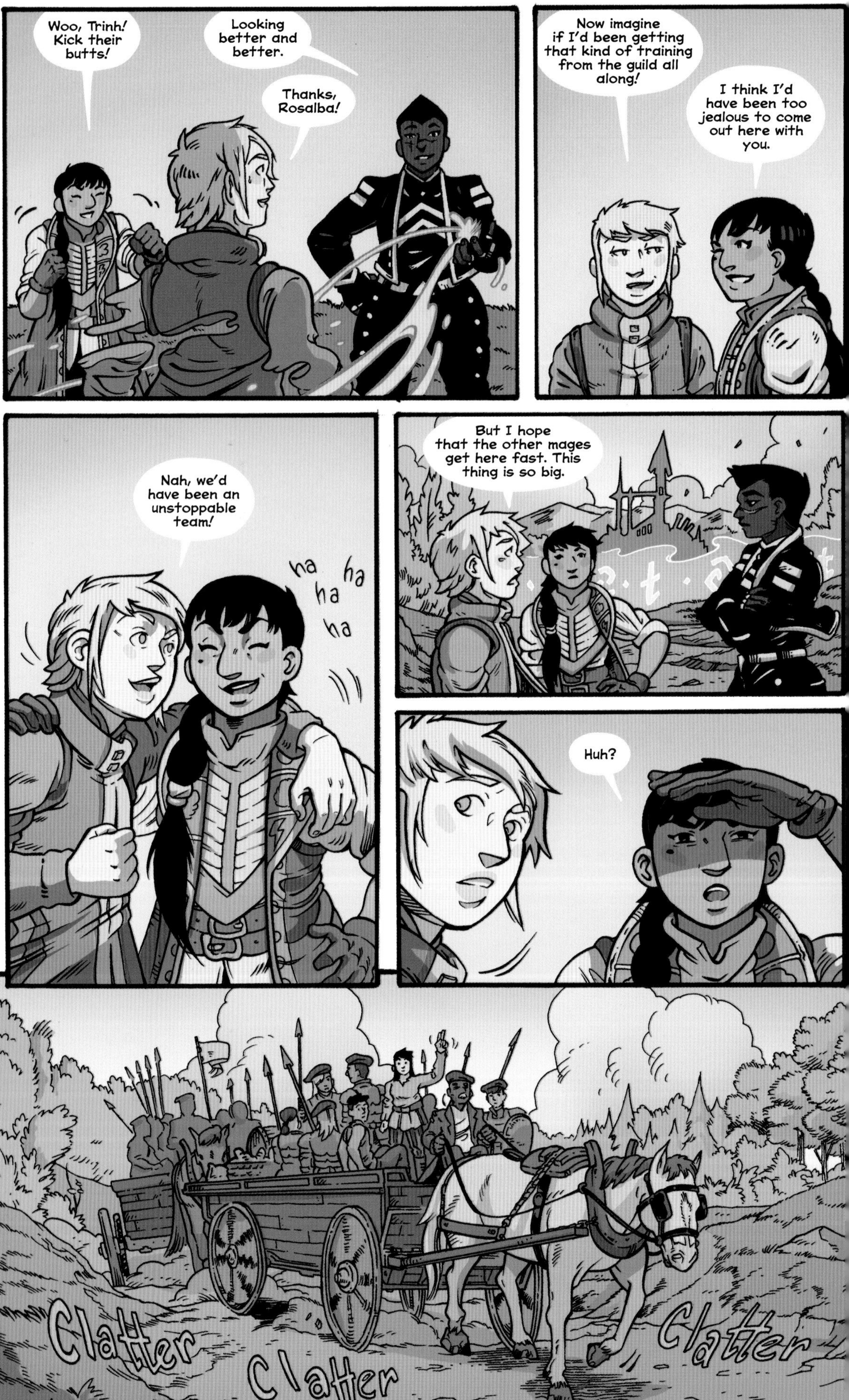
Woo, Trinh! Kick their butts!
Looking better and better.
Thanks, Rosalba!
Now imagine if I'd been getting that kind of training from the guild all along!
I think I'd have been too jealous to come out here with you.
Nah, we'd have been an unstoppable team!
ha ha ha ha
But I hope that the other mages get here fast. This thing is so big.
Huh?
Clatter
Clatter
Clatter

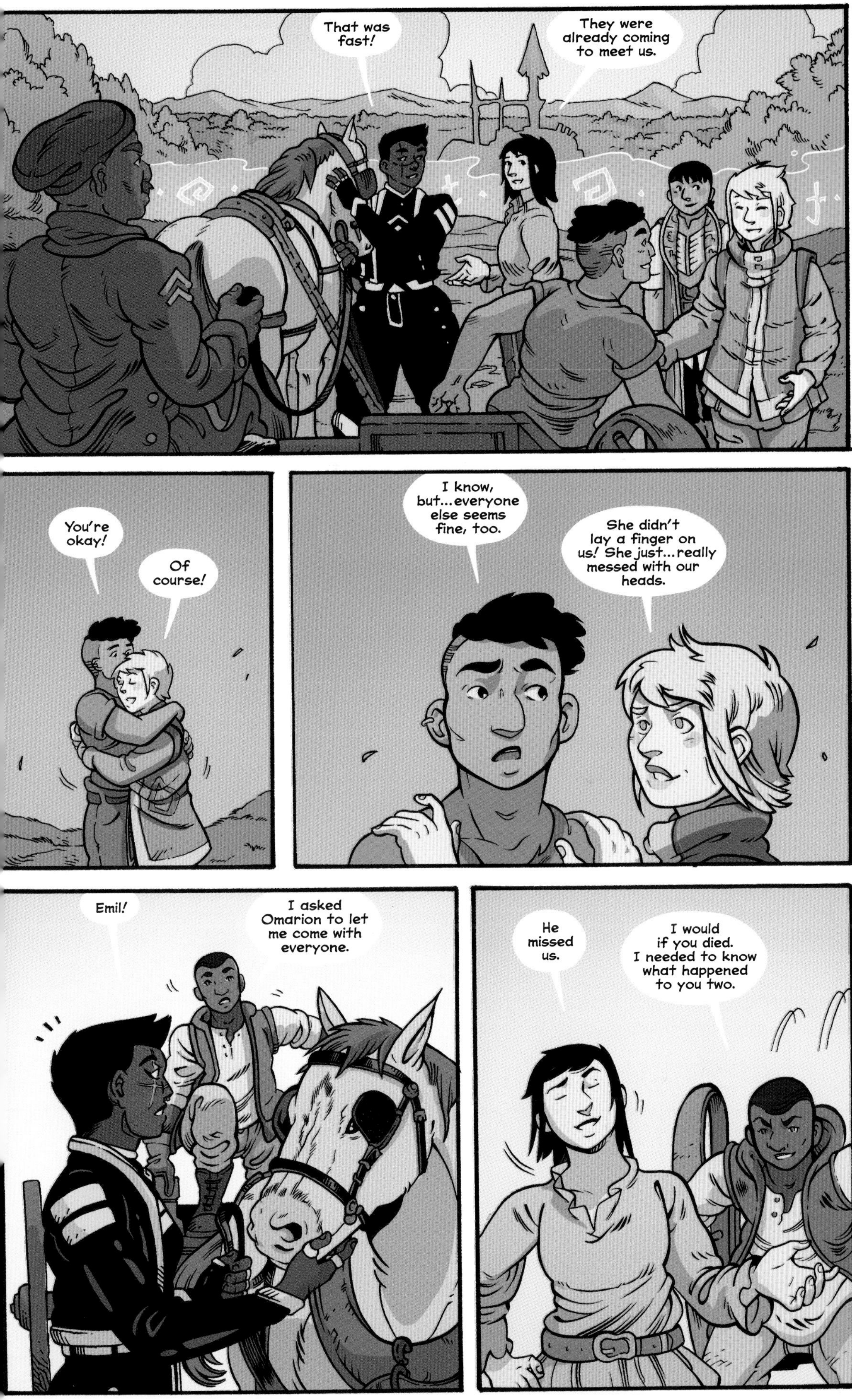
That was fast!
They were already coming to meet us.
You're okay!
Of course!
I know, but...everyone else seems fine, too.
She didn't lay a finger on us! She just...really messed with our heads.
Emil!
I asked Omarion to let me come with everyone.
He missed us.
I would if you died. I needed to know what happened to you two.

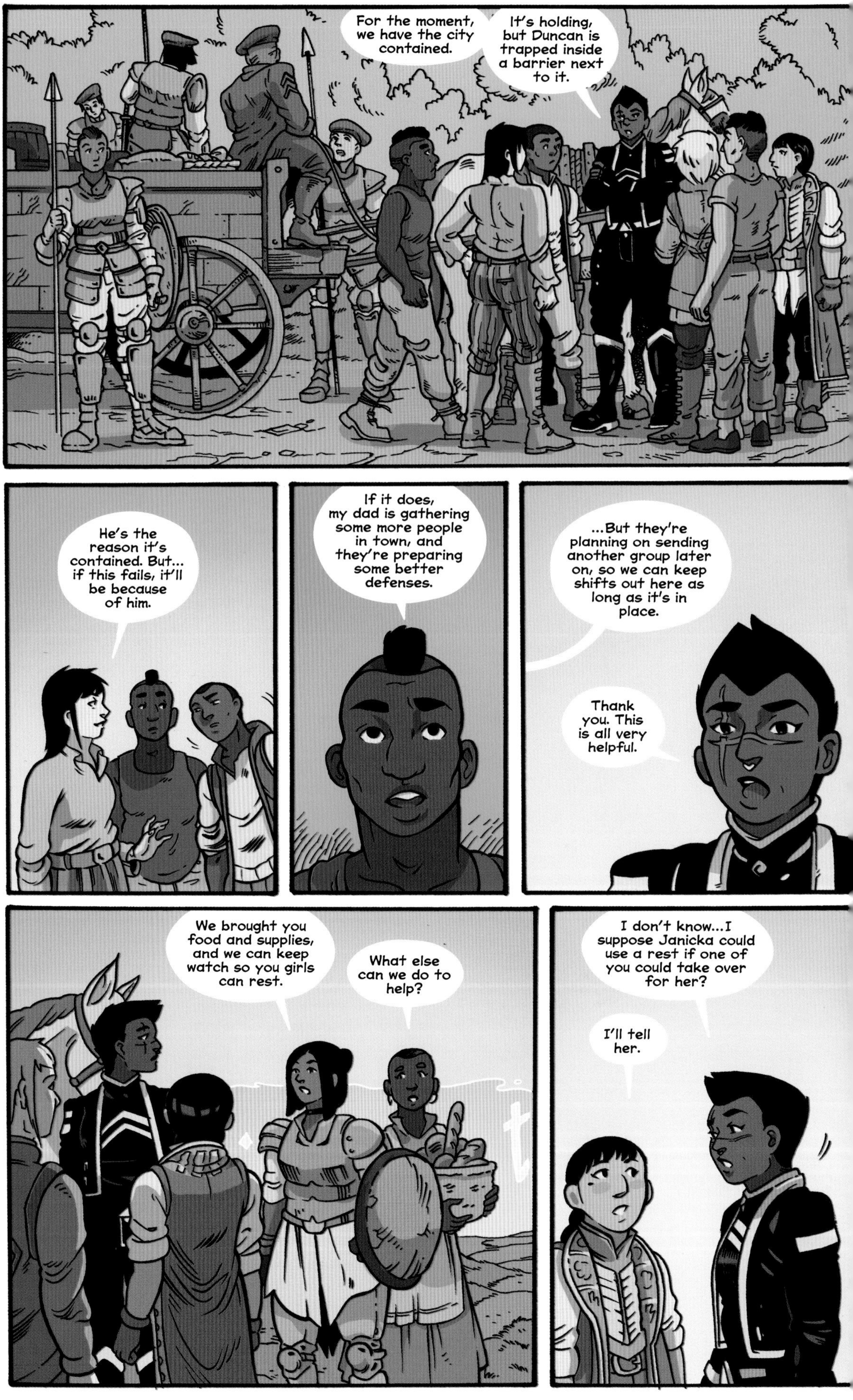
For the moment, we have the city contained.
It's holding, but Duncan is trapped inside a barrier next to it.
He's the reason it's contained. But... if this fails, it'll be because of him.
If it does, my dad is gathering some more people in town, and they're preparing some better defenses.
...But they're planning on sending another group later on, so we can keep shifts out here as long as it's in place.
Thank you. This is all very helpful.
We brought you food and supplies, and we can keep watch so you girls can rest.
What else can we do to help?
I don't know...I suppose Janicka could use a rest if one of you could take over for her?
I'll tell her.

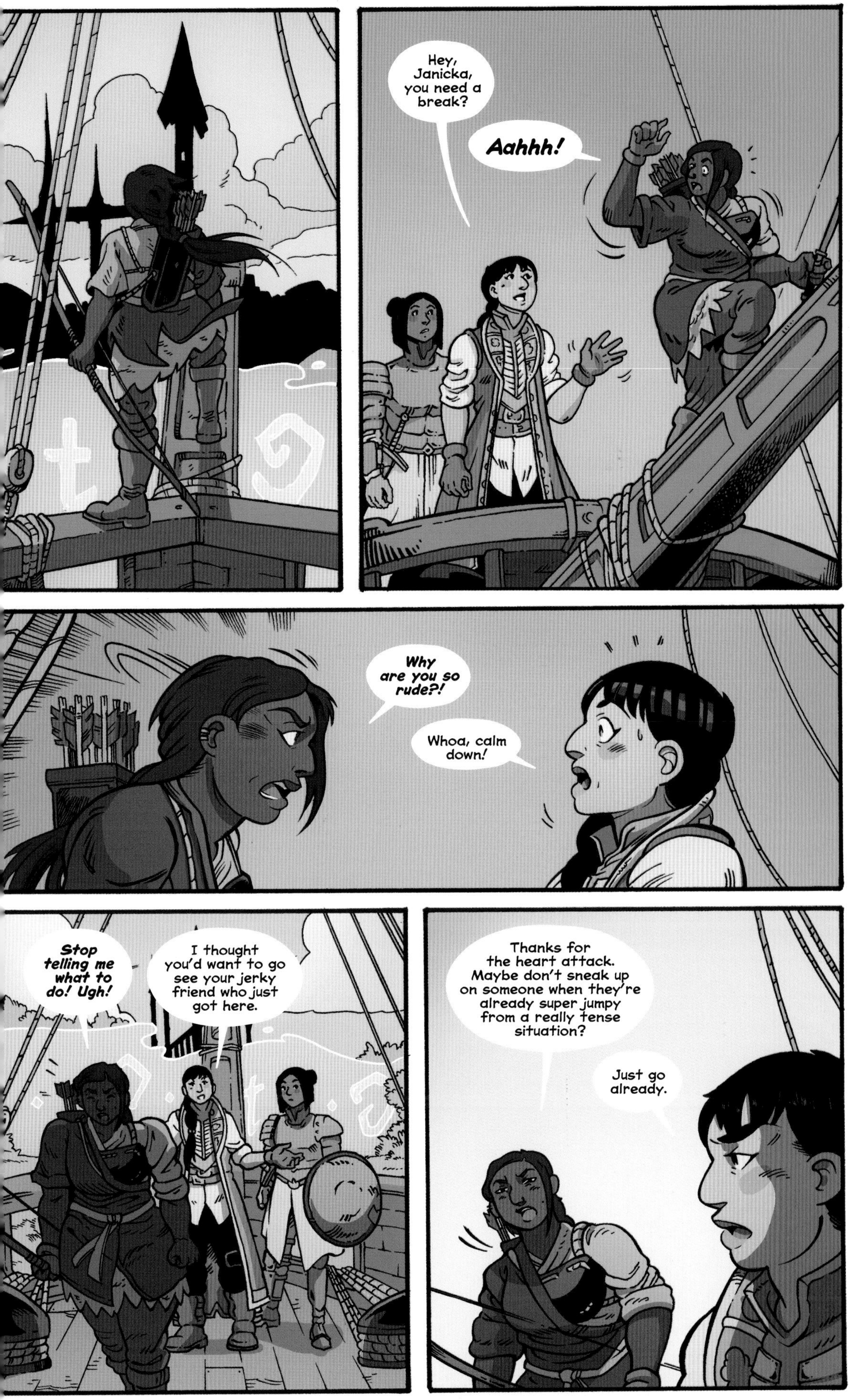
Hey, Janicka, you need a break?
Aahhh!
Why are you so rude?!
Whoa, calm down!
Stop telling me what to do! Ugh!
I thought you'd want to go see your jerky friend who just got here.
Thanks for the heart attack. Maybe don't sneak up on someone when they're already super jumpy from a really tense situation?
Just go already.

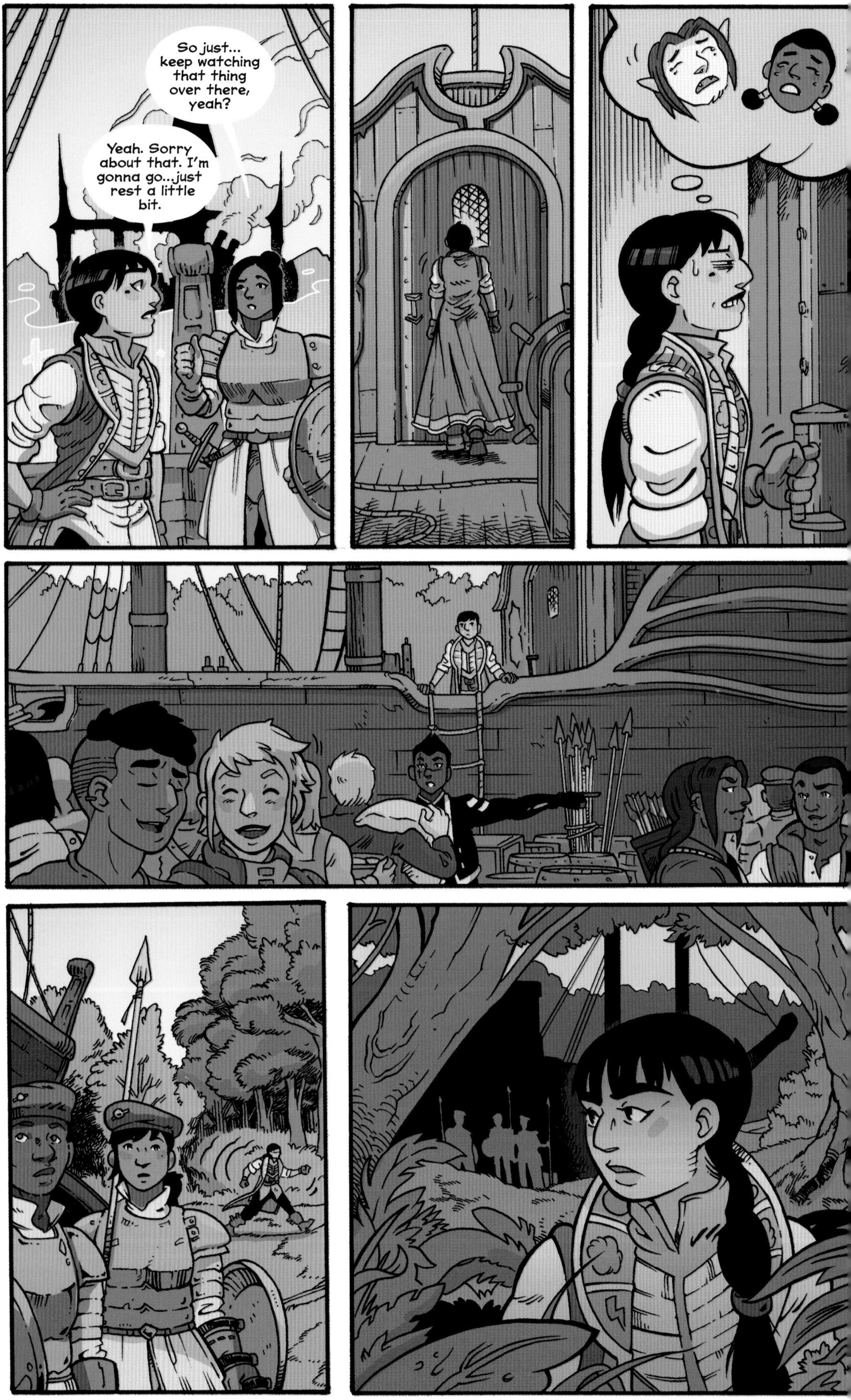
So just... keep watching that thing over there, yeah?
Yeah. Sorry about that. I'm gonna go...just rest a little bit.

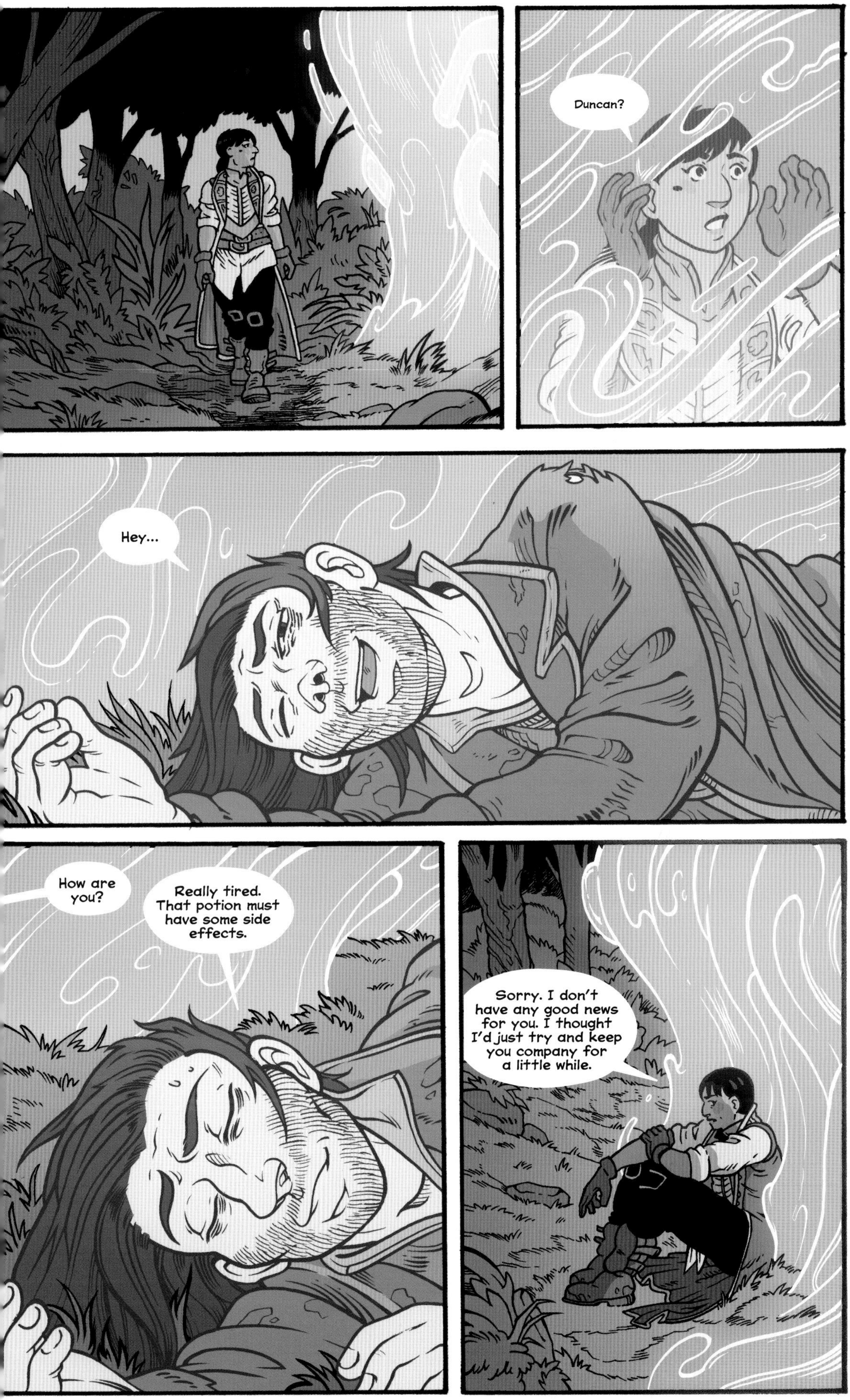
Duncan?
Hey...
How are you?
Really tired. That potion must have some side effects.
Sorry. I don't have any good news for you. I thought I'd just try and keep you company for a little while.

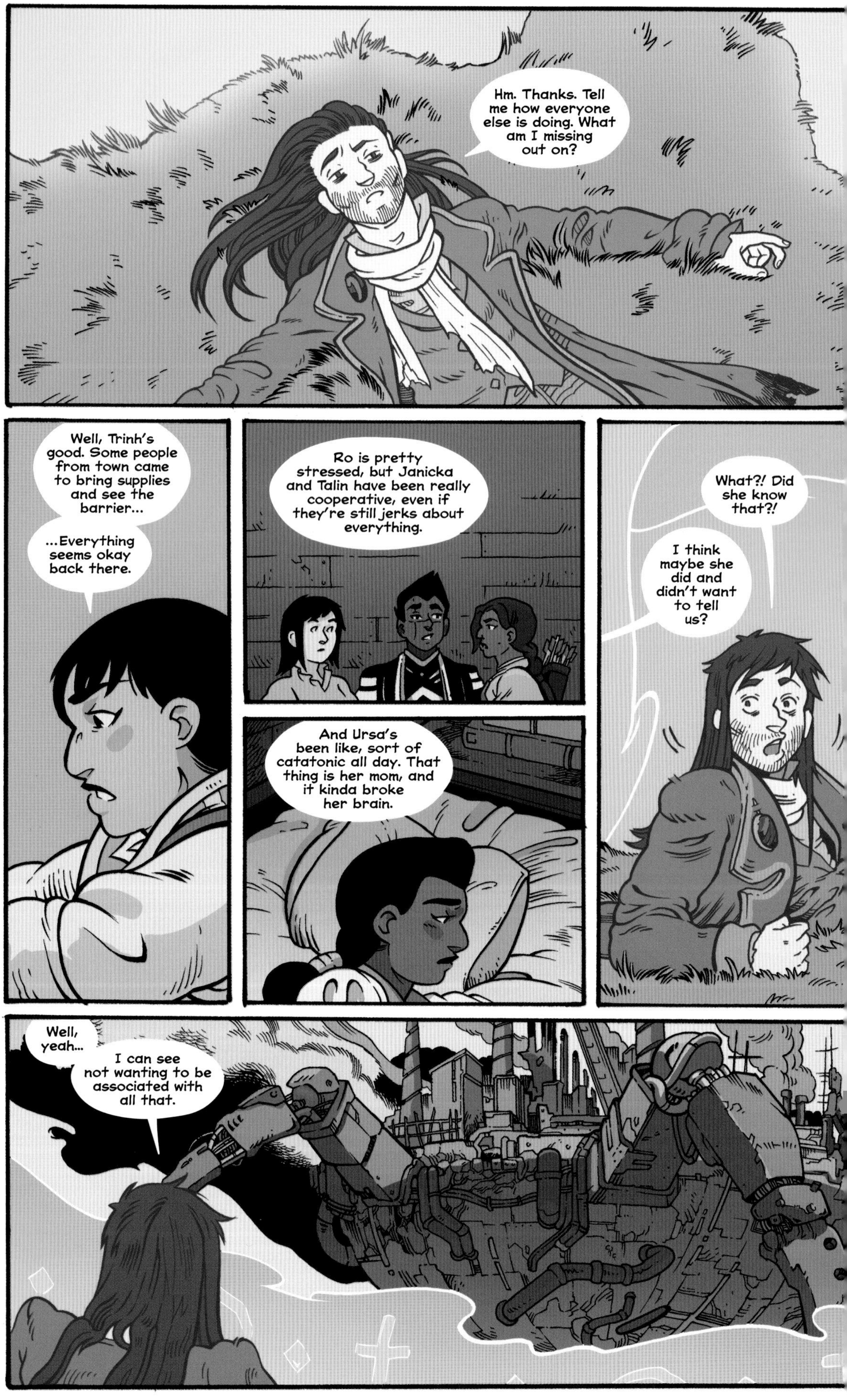

Hm. Thanks. Tell me how everyone else is doing. What am I missing out on?
Well, Trinh's good. Some people from town came to bring supplies and see the barrier...
...Everything seems okay back there.
Ro is pretty stressed, but Janicka and Talin have been really cooperative, even if they're still jerks about everything.
And Ursa's been like, sort of catatonic all day. That thing is her mom, and it kinda broke her brain.
What?! Did she know that?!
I think maybe she did and didn't want to tell us?
Well, yeah...
I can see not wanting to be associated with all that.

Yeah. I feel dumb for not realizing it sooner.

I've been feeling pretty dumb lately.

I don't know what I'm doing out here.

When we left, I didn't know what Ursa and Trinh could do, and I thought they were gonna hold me back.

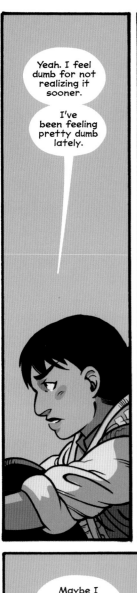

But they can kick everything's butt without me. They don't look it, but they're really strong.

Maybe I should be doing something else. I don't know if they need me.

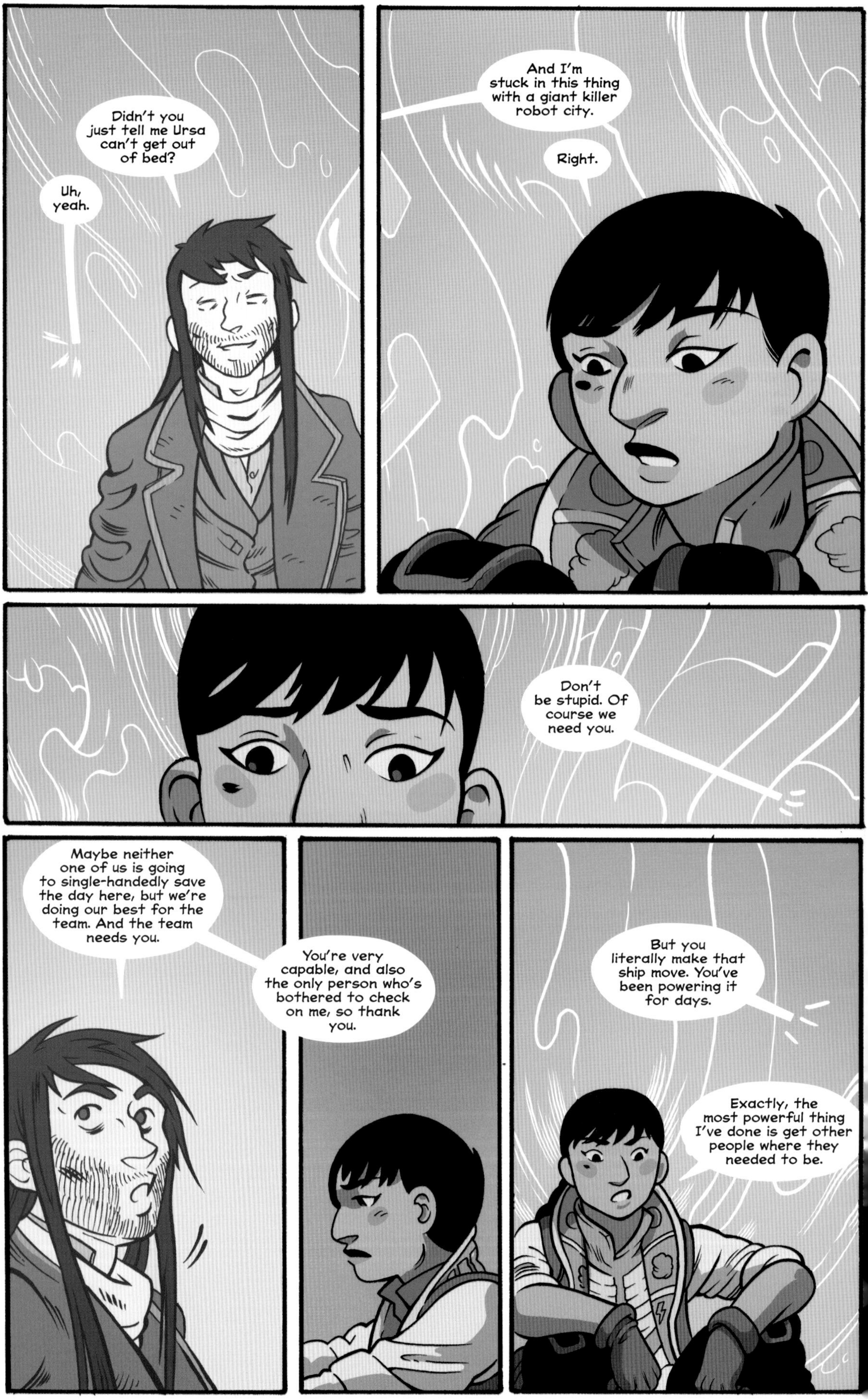
Didn't you just tell me Ursa can't get out of bed?
Uh, yeah.
And I'm stuck in this thing with a giant killer robot city.
Right.
Don't be stupid. Of course we need you.
Maybe neither one of us is going to single-handedly save the day here, but we're doing our best for the team. And the team needs you.
You're very capable, and also the only person who's bothered to check on me, so thank you.
But you literally make that ship move. You've been powering it for days.
Exactly, the most powerful thing I've done is get other people where they needed to be.

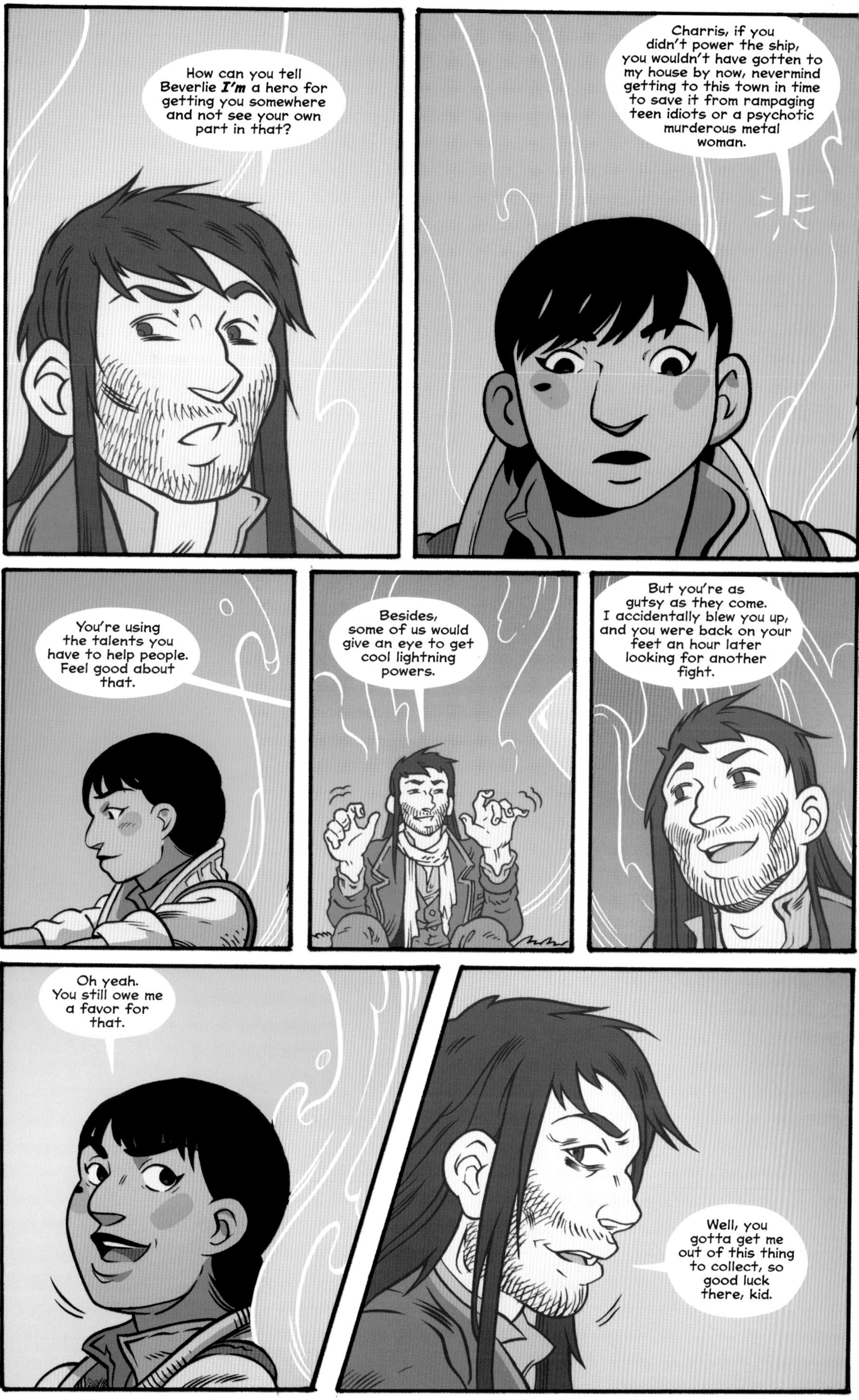

How can you tell Beverlie *I'm* a hero for getting you somewhere and not see your own part in that?
Charris, if you didn't power the ship, you wouldn't have gotten to my house by now, nevermind getting to this town in time to save it from rampaging teen idiots or a psychotic murderous metal woman.
You're using the talents you have to help people. Feel good about that.
Besides, some of us would give an eye to get cool lightning powers.
But you're as gutsy as they come. I accidentally blew you up, and you were back on your feet an hour later looking for another fight.
Oh yeah. You still owe me a favor for that.
Well, you gotta get me out of this thing to collect, so good luck there, kid.

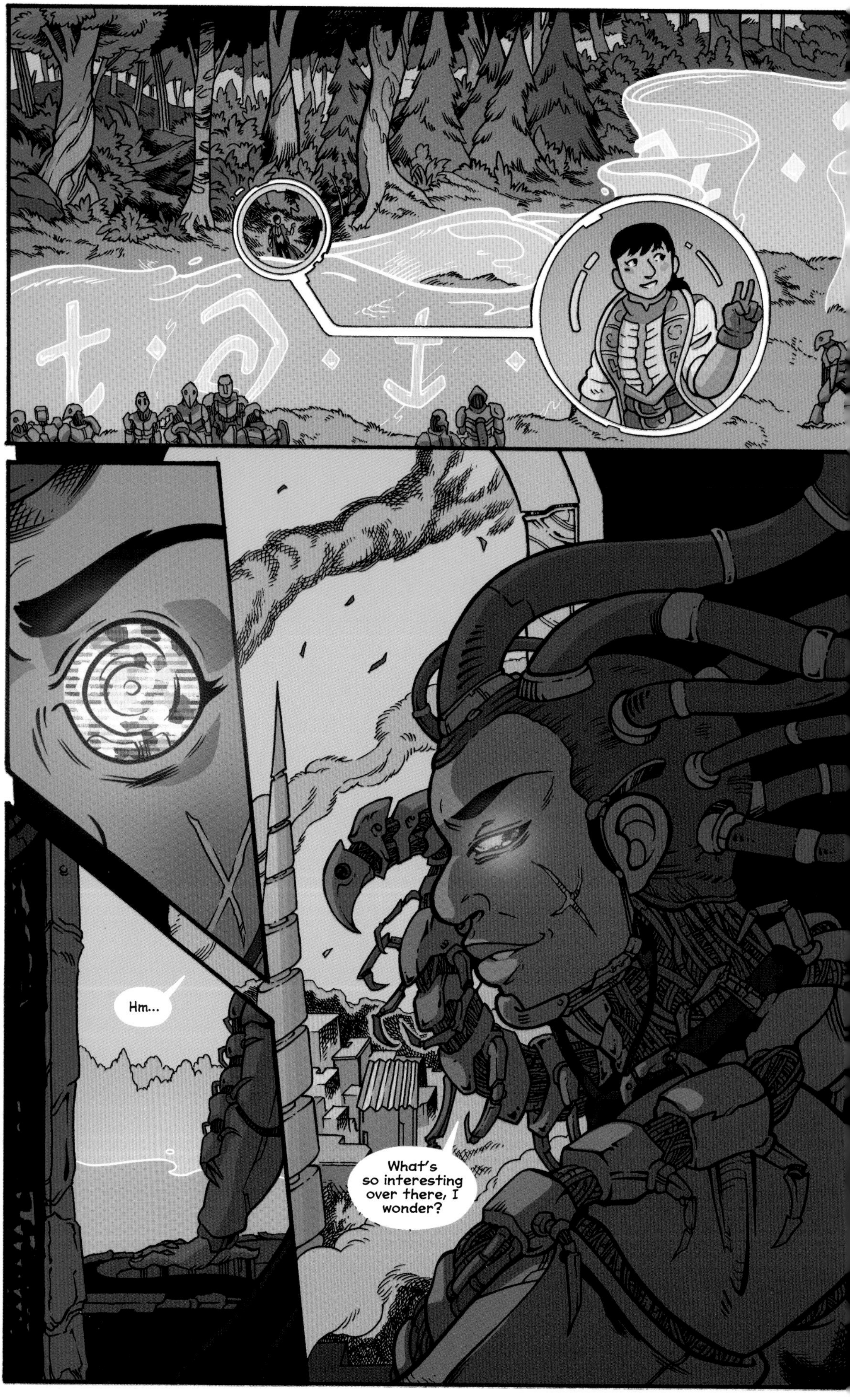
Hm...
What's so interesting over there, I wonder?

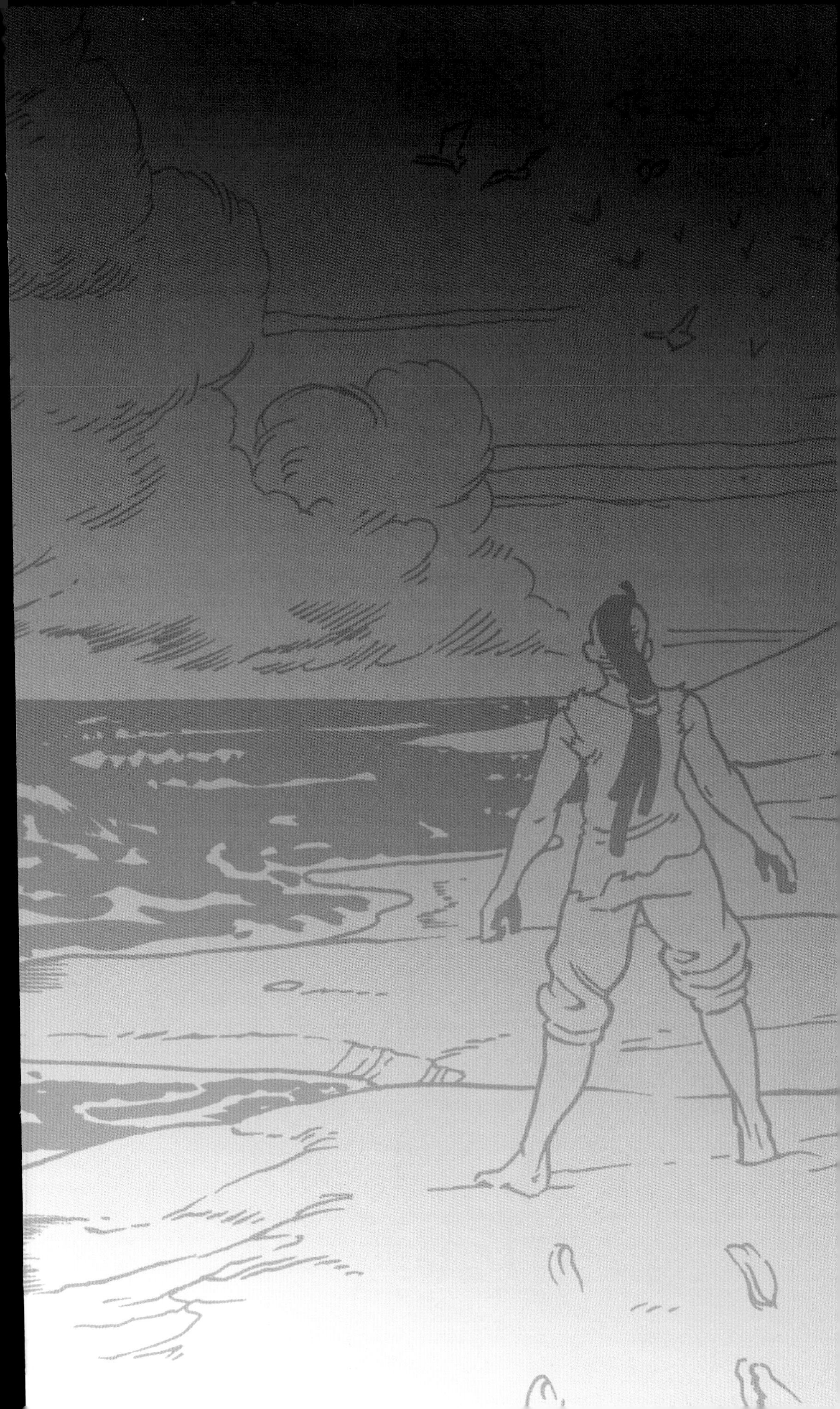

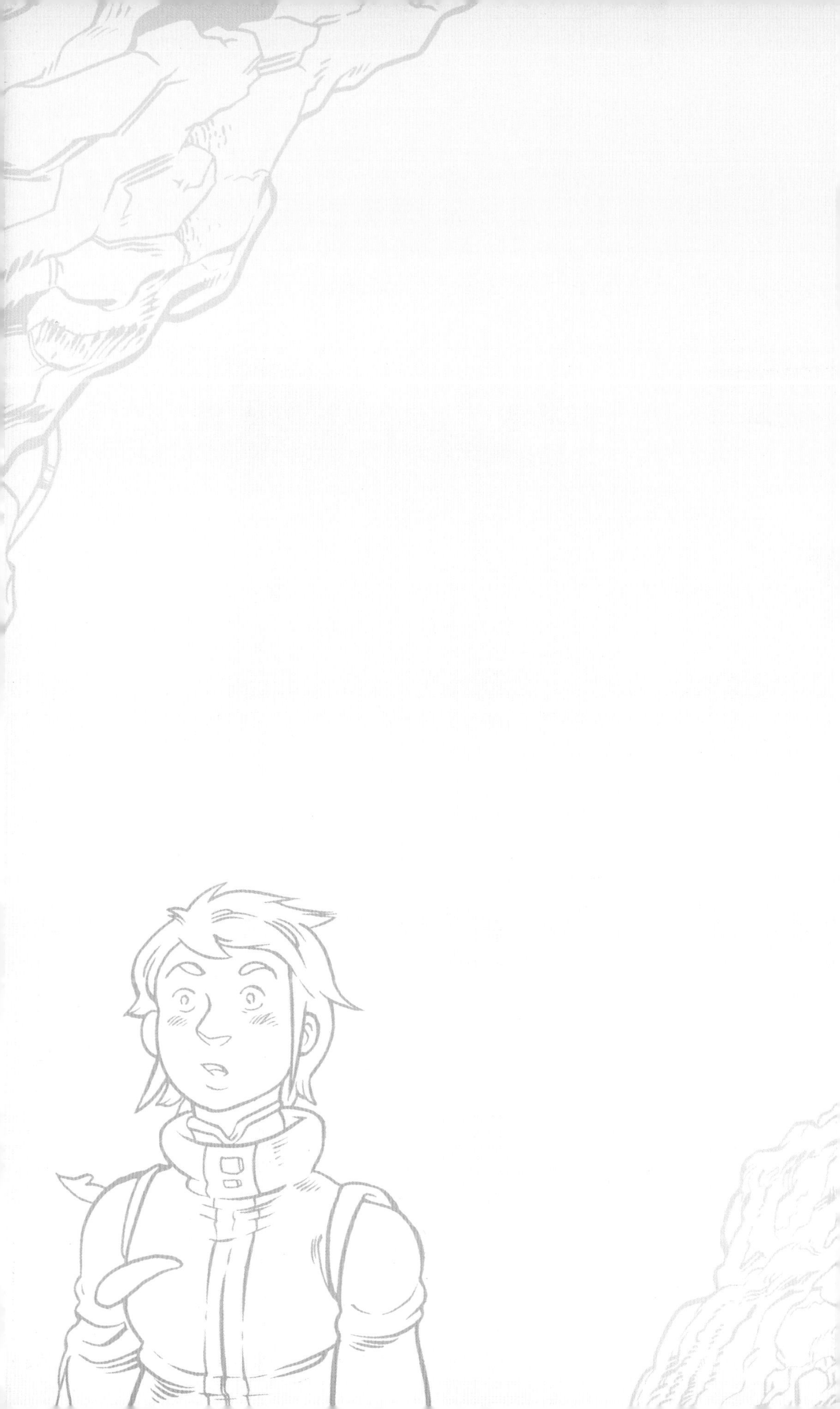

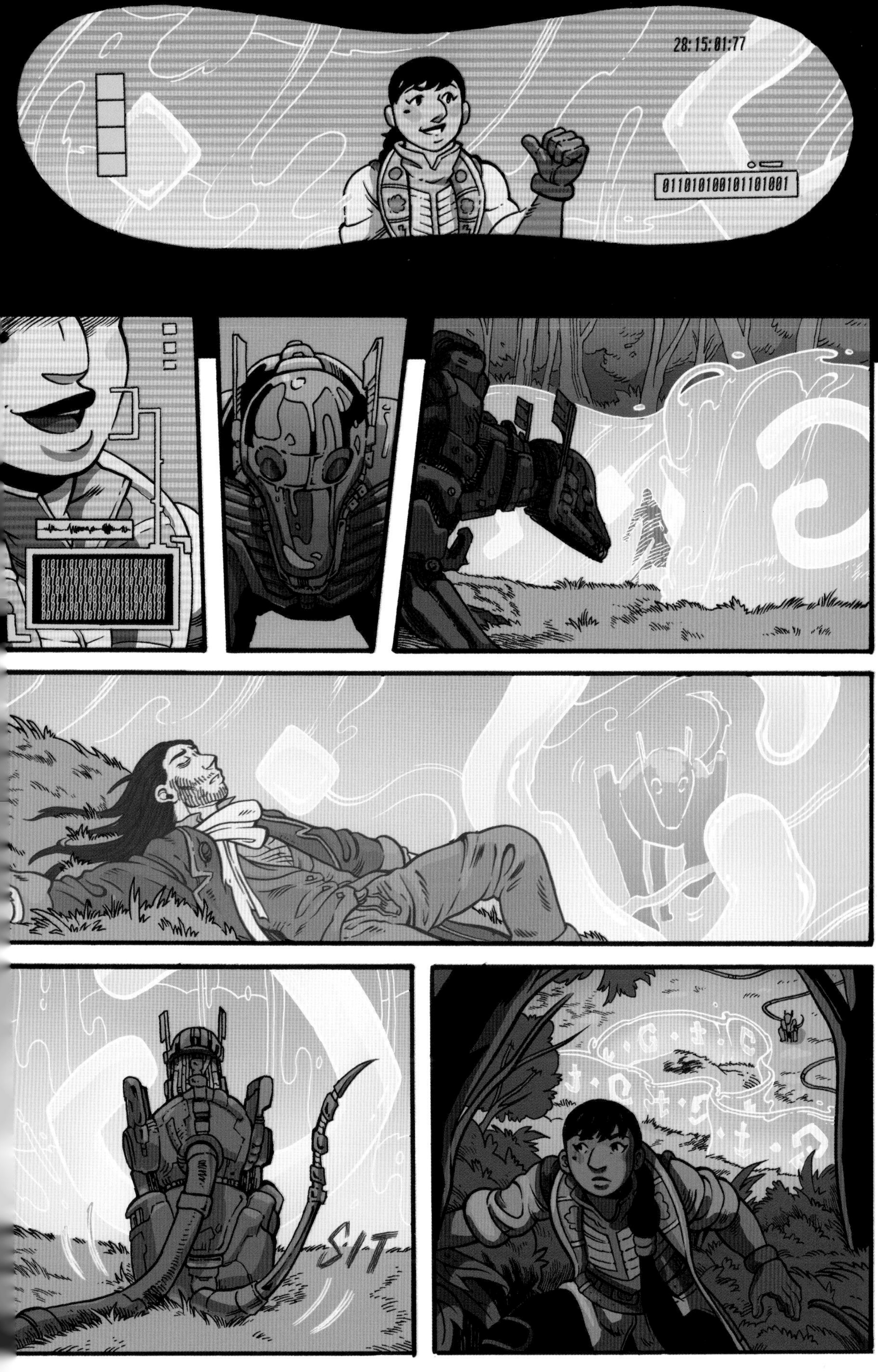
28:15:01:77
011010100101101001
SIT

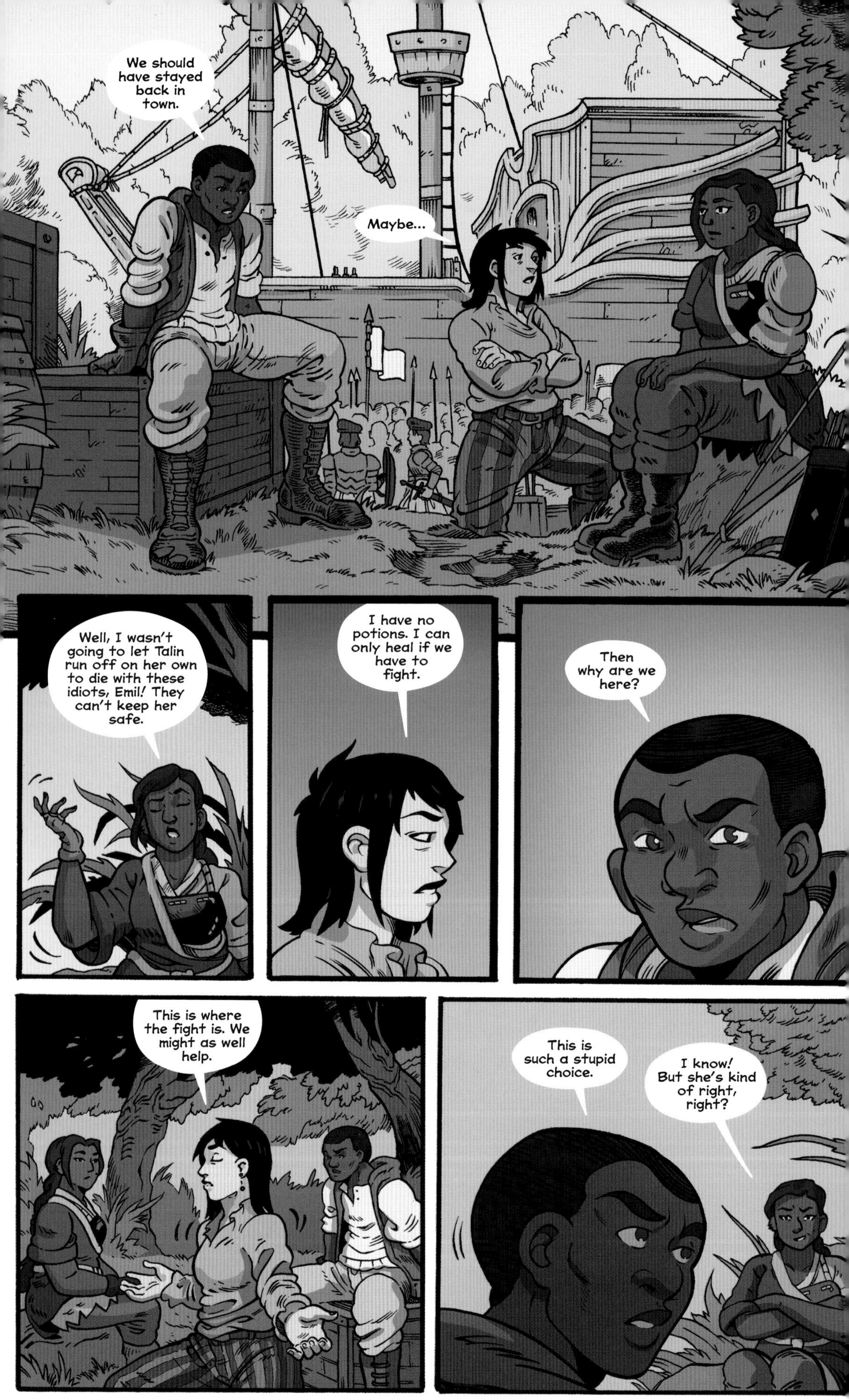
We should have stayed back in town.
Maybe...
Well, I wasn't going to let Talin run off on her own to die with these idiots, Emil! They can't keep her safe.
I have no potions. I can only heal if we have to fight.
Then why are we here?
This is where the fight is. We might as well help.
This is such a stupid choice.
I know! But she's kind of right, right?

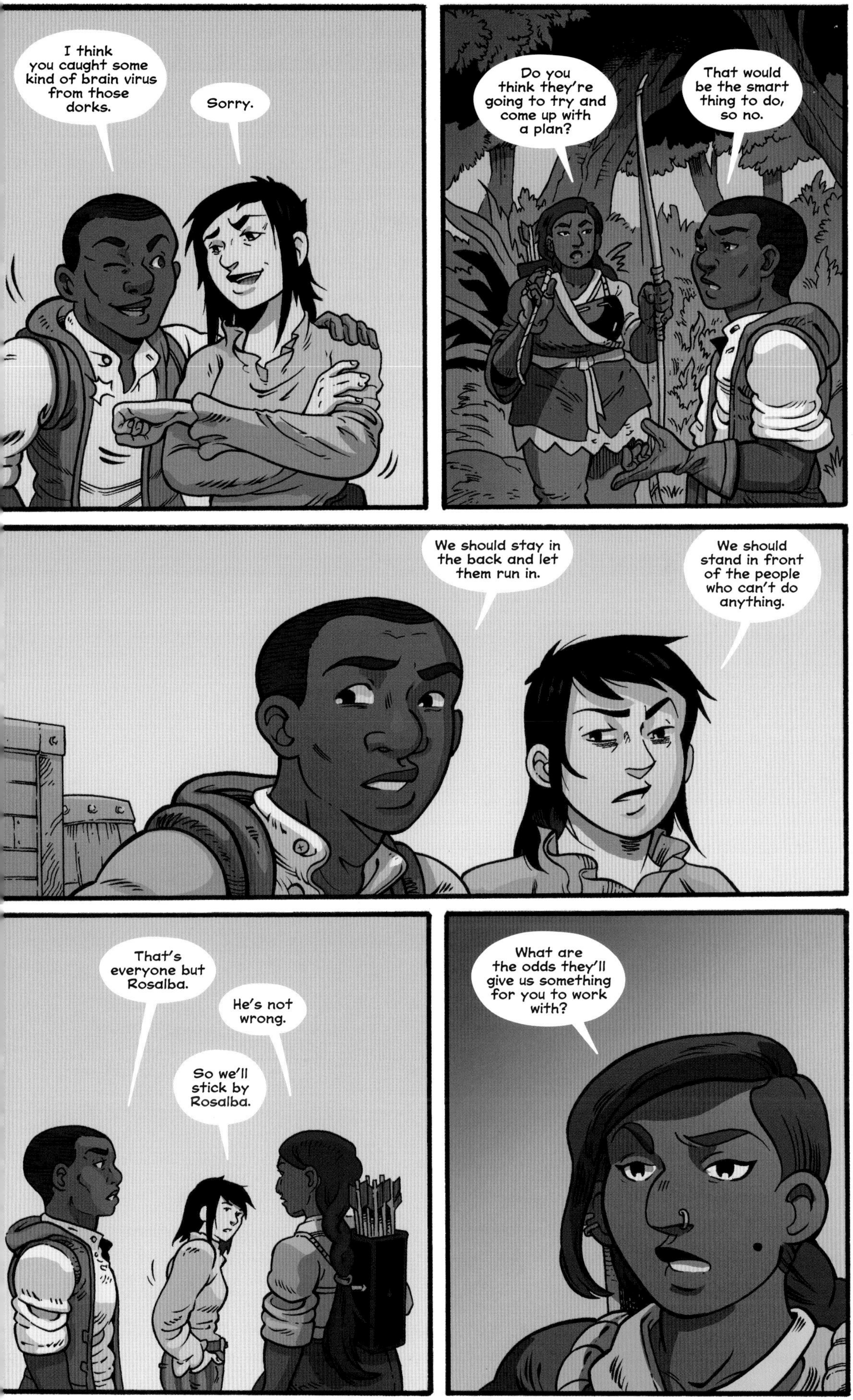
I think you caught some kind of brain virus from those dorks.
Sorry.
Do you think they're going to try and come up with a plan?
That would be the smart thing to do, so no.
We should stay in the back and let them run in.
We should stand in front of the people who can't do anything.
That's everyone but Rosalba.
He's not wrong.
So we'll stick by Rosalba.
What are the odds they'll give us something for you to work with?

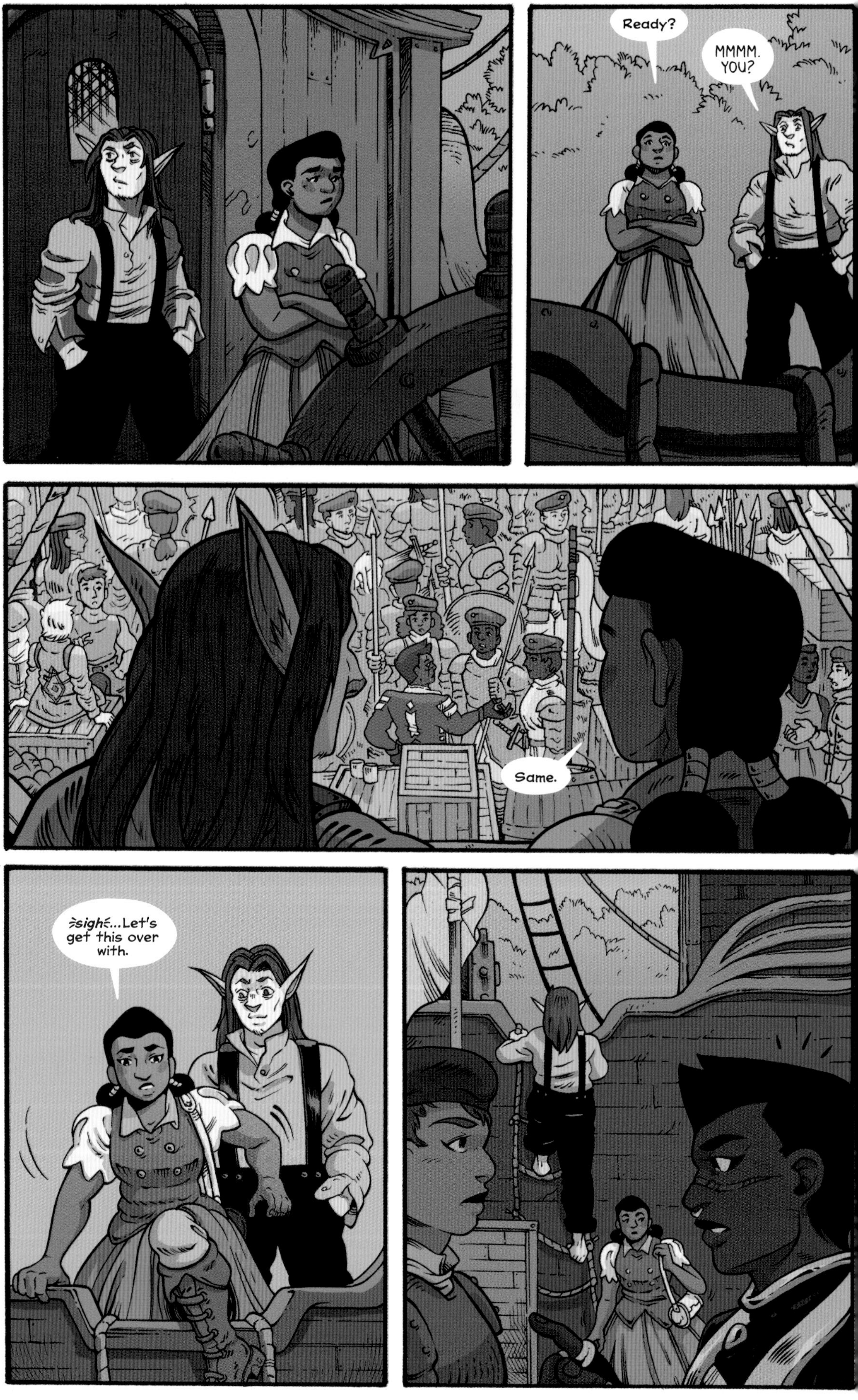
Ready?
MMMM. YOU?
Same.
≥sigh≤...Let's get this over with.

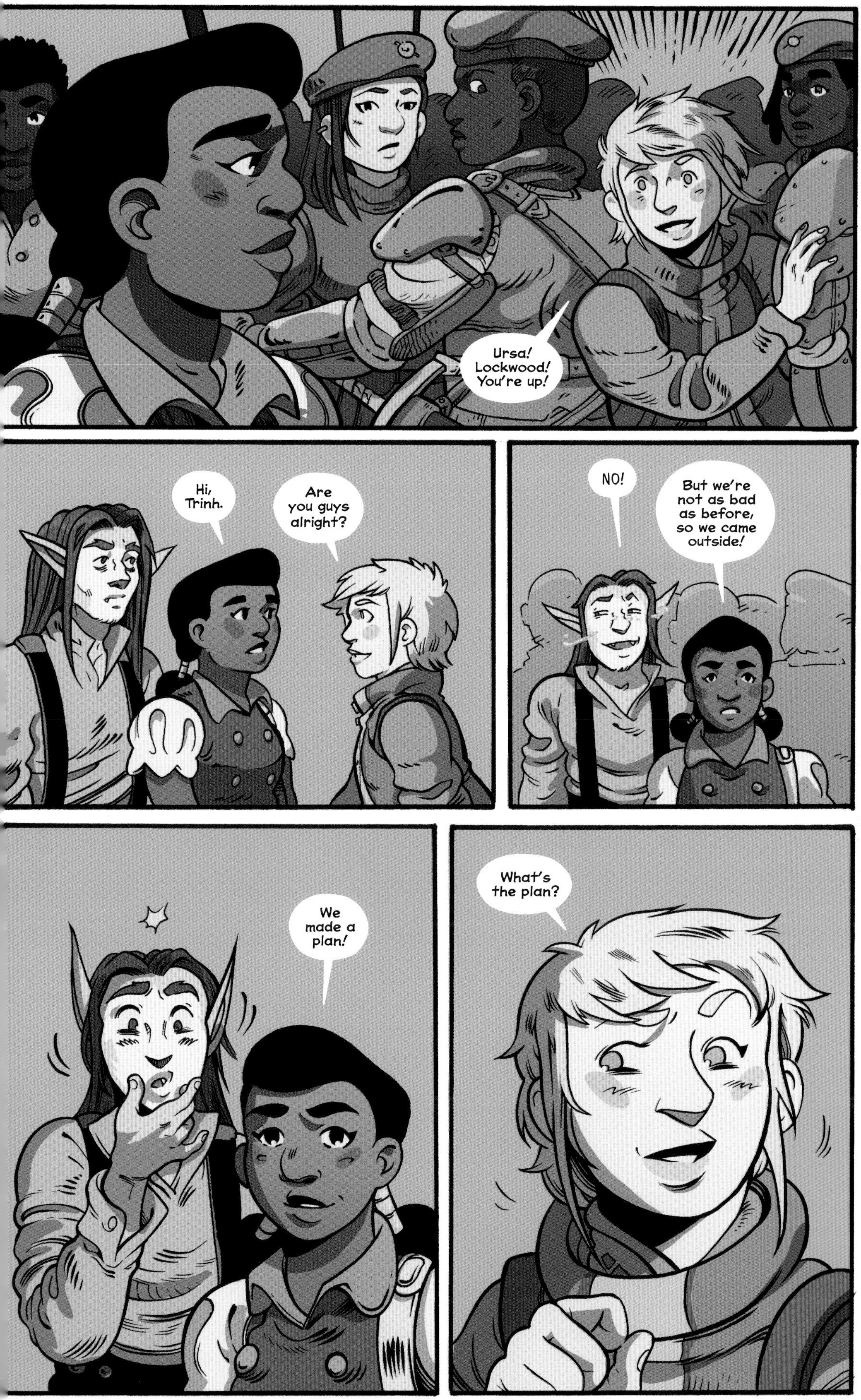

Ursa! Lockwood! You're up!
Hi, Trinh.
Are you guys alright?
NO!
But we're not as bad as before, so we came outside!
We made a plan!
What's the plan?

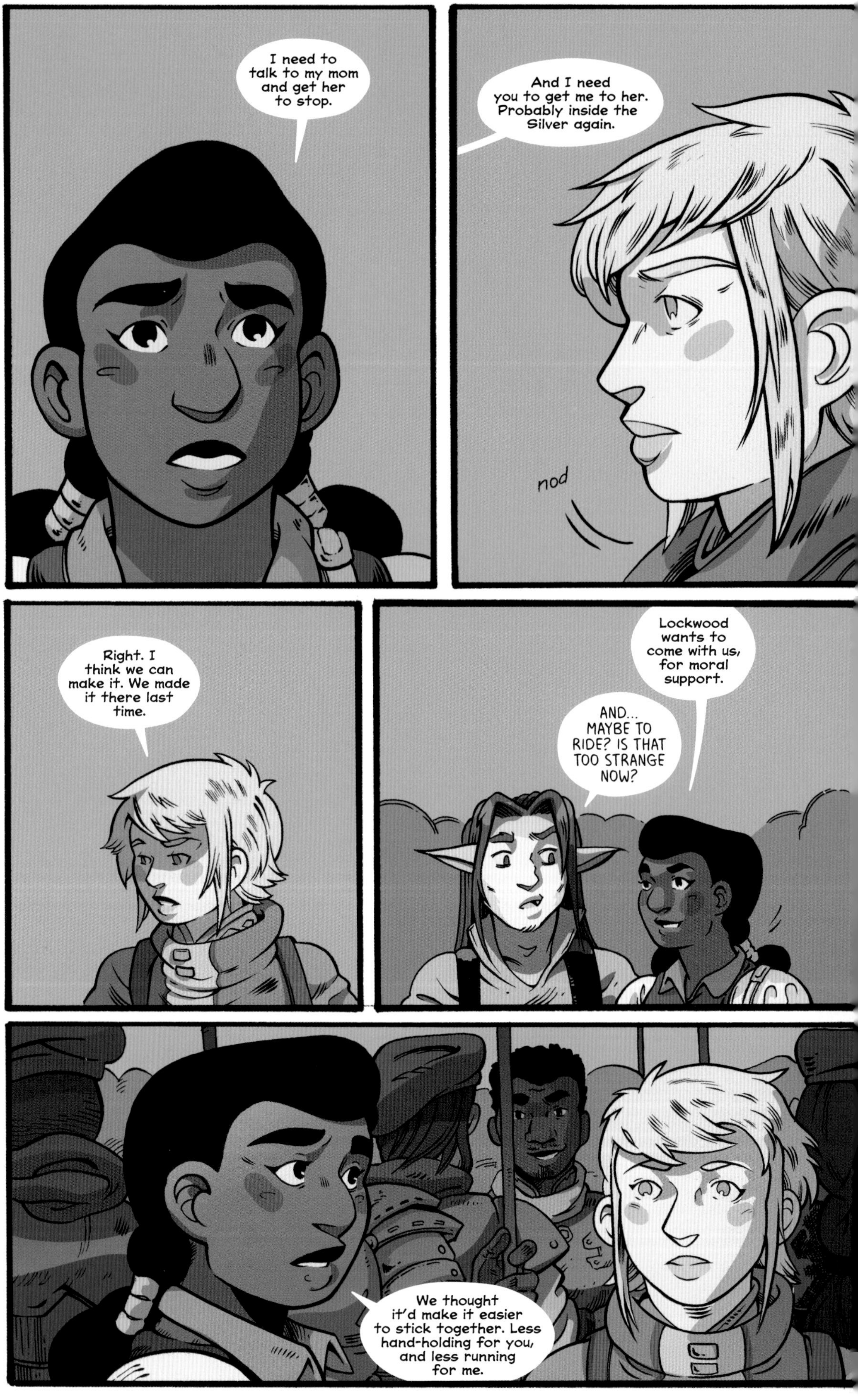
I need to talk to my mom and get her to stop.
And I need you to get me to her. Probably inside the Silver again.
nod
Right. I think we can make it. We made it there last time.
Lockwood wants to come with us, for moral support.
AND... MAYBE TO RIDE? IS THAT TOO STRANGE NOW?
We thought it'd make it easier to stick together. Less hand-holding for you, and less running for me.

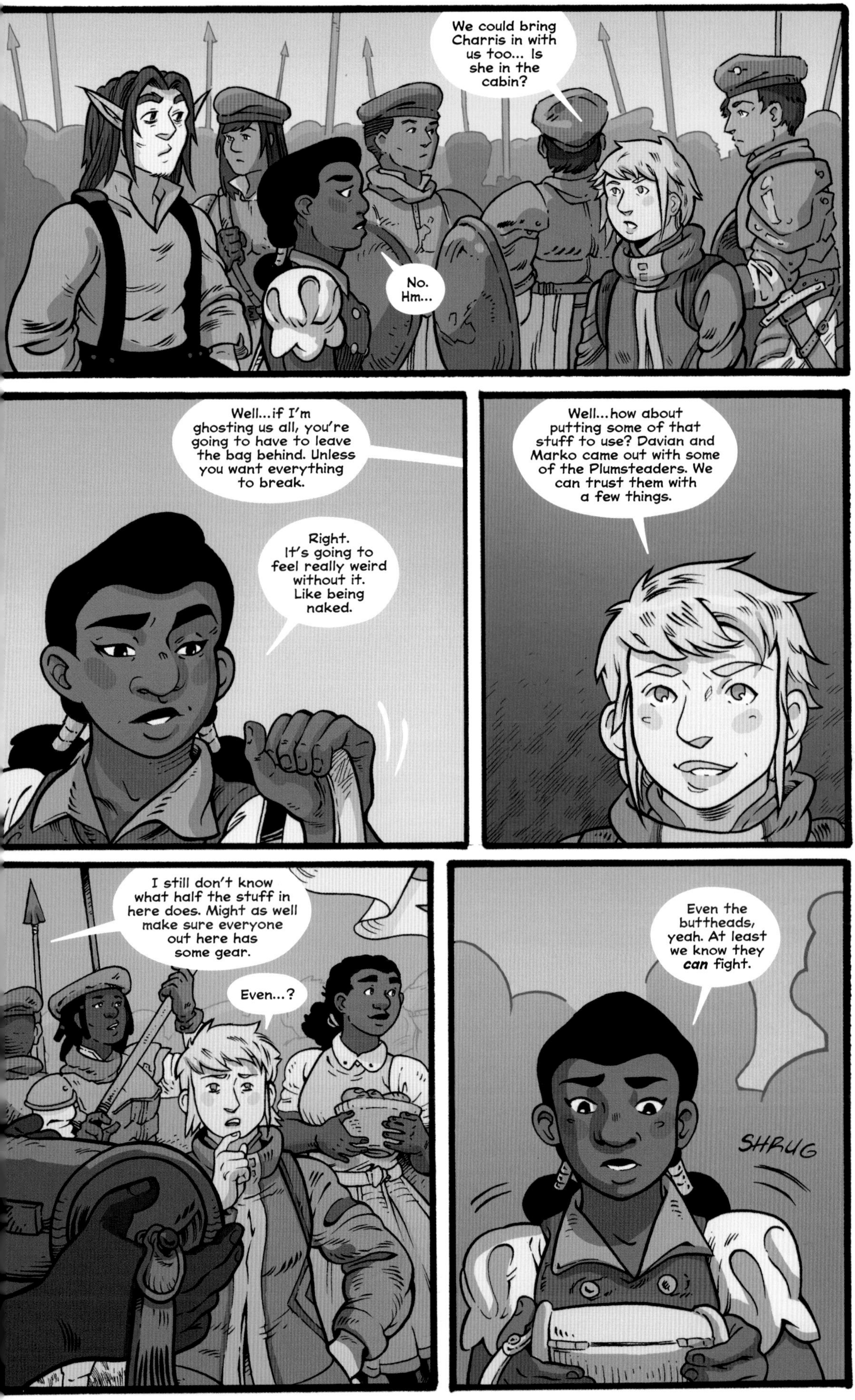
We could bring Charris in with us too... Is she in the cabin?
No. Hm...
Well...if I'm ghosting us all, you're going to have to leave the bag behind. Unless you want everything to break.
Right. It's going to feel really weird without it. Like being naked.
Well...how about putting some of that stuff to use? Davian and Marko came out with some of the Plumsteaders. We can trust them with a few things.
I still don't know what half the stuff in here does. Might as well make sure everyone out here has some gear.
Even...?
Even the buttheads, yeah. At least we know they *can* fight.
SHRUG

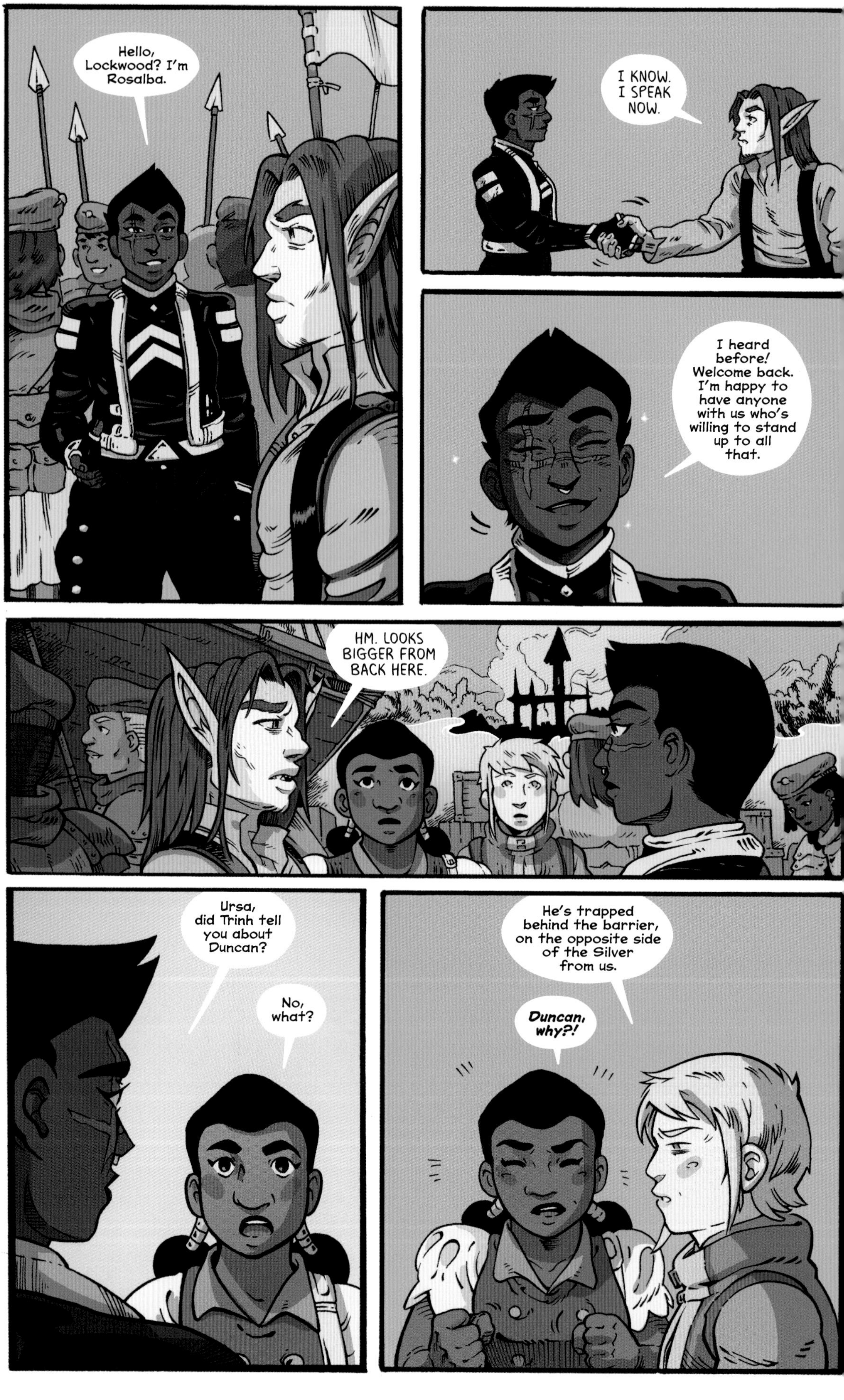
Hello, Lockwood? I'm Rosalba.
I KNOW. I SPEAK NOW.
I heard before! Welcome back. I'm happy to have anyone with us who's willing to stand up to all that.
HM. LOOKS BIGGER FROM BACK HERE.
Ursa, did Trinh tell you about Duncan?
No, what?
He's trapped behind the barrier, on the opposite side of the Silver from us.
Duncan, why?!

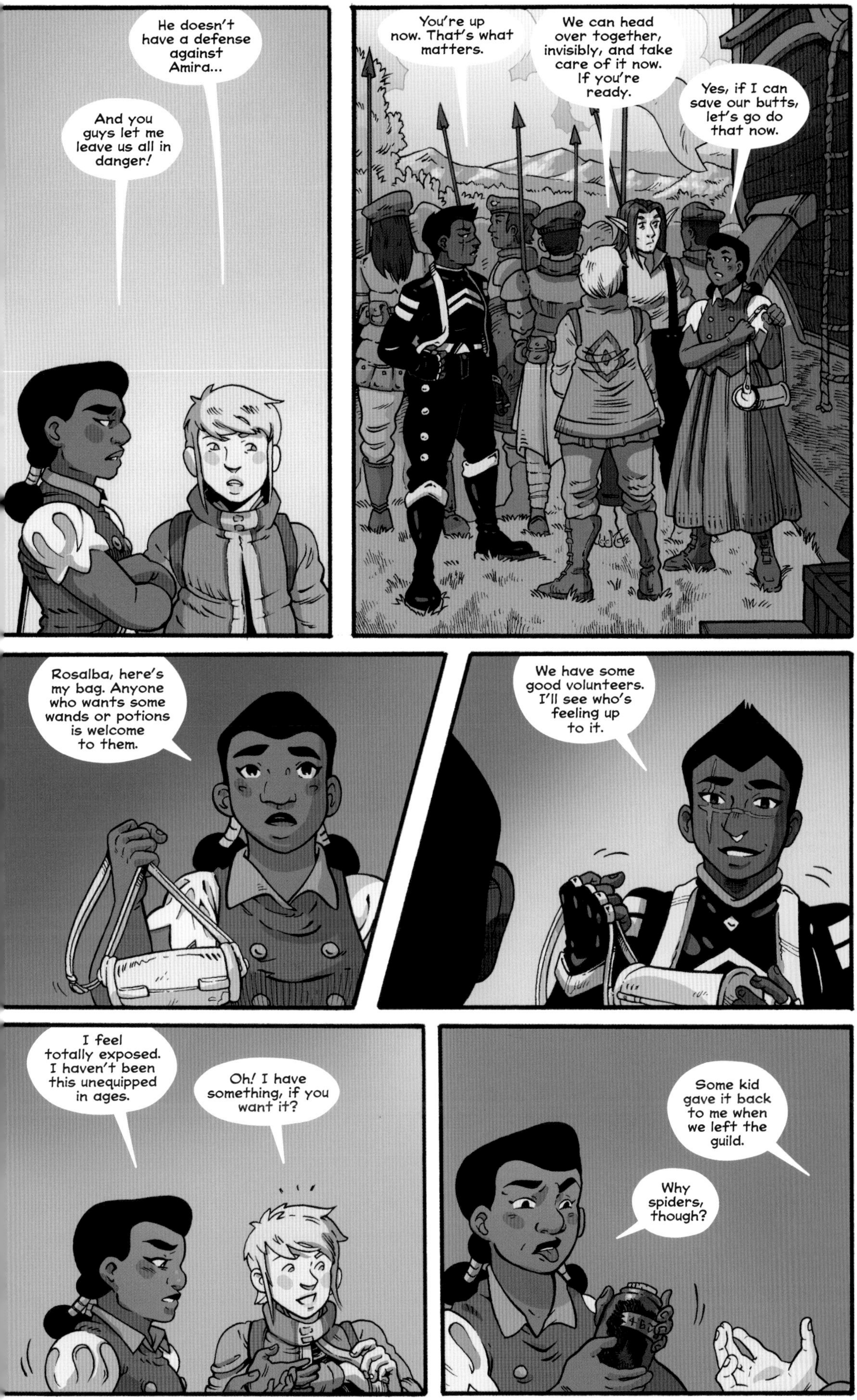

He doesn't have a defense against Amira...
And you guys let me leave us all in danger!
You're up now. That's what matters.
We can head over together, invisibly, and take care of it now. If you're ready.
Yes, if I can save our butts, let's go do that now.
Rosalba, here's my bag. Anyone who wants some wands or potions is welcome to them.
We have some good volunteers. I'll see who's feeling up to it.
I feel totally exposed. I haven't been this unequipped in ages.
Oh! I have something, if you want it?
Some kid gave it back to me when we left the guild.
Why spiders, though?

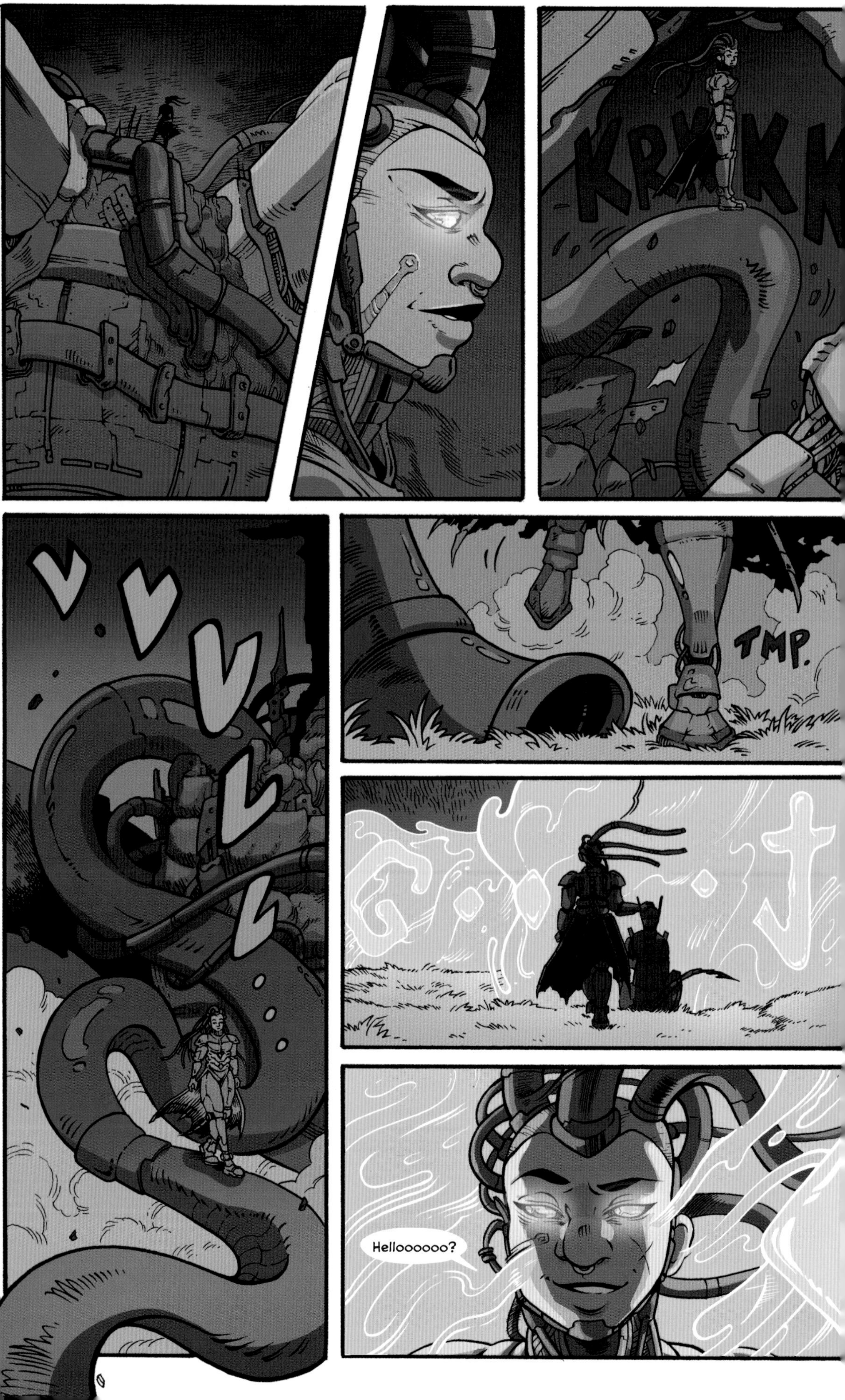
TMP.
Helloooooo?

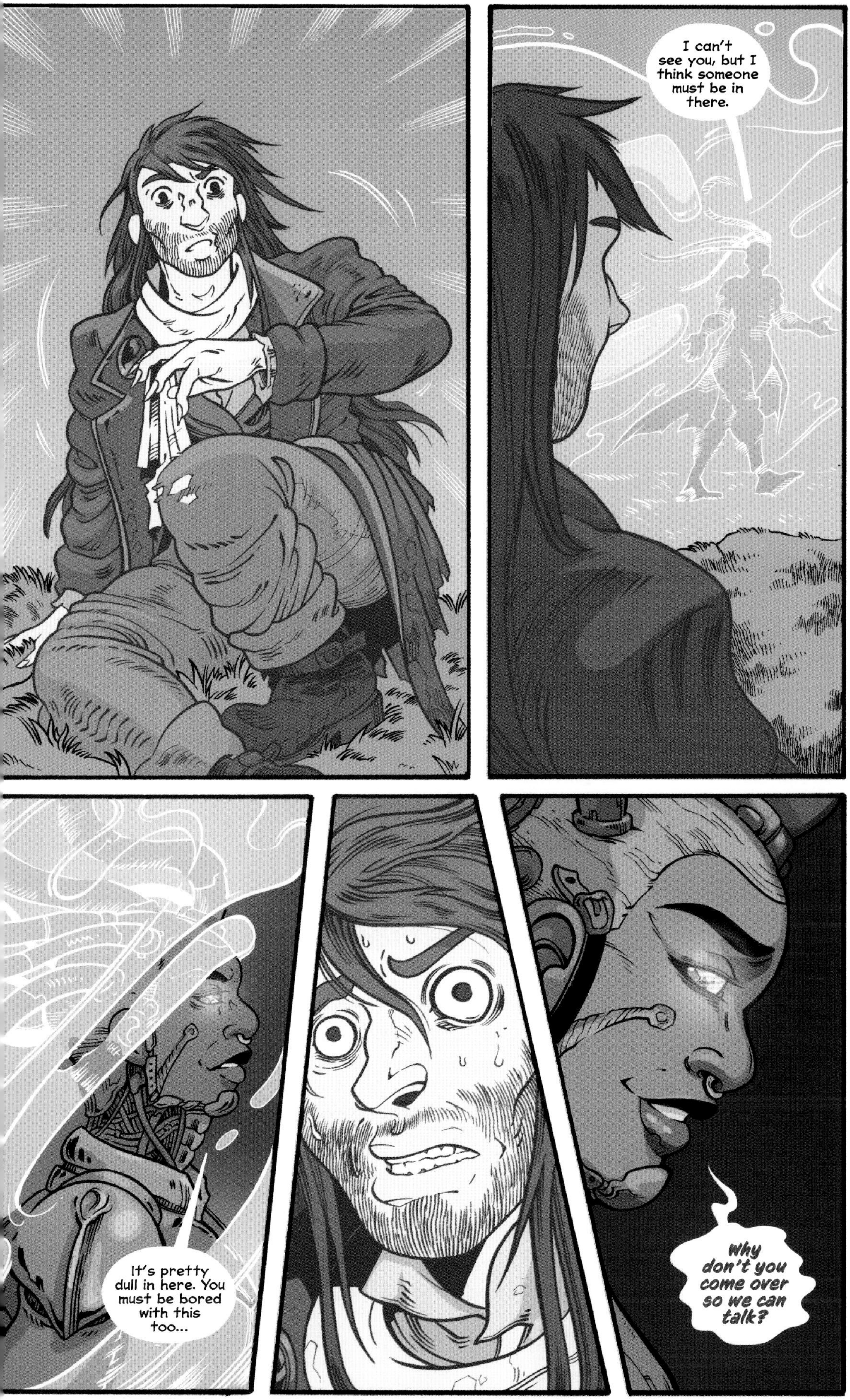
I can't see you, but I think someone must be in there.
It's pretty dull in here. You must be bored with this too...
Why don't you come over so we can talk?

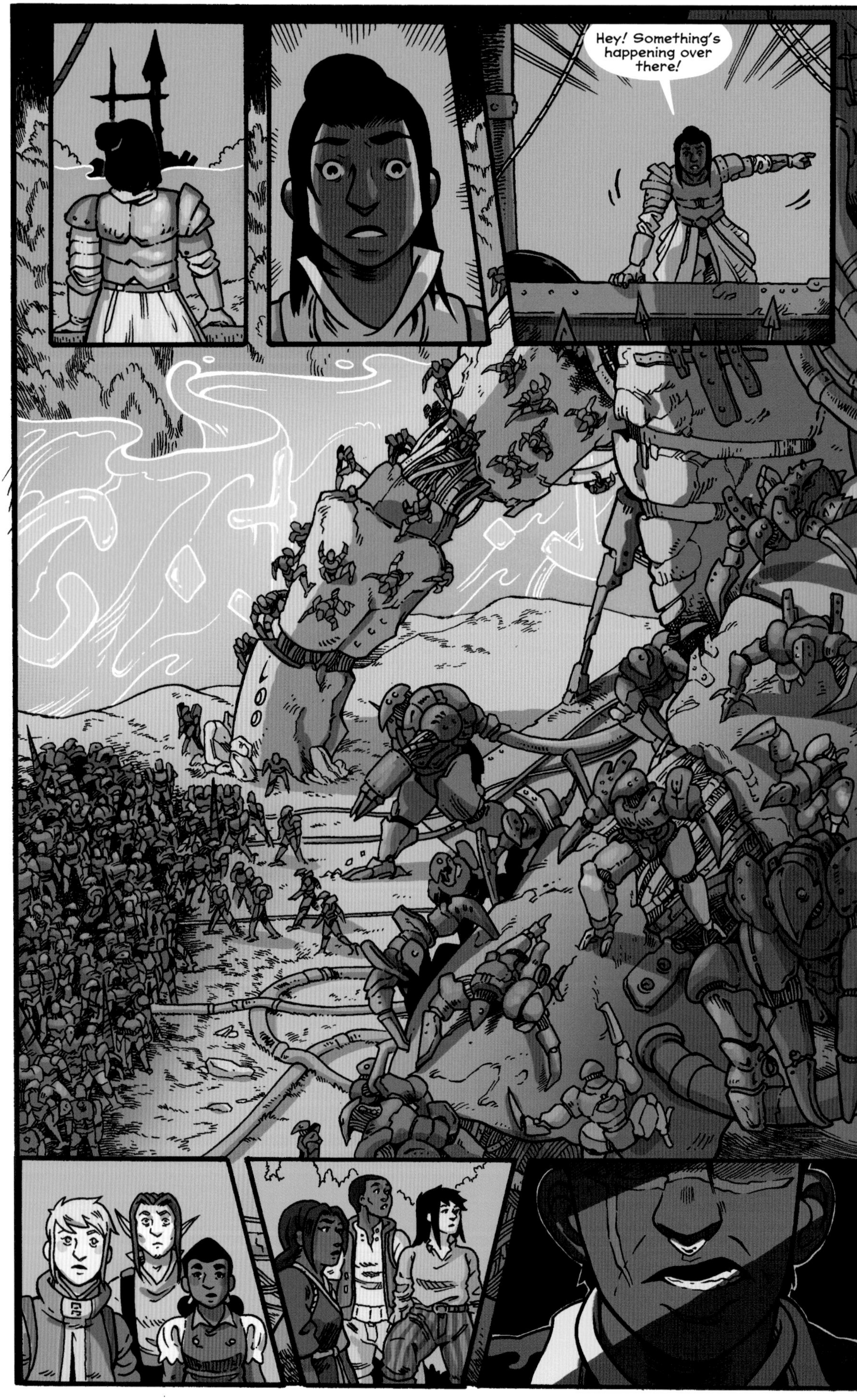
Hey! Something's happening over there!

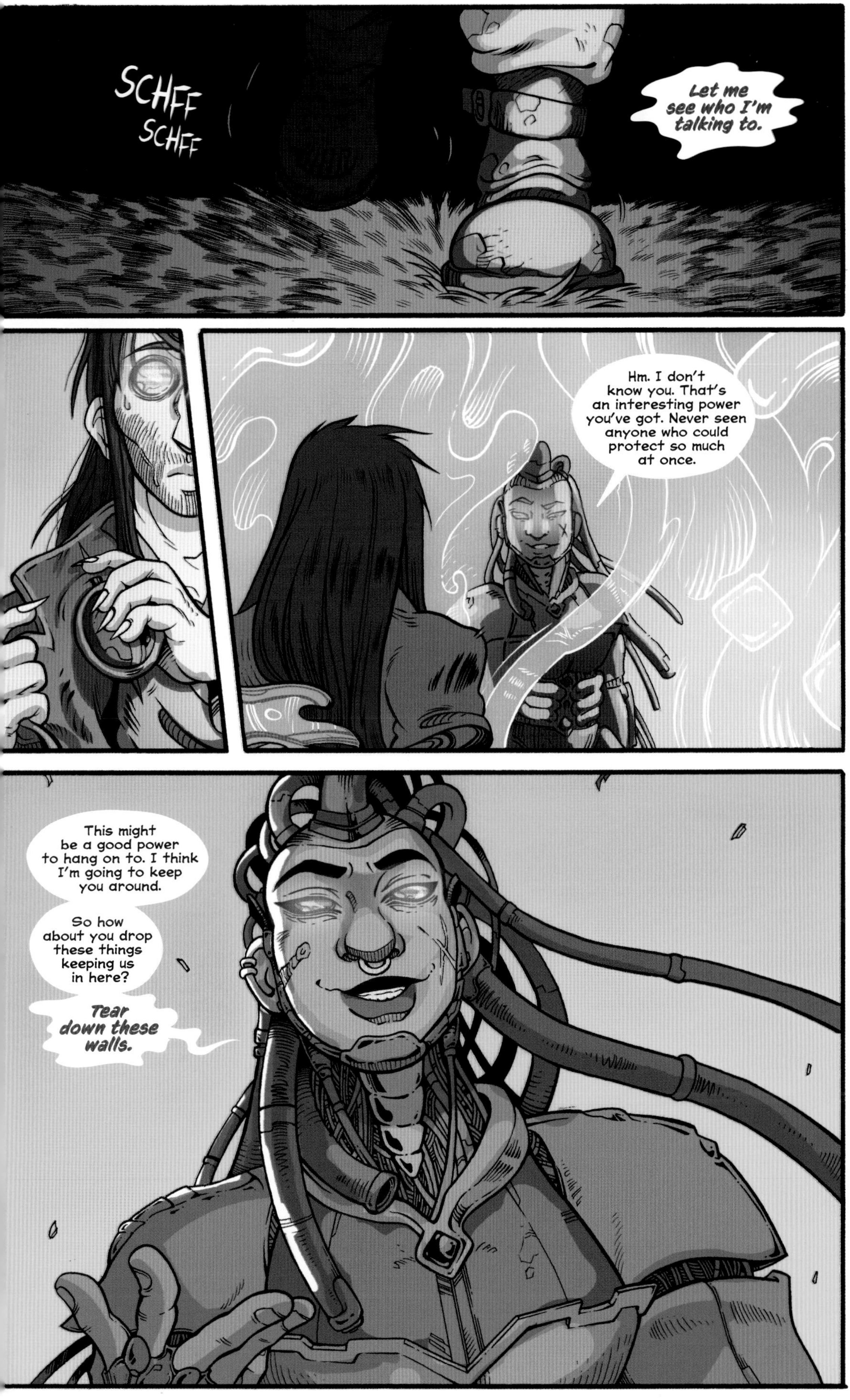
SCHFF
SCHFF
Let me see who I'm talking to.
Hm. I don't know you. That's an interesting power you've got. Never seen anyone who could protect so much at once.
This might be a good power to hang on to. I think I'm going to keep you around.
So how about you drop these things keeping us in here?
Tear down these walls.

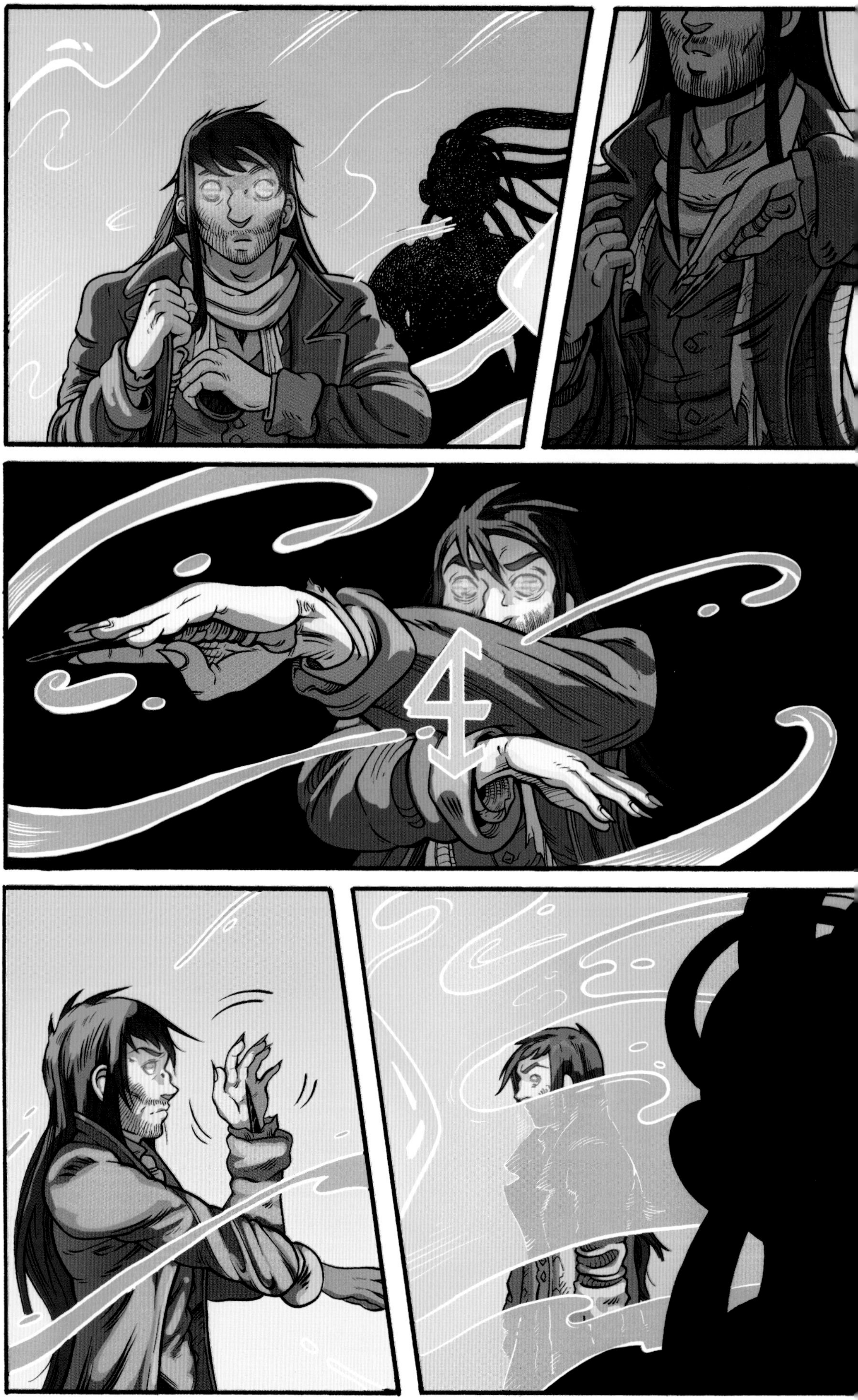

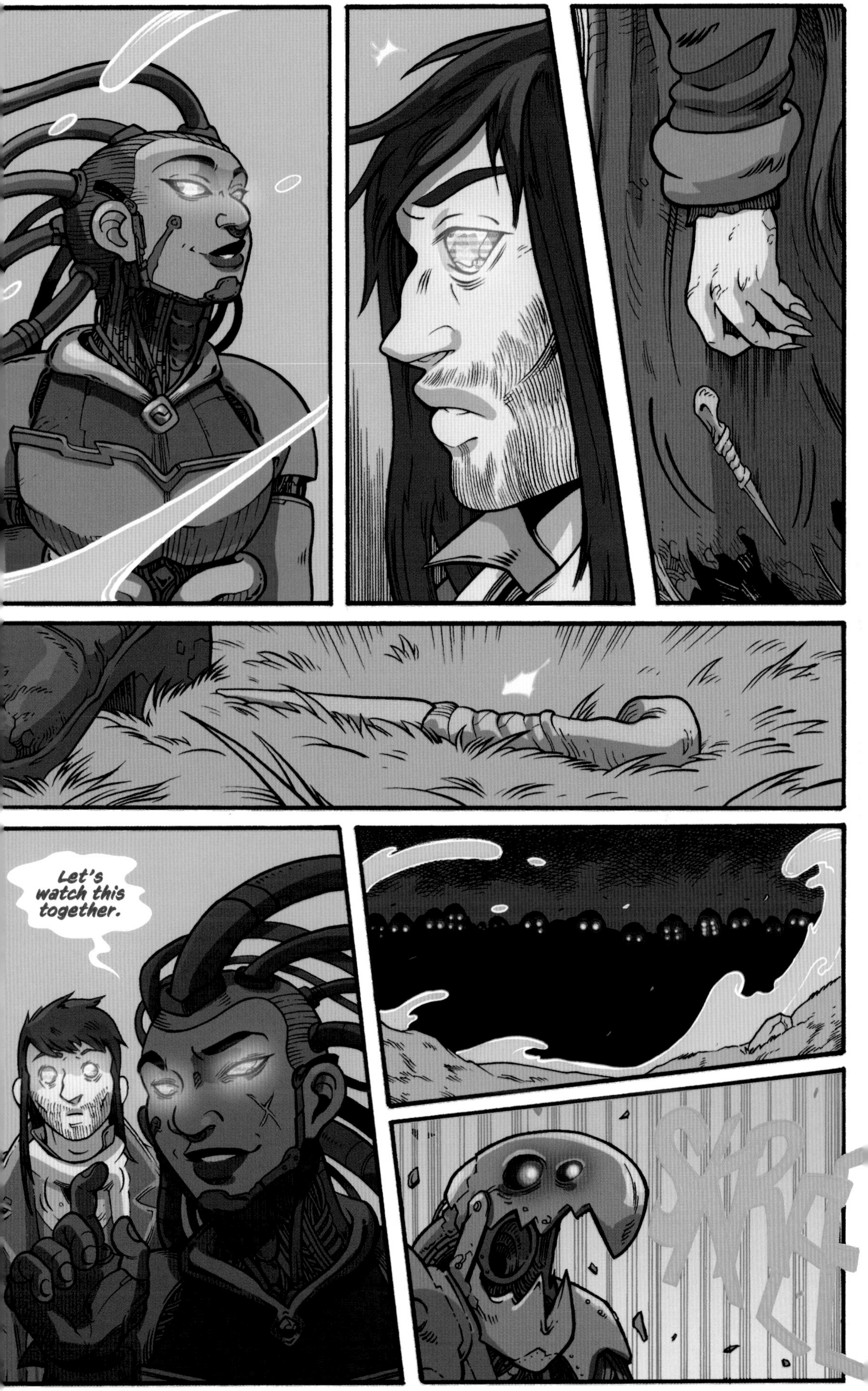
Let's watch this together.

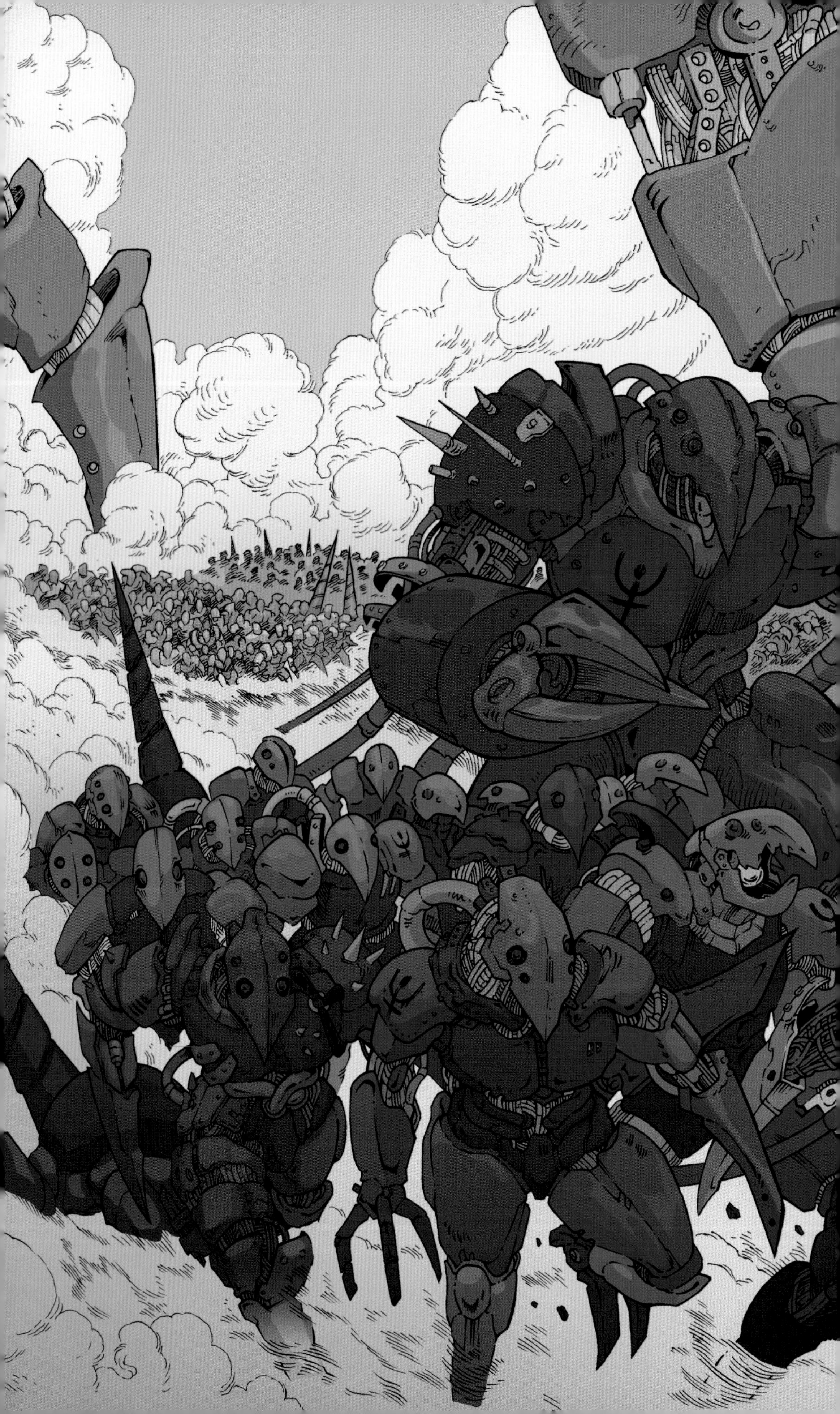

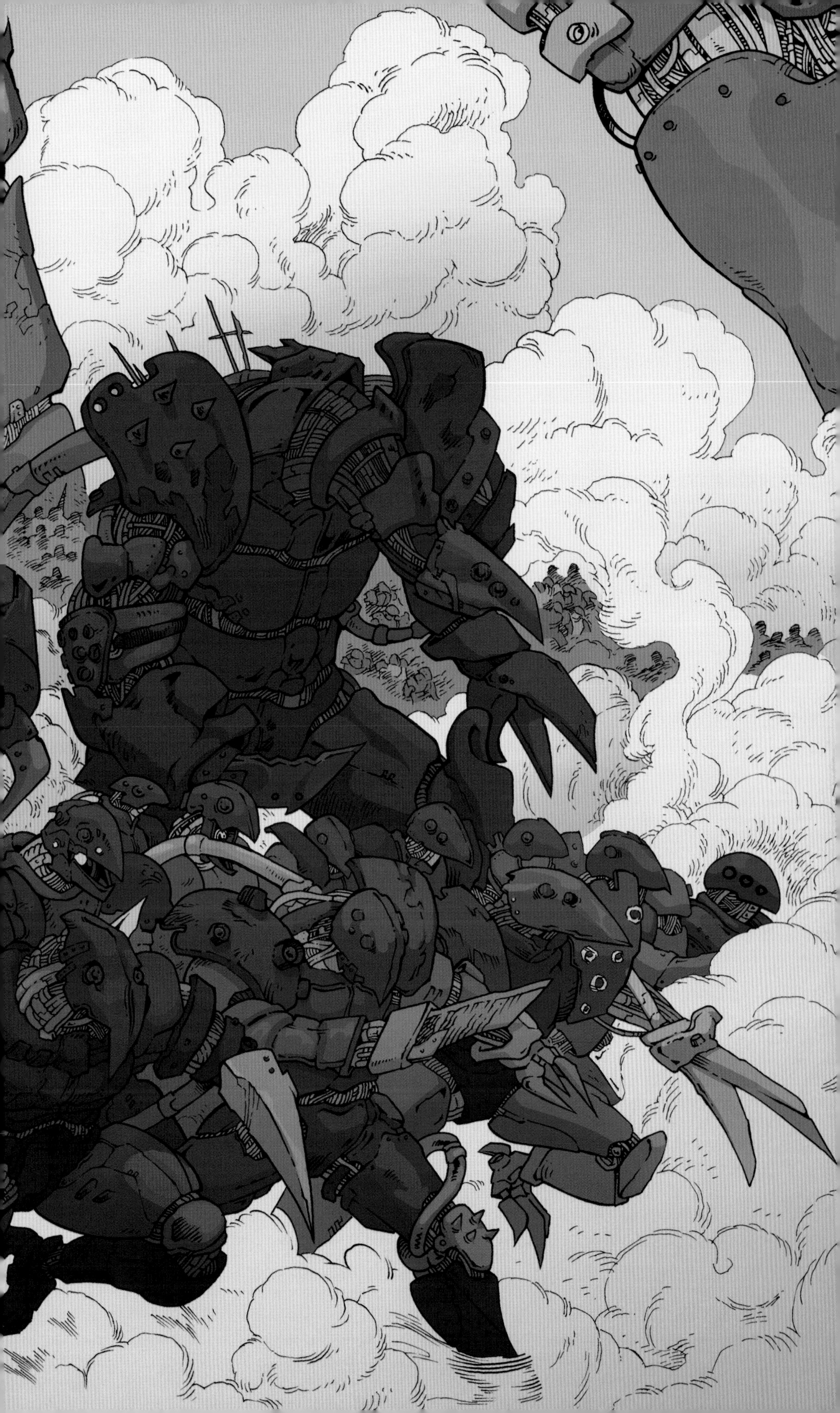

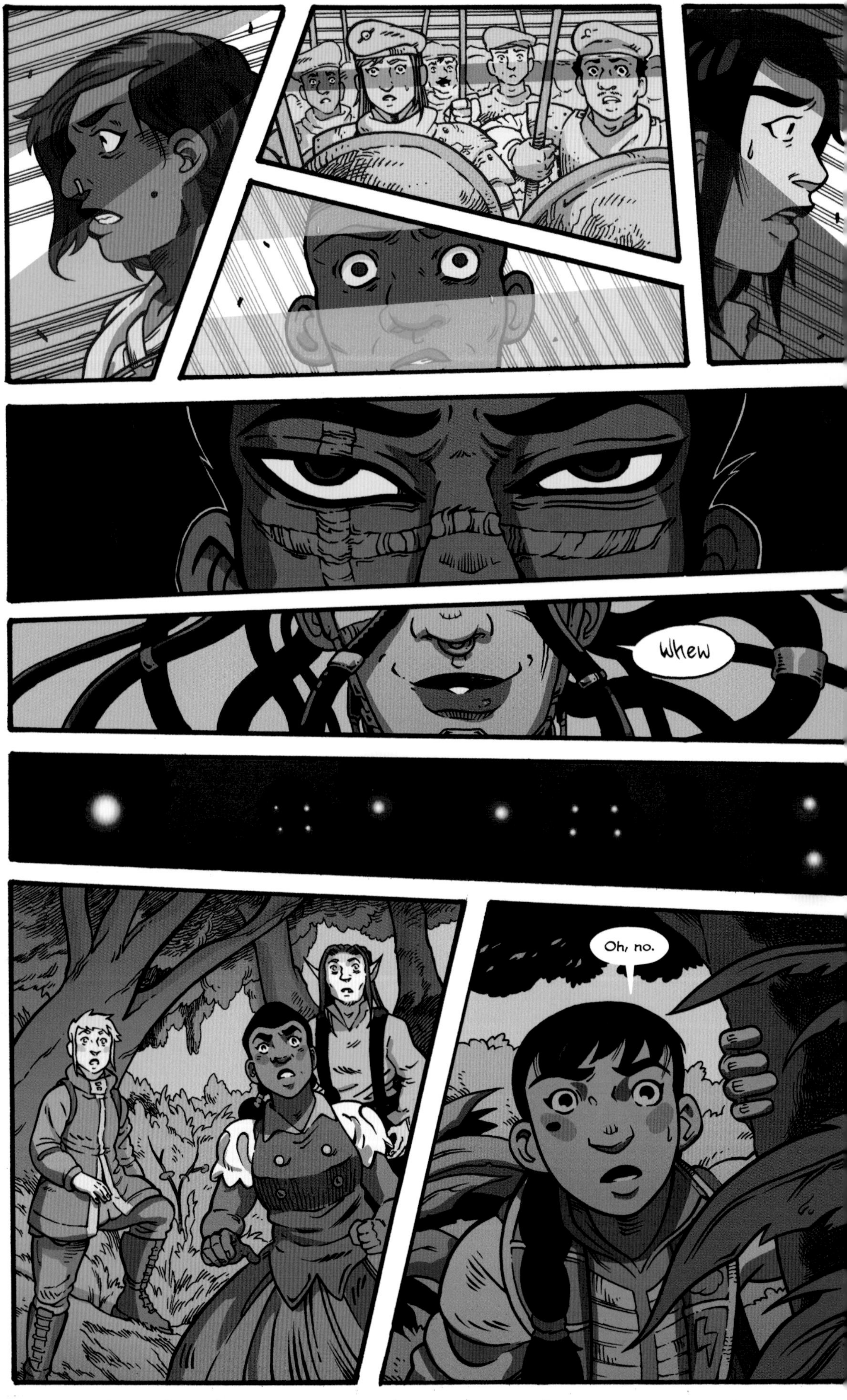
Whew
Oh, no.

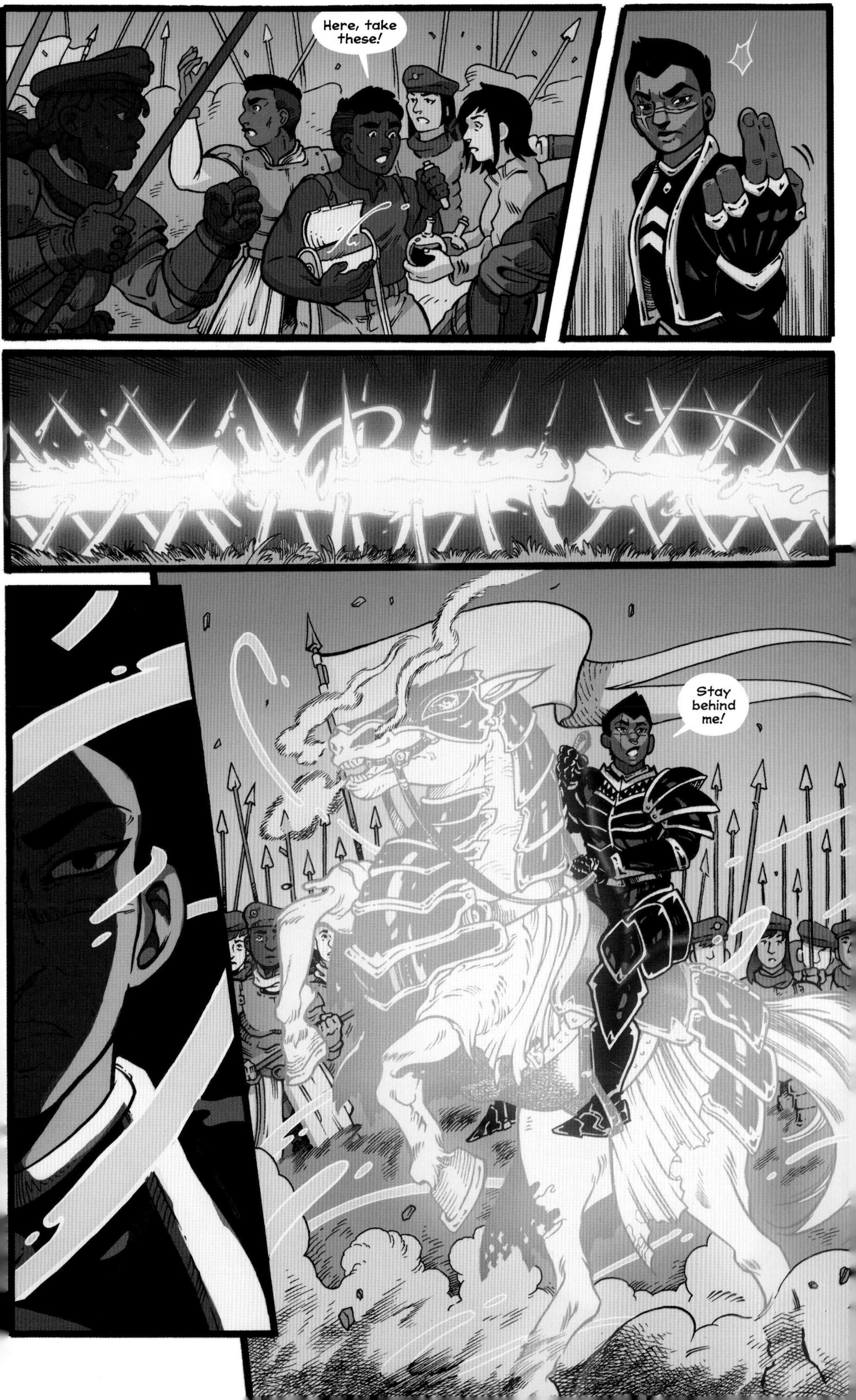
Here, take these!
Stay behind me!

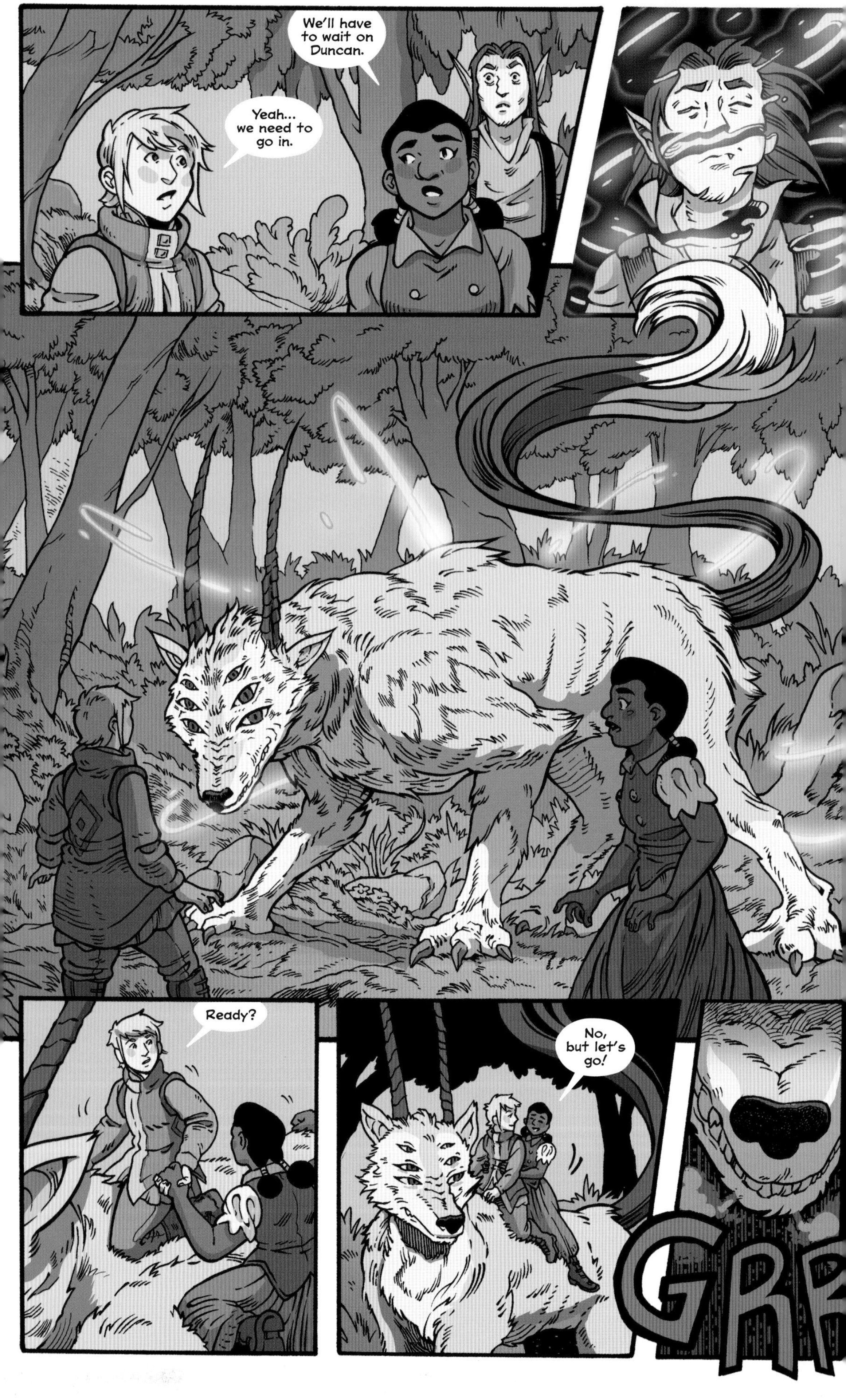
We'll have to wait on Duncan.
Yeah... we need to go in.
Ready?
No, but let's go!
GRR

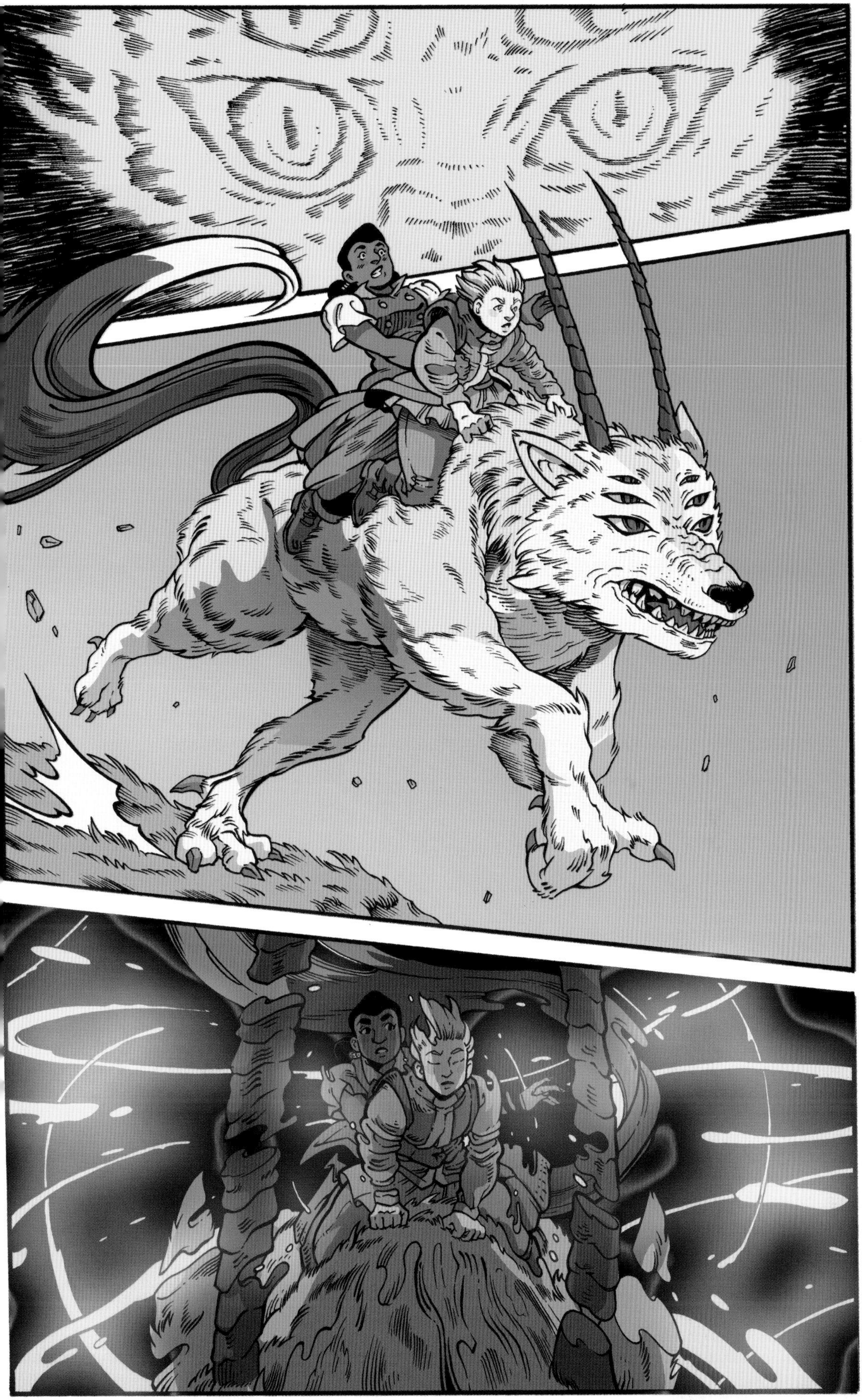

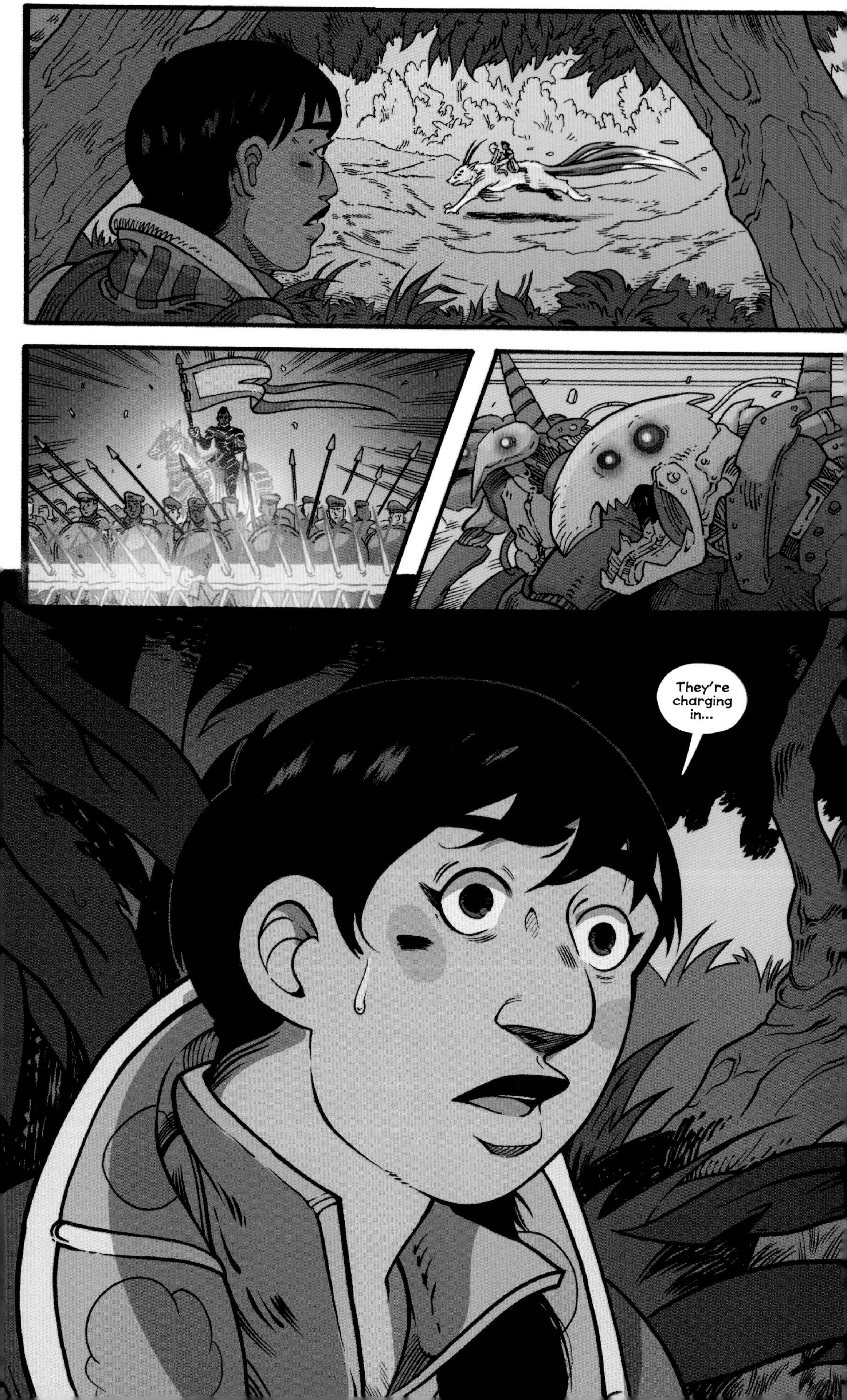
They're
charging
in...

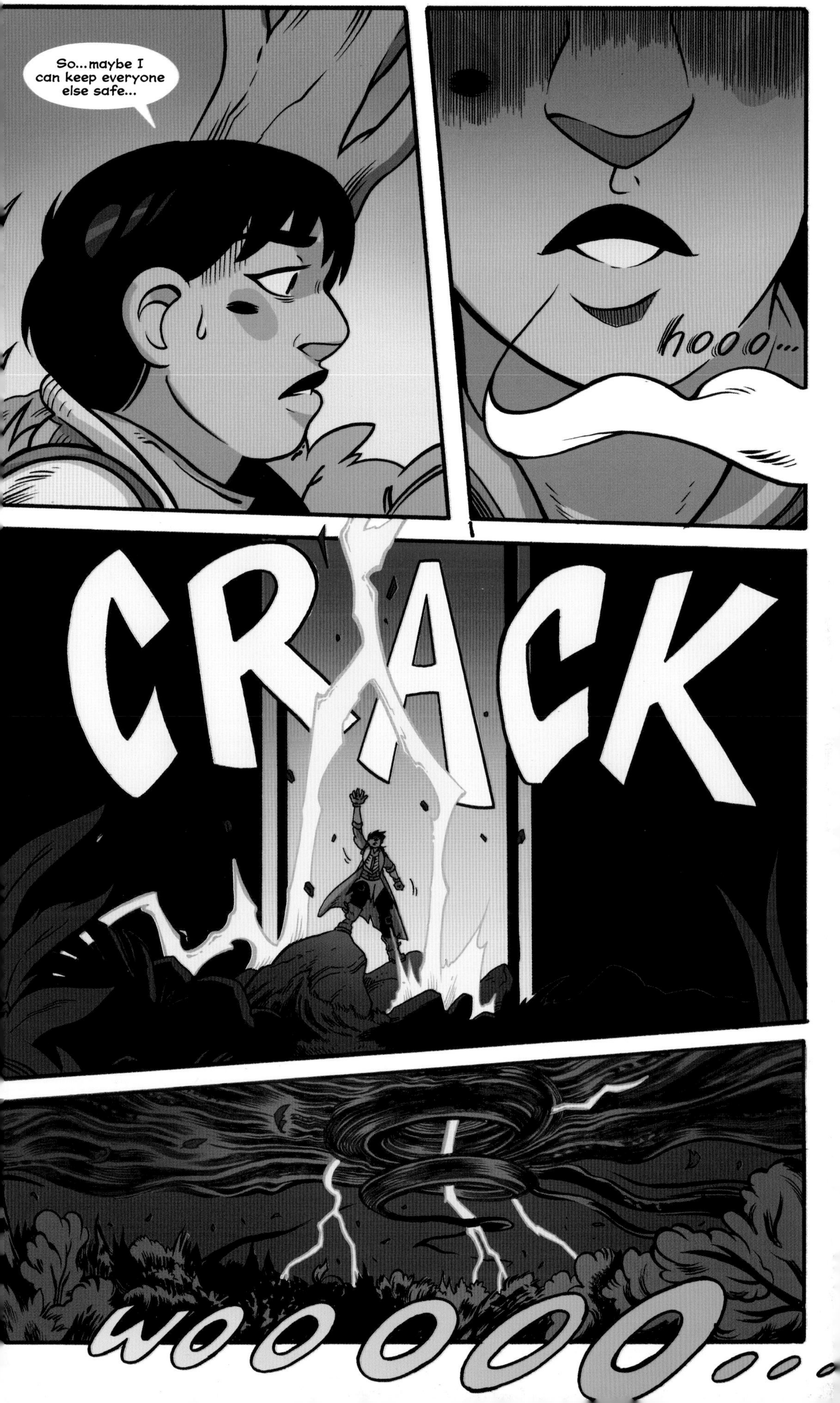
So...maybe I can keep everyone else safe...
hooo...
CRACK
WOO OOOO...

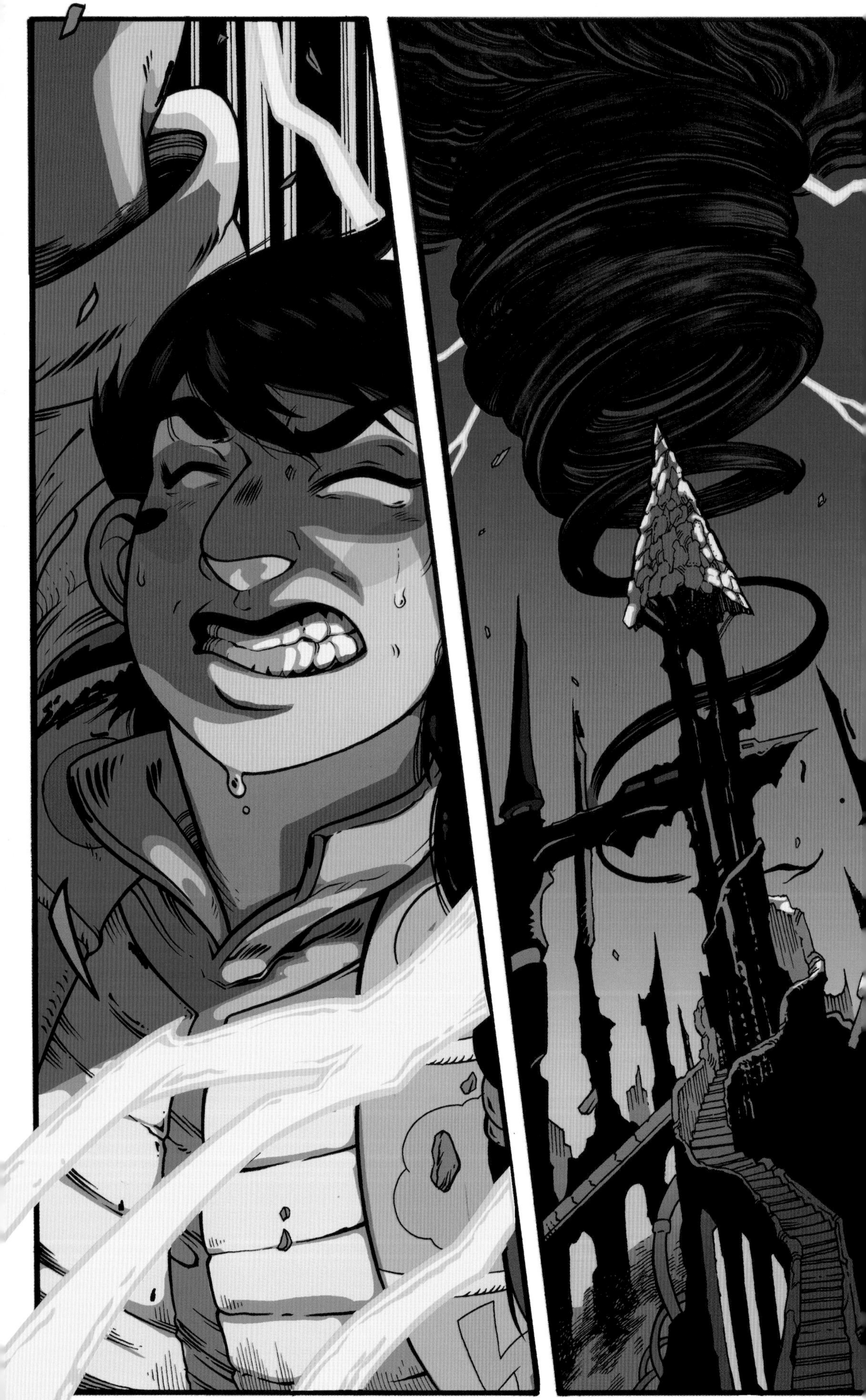

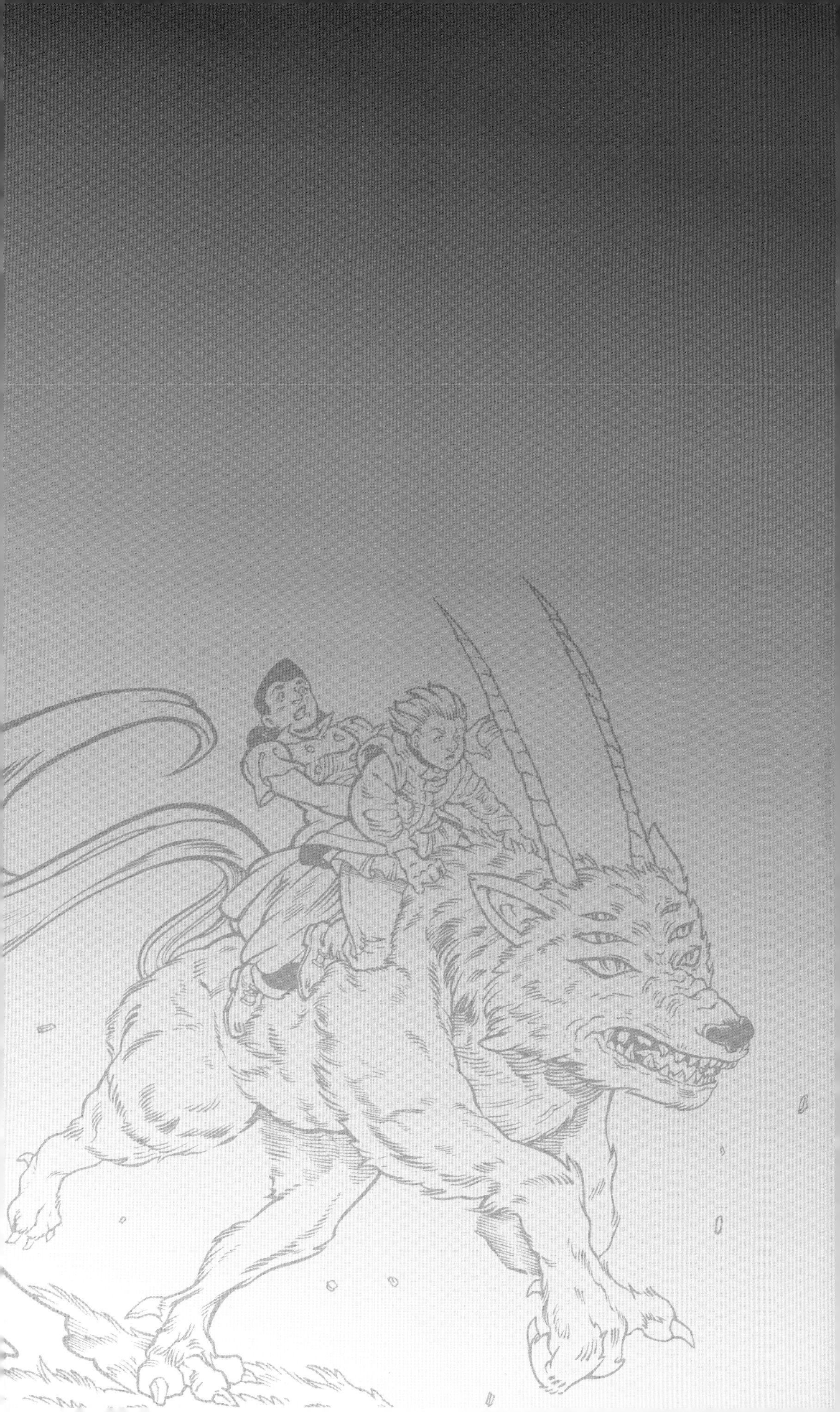

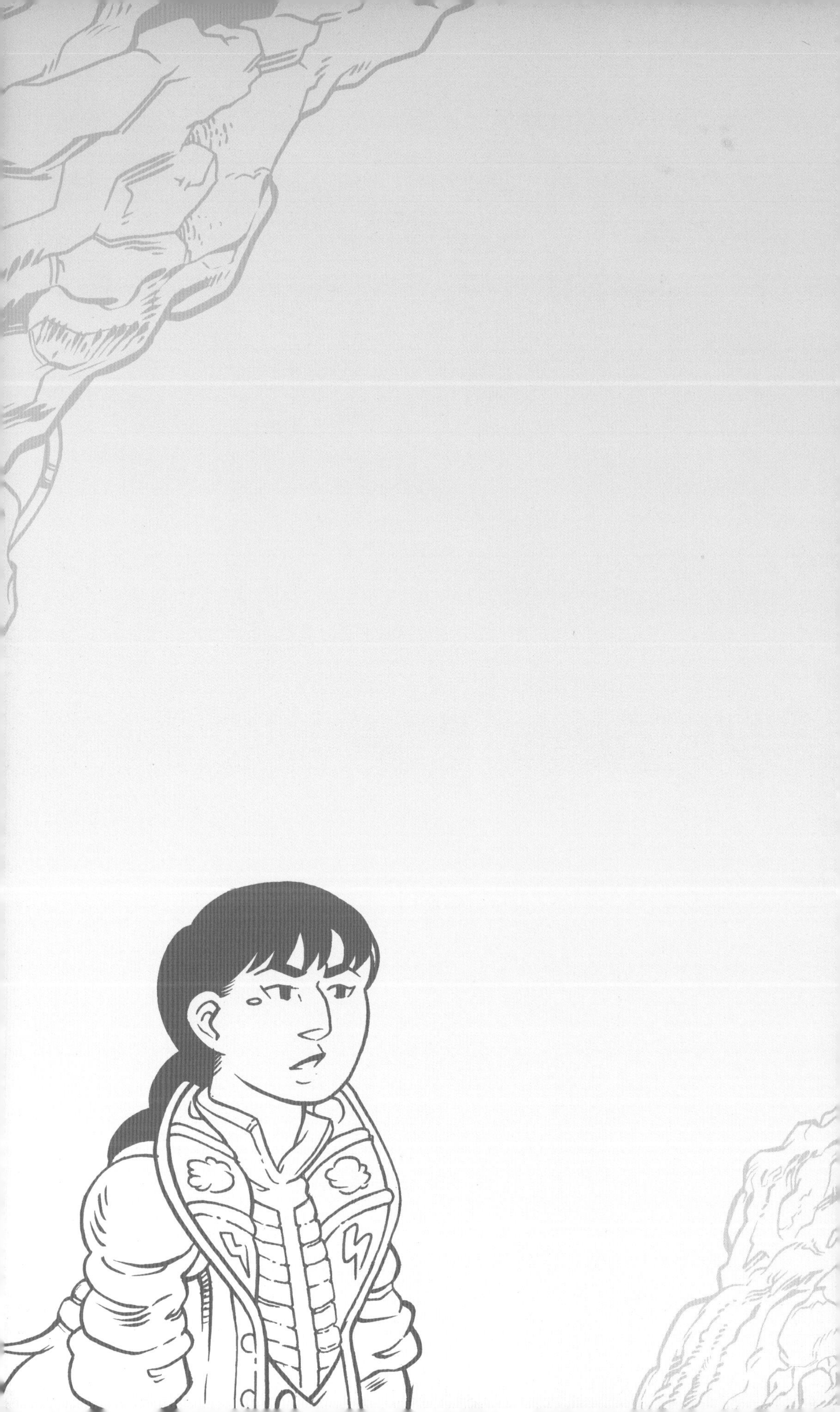

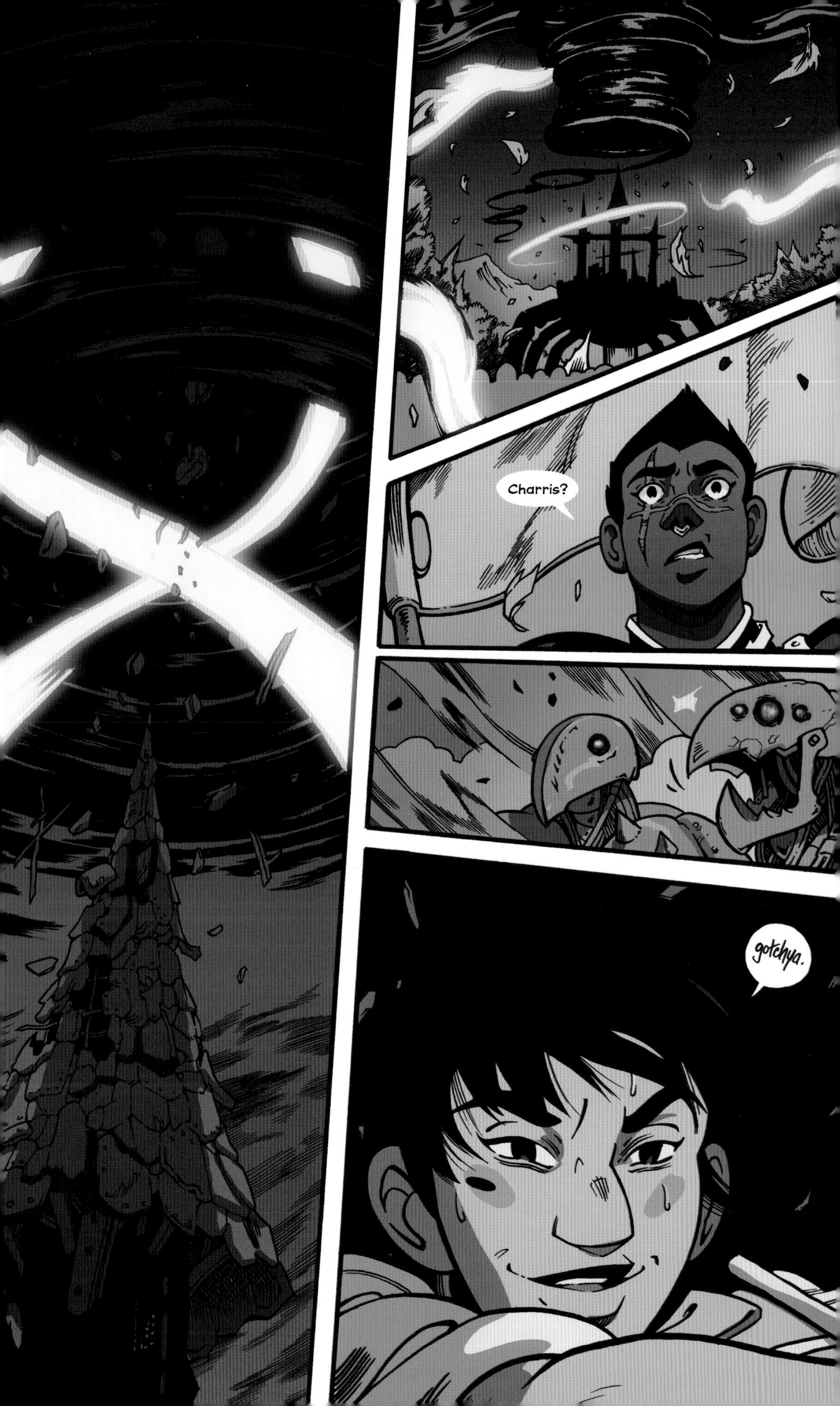
Charris?
gotchya.

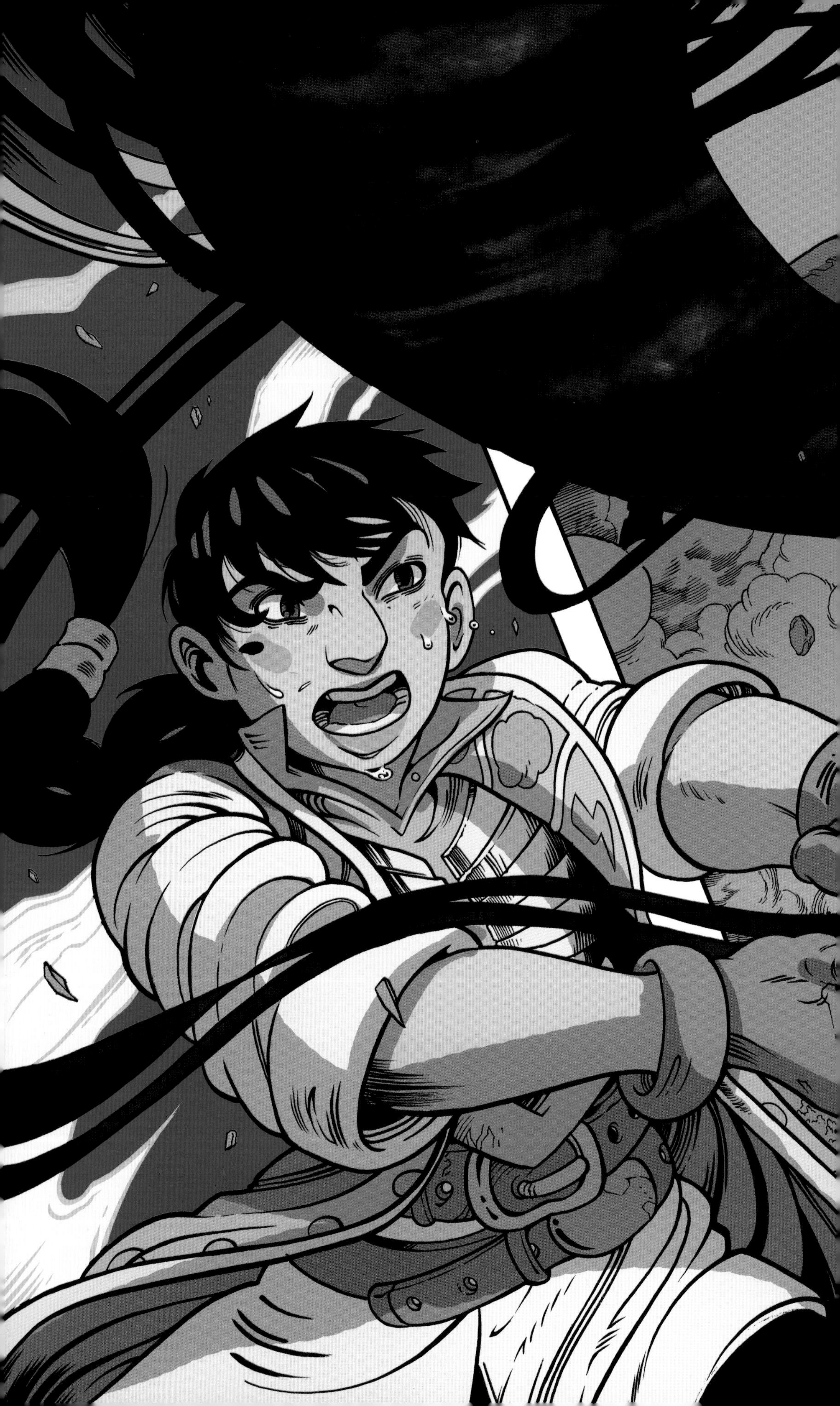

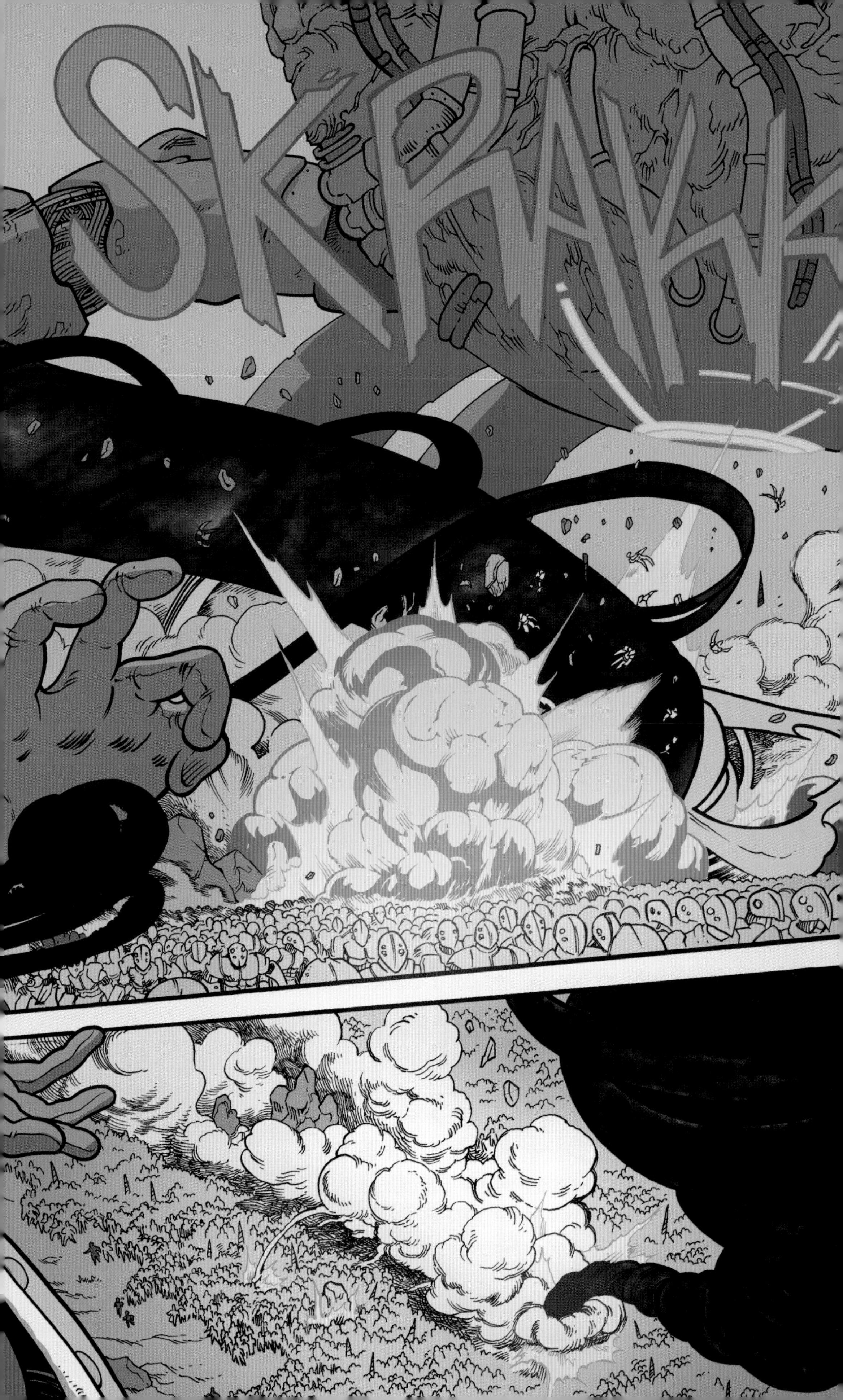
SKRAKK

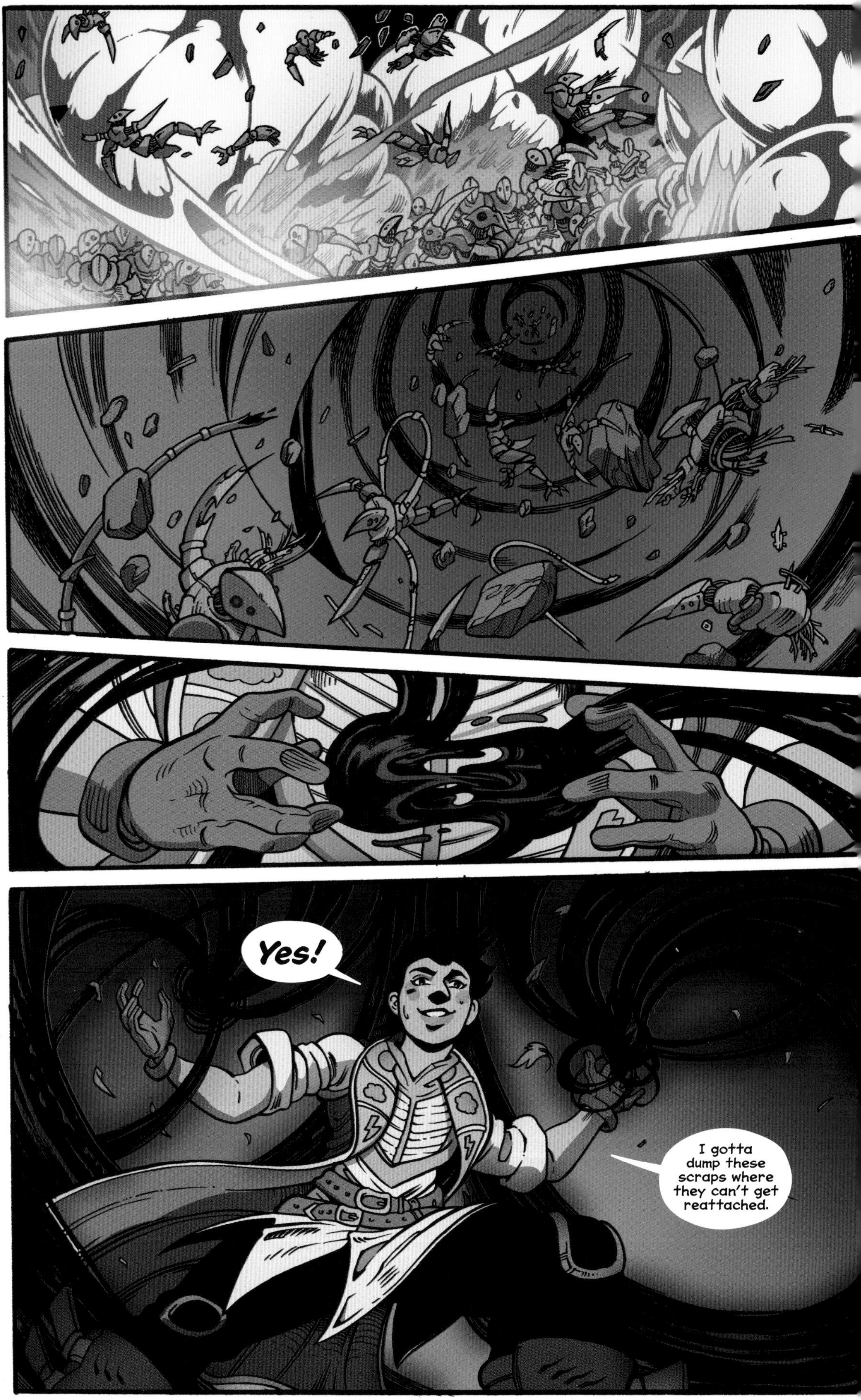
Yes!
I gotta dump these scraps where they can't get reattached.

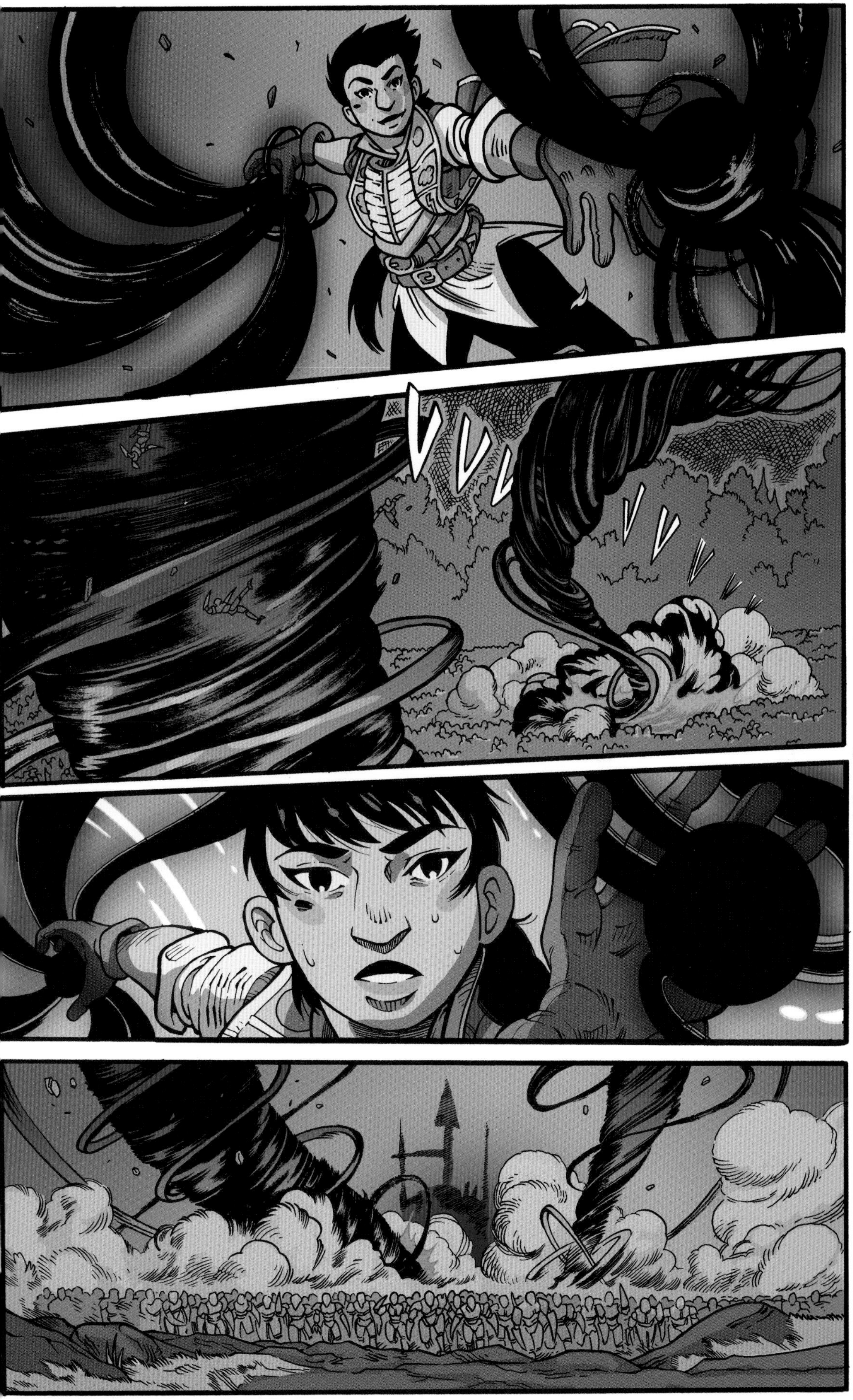

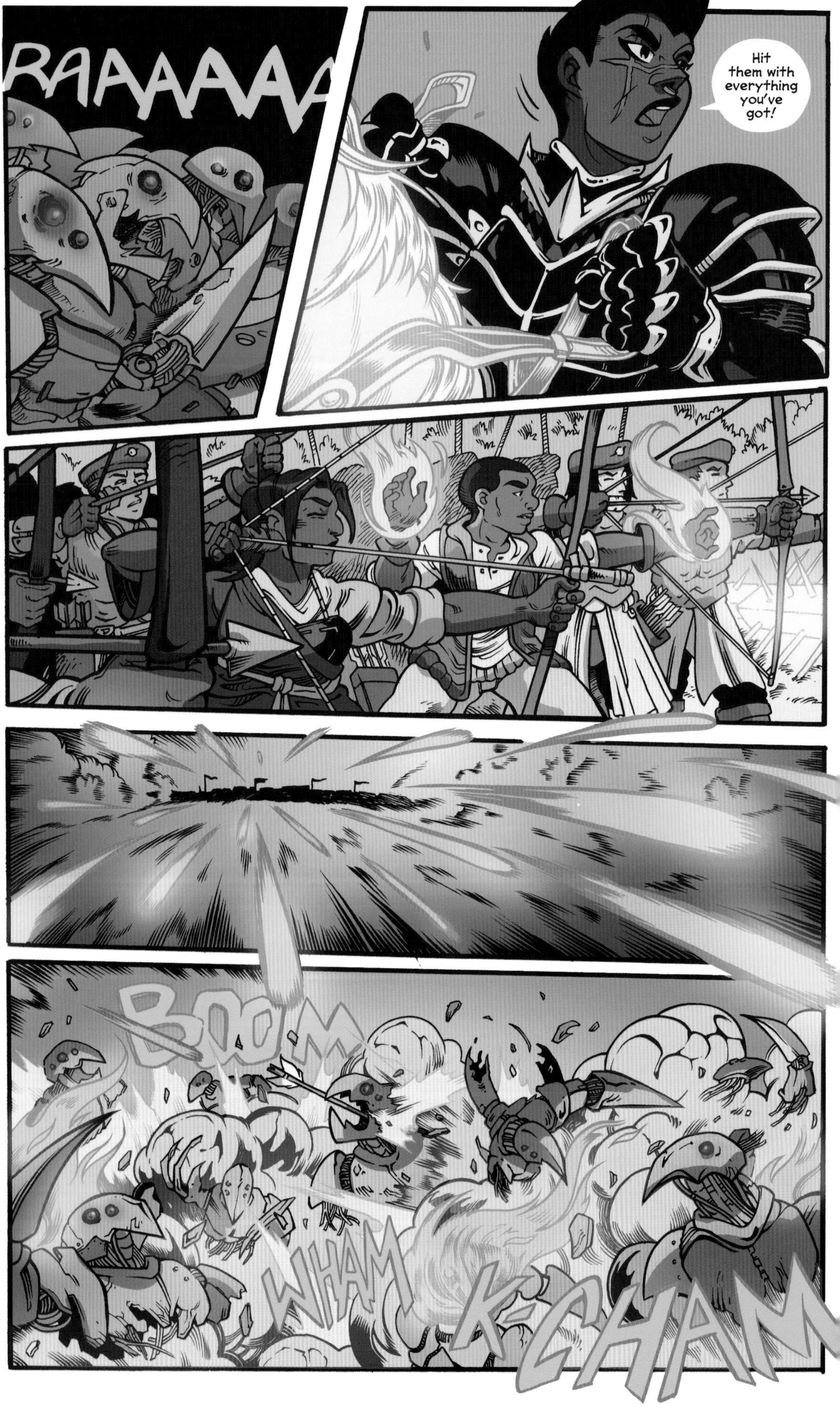
RAAAAAA
Hit them with everything you've got!
BOOM
WHAM
K-CHAM

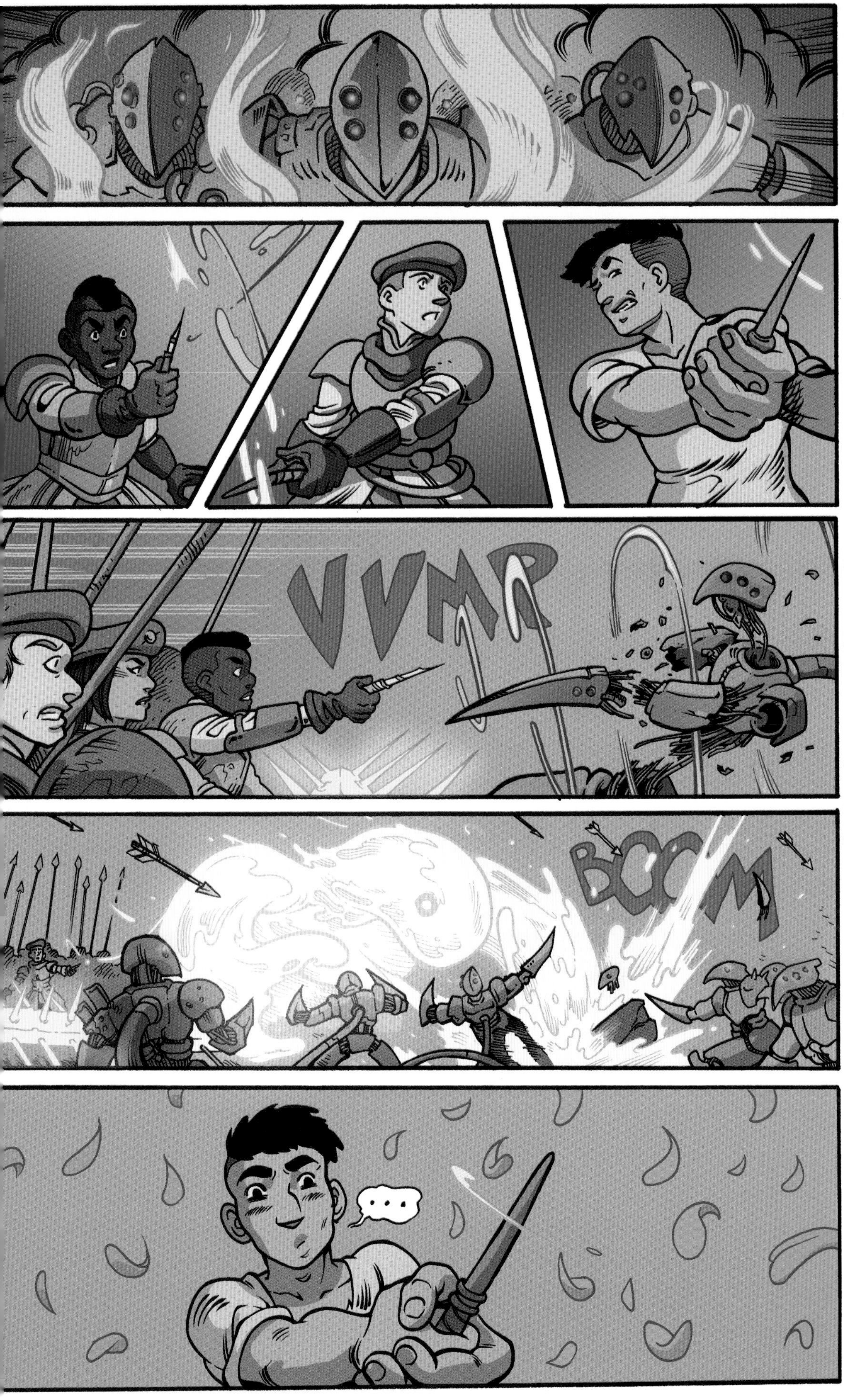
VVMP
BOOM
...

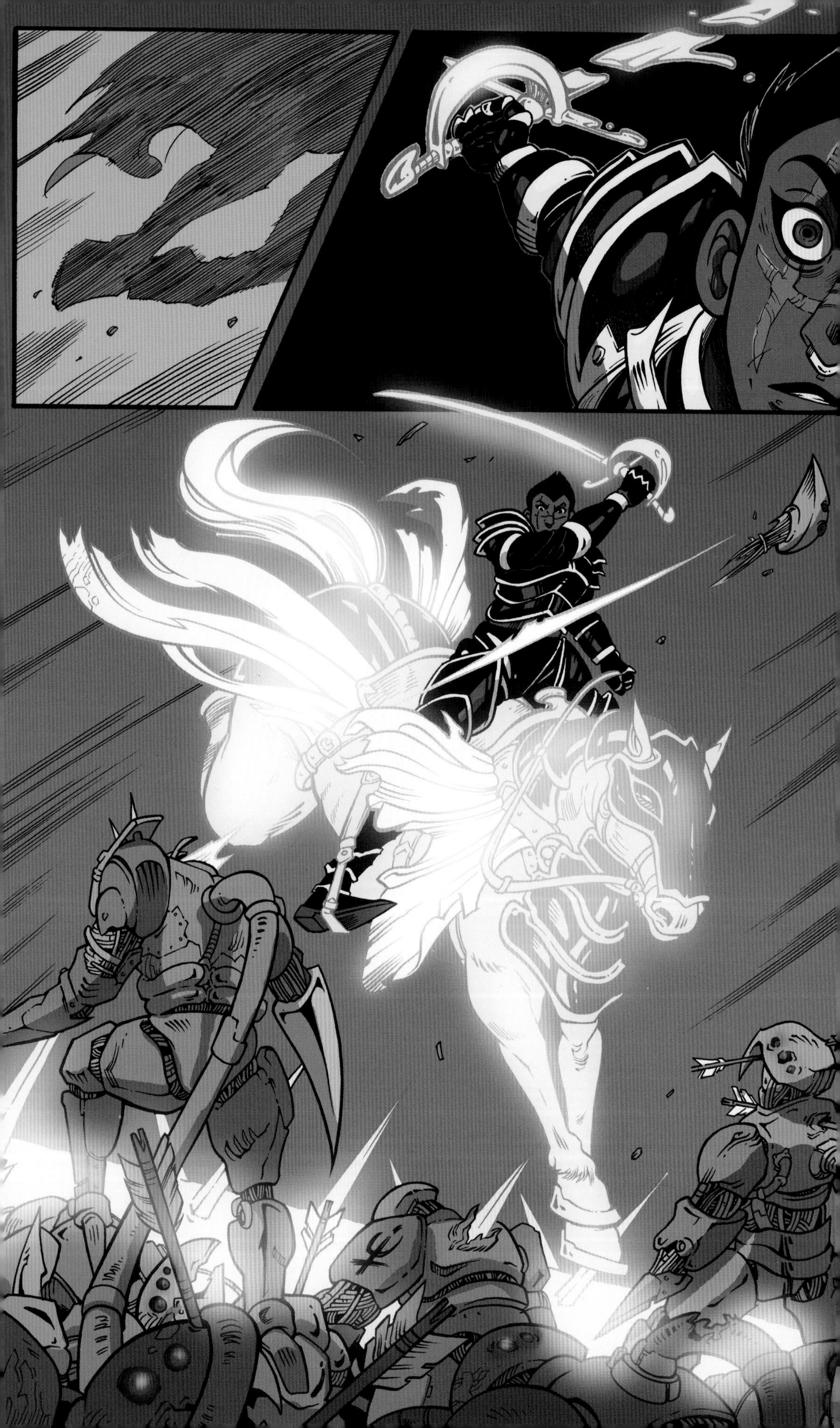

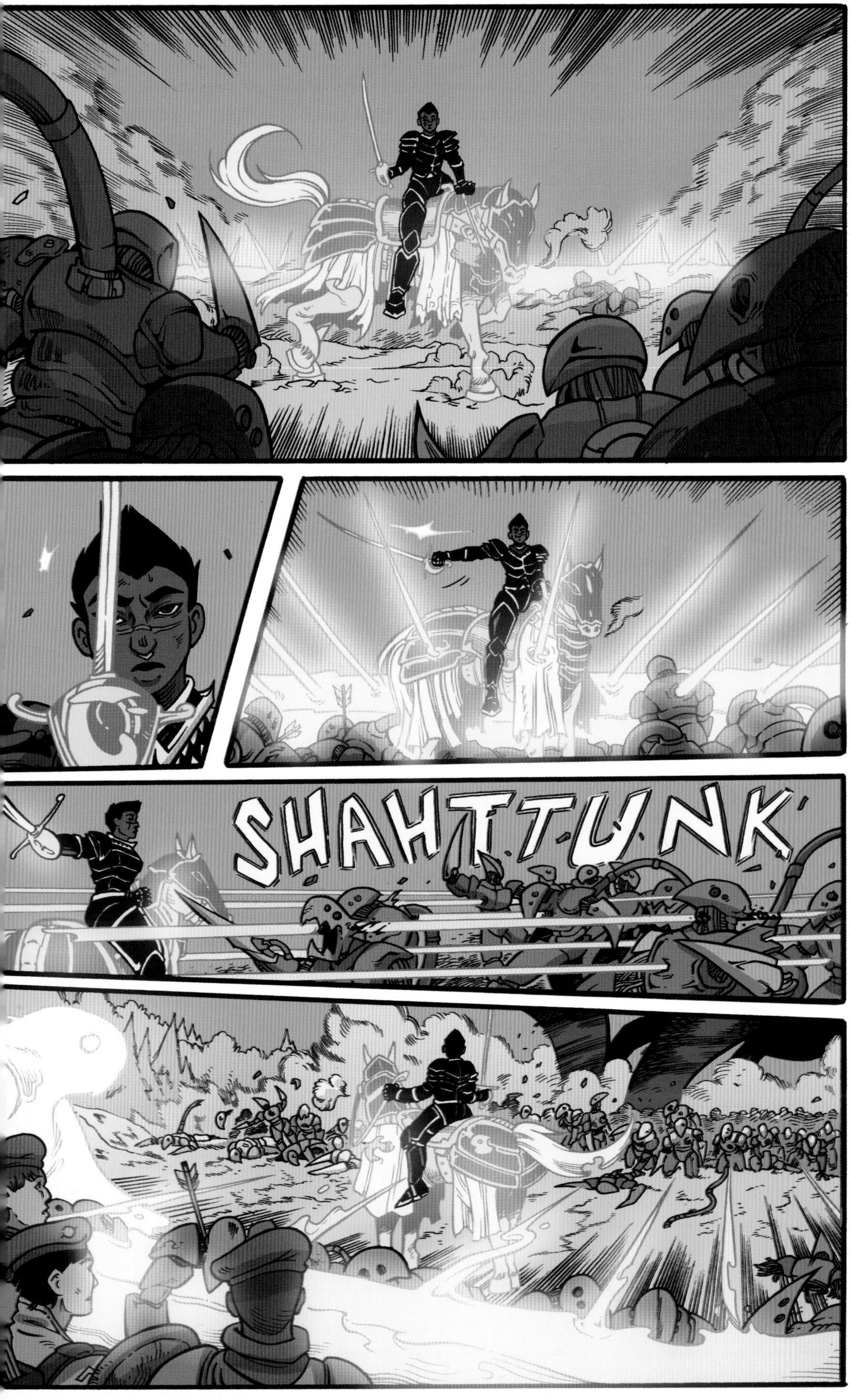
SHAHTTUNK

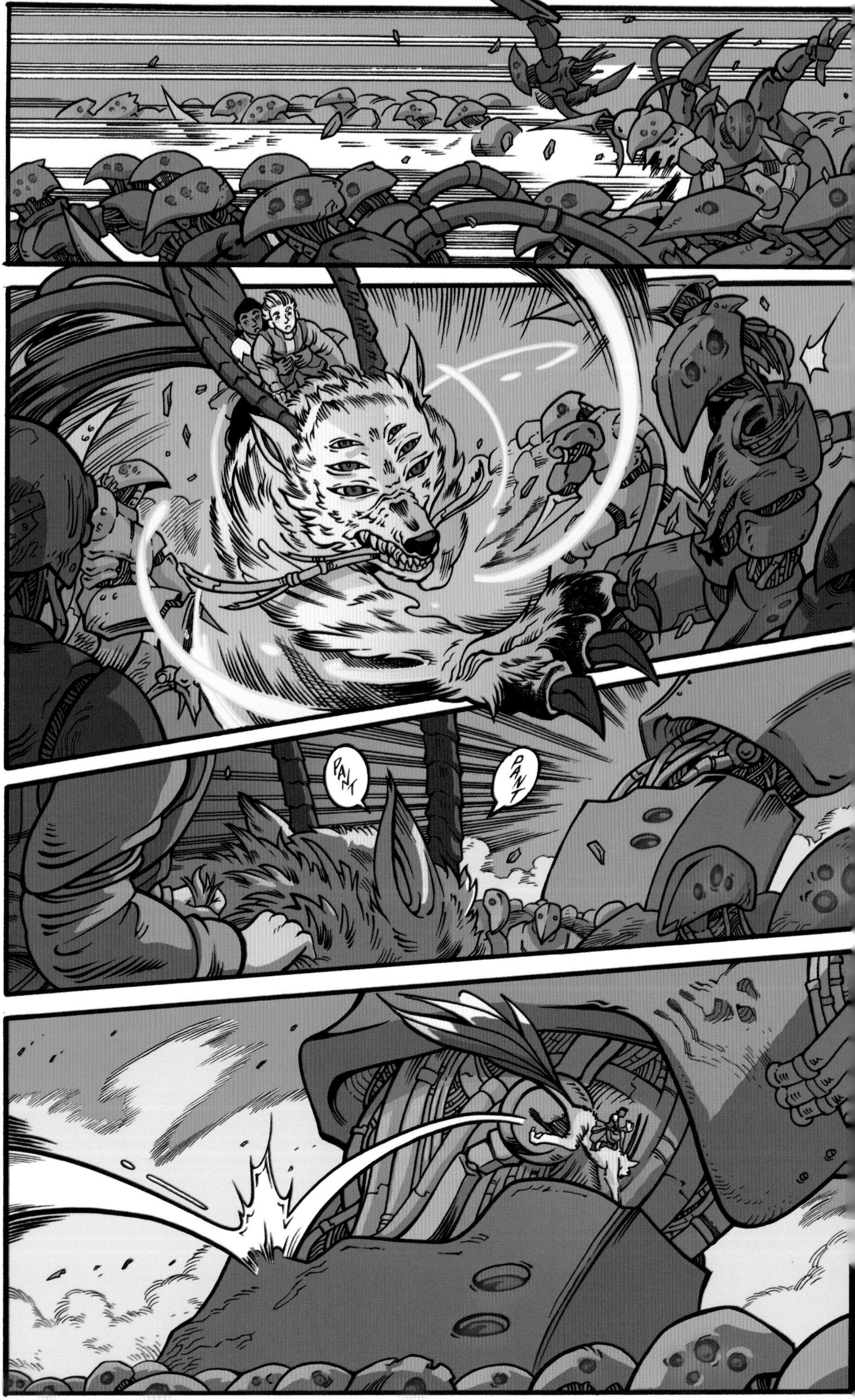
PANT
PANT

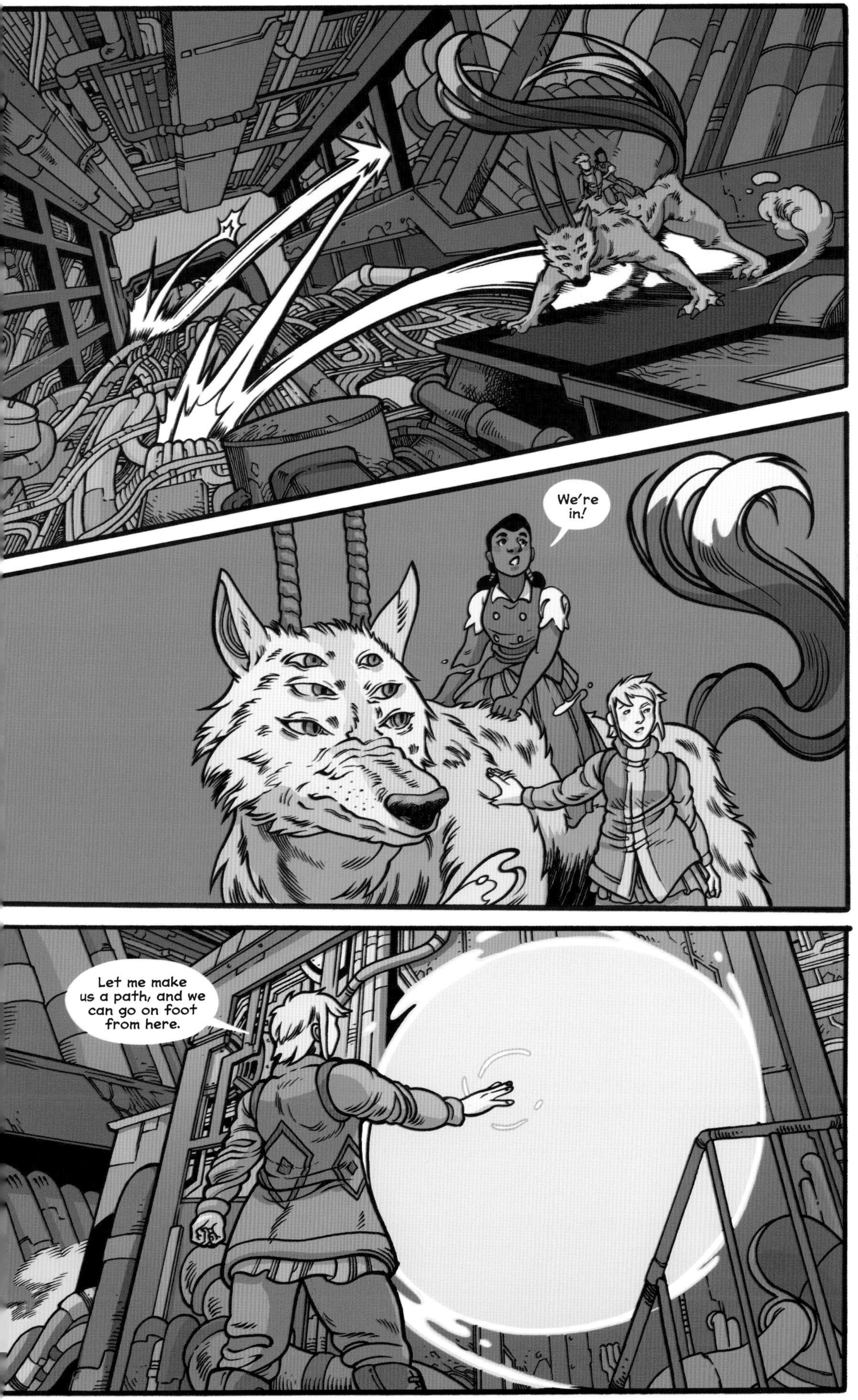
We're in!
Let me make us a path, and we can go on foot from here.

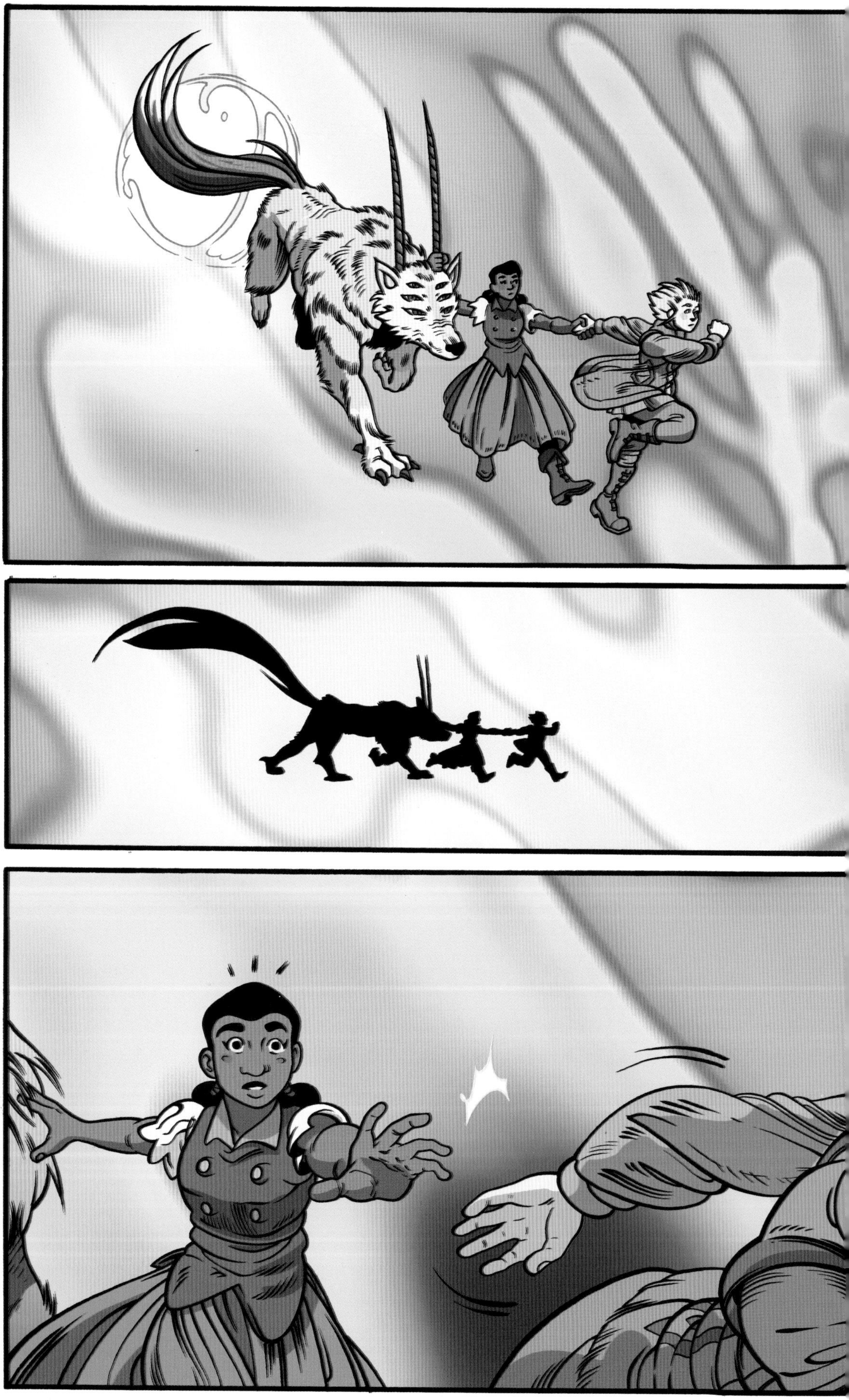

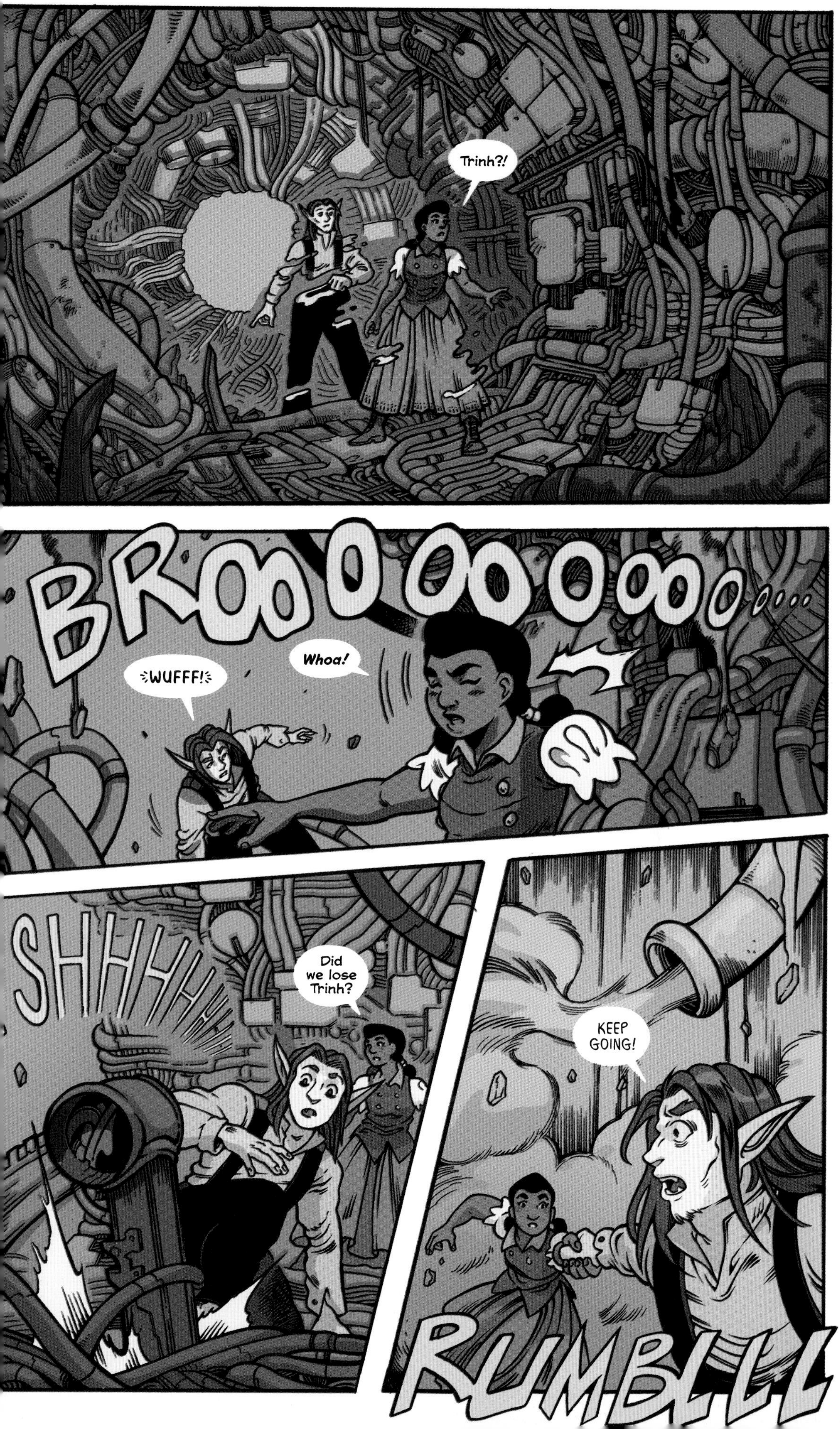
Trinh?!
BROOOOOOOO...
WUFFF!
Whoa!
SHHHHH
Did we lose Trinh?
KEEP GOING!
RUMBLLL

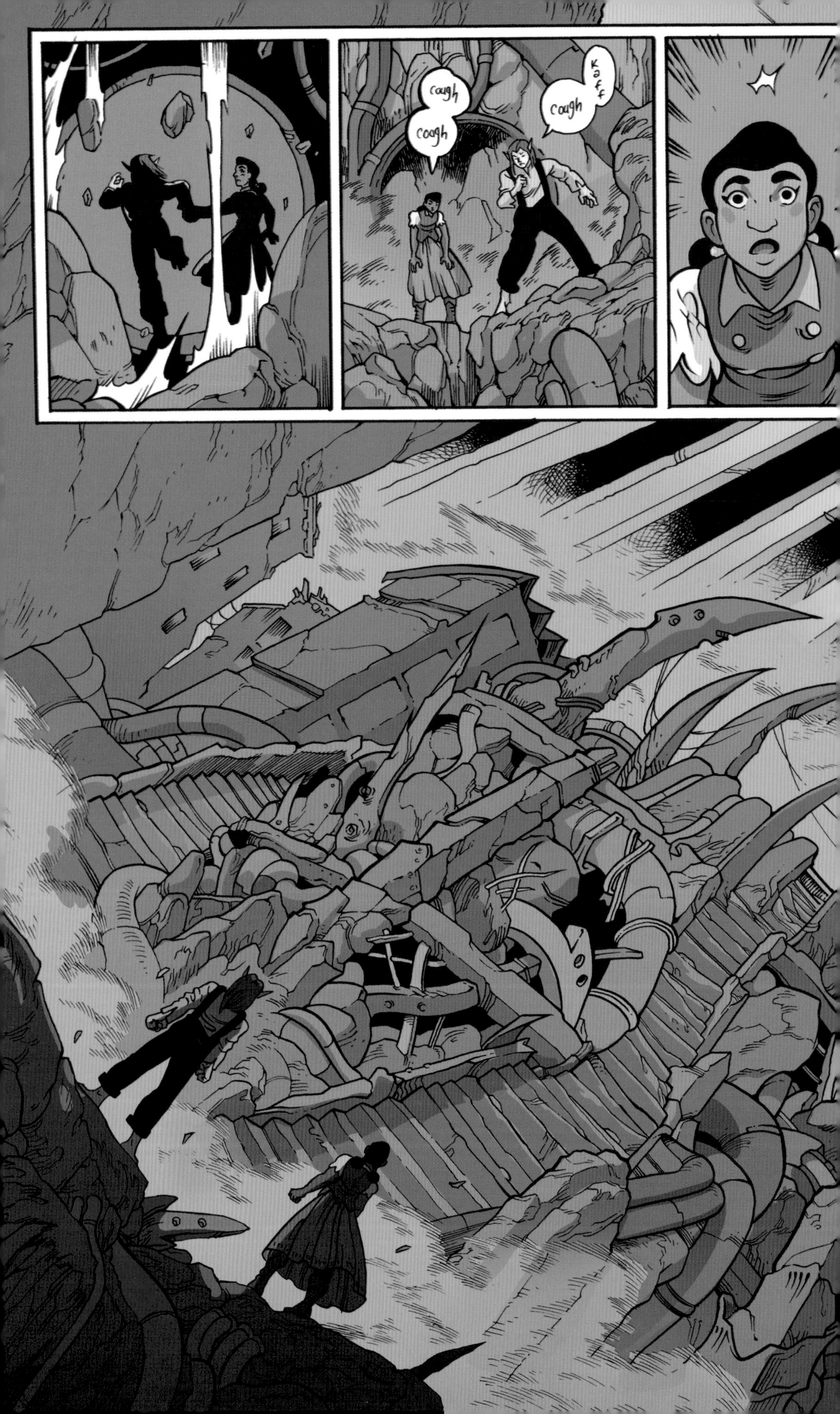
cough
cough
cough
Kaff

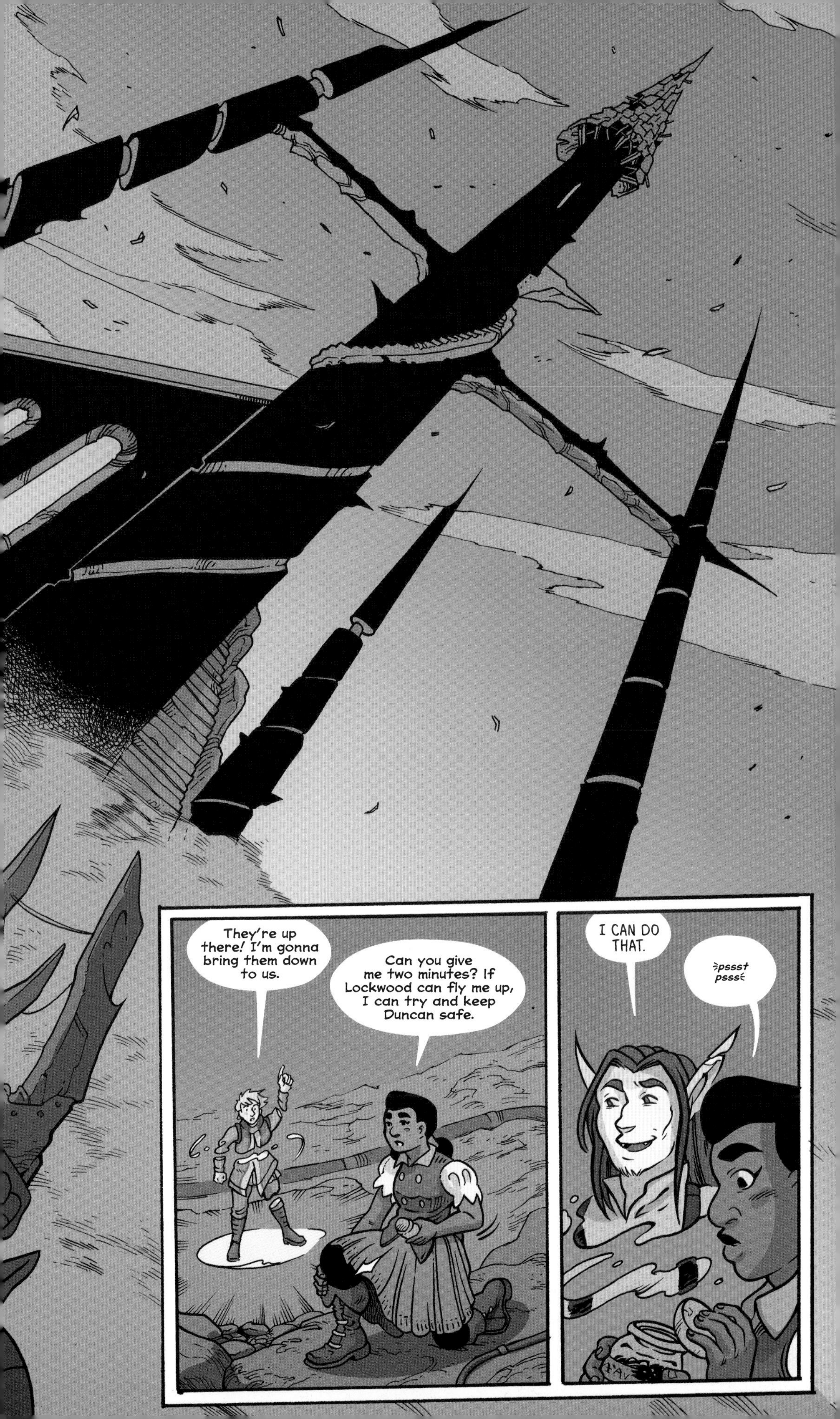
They're up there! I'm gonna bring them down to us.
Can you give me two minutes? If Lockwood can fly me up, I can try and keep Duncan safe.
I CAN DO THAT.
pssst psss

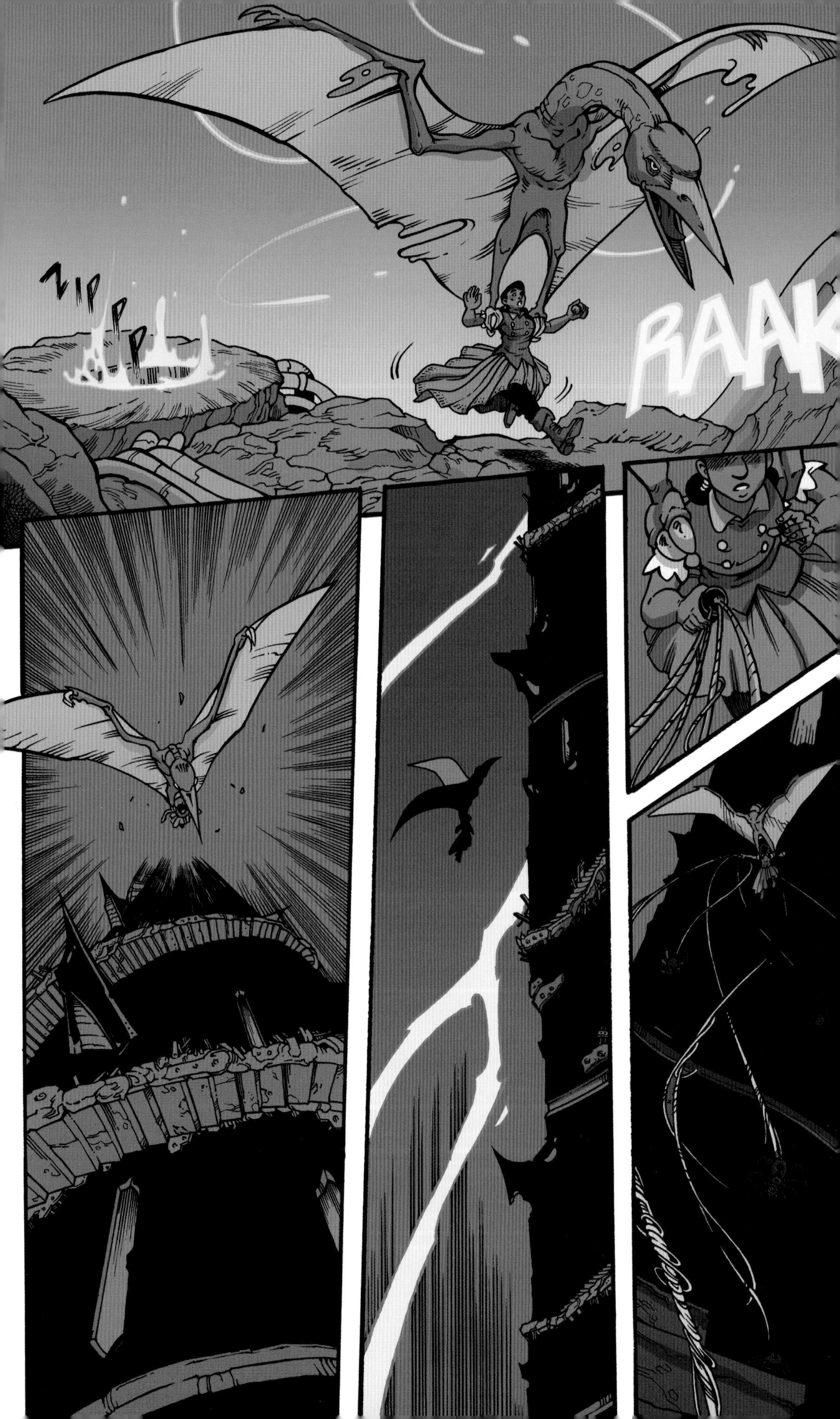
ZIPPP
RAAK

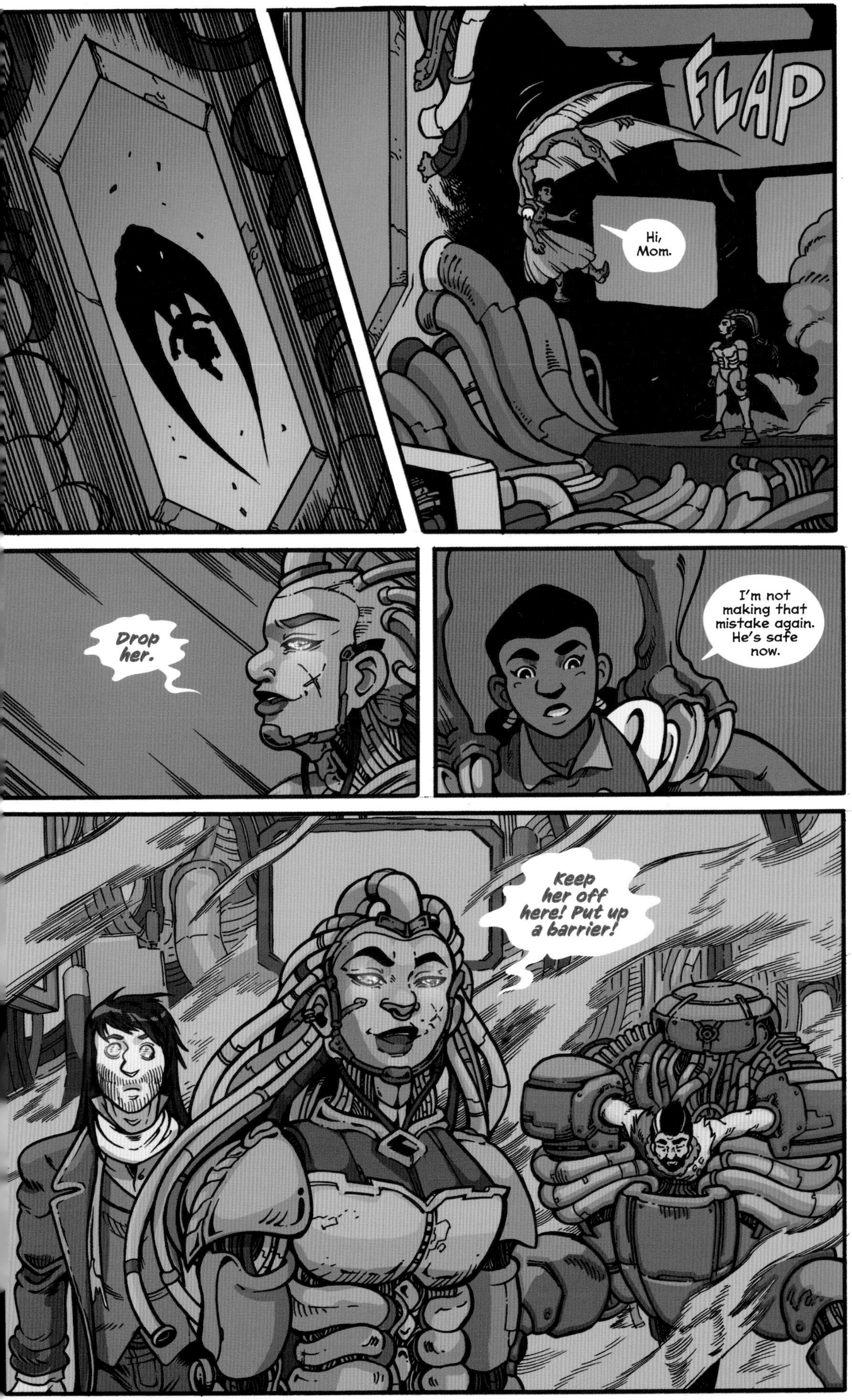
FLAP
Hi, Mom.
Drop her.
I'm not making that mistake again. He's safe now.
Keep her off here! Put up a barrier!

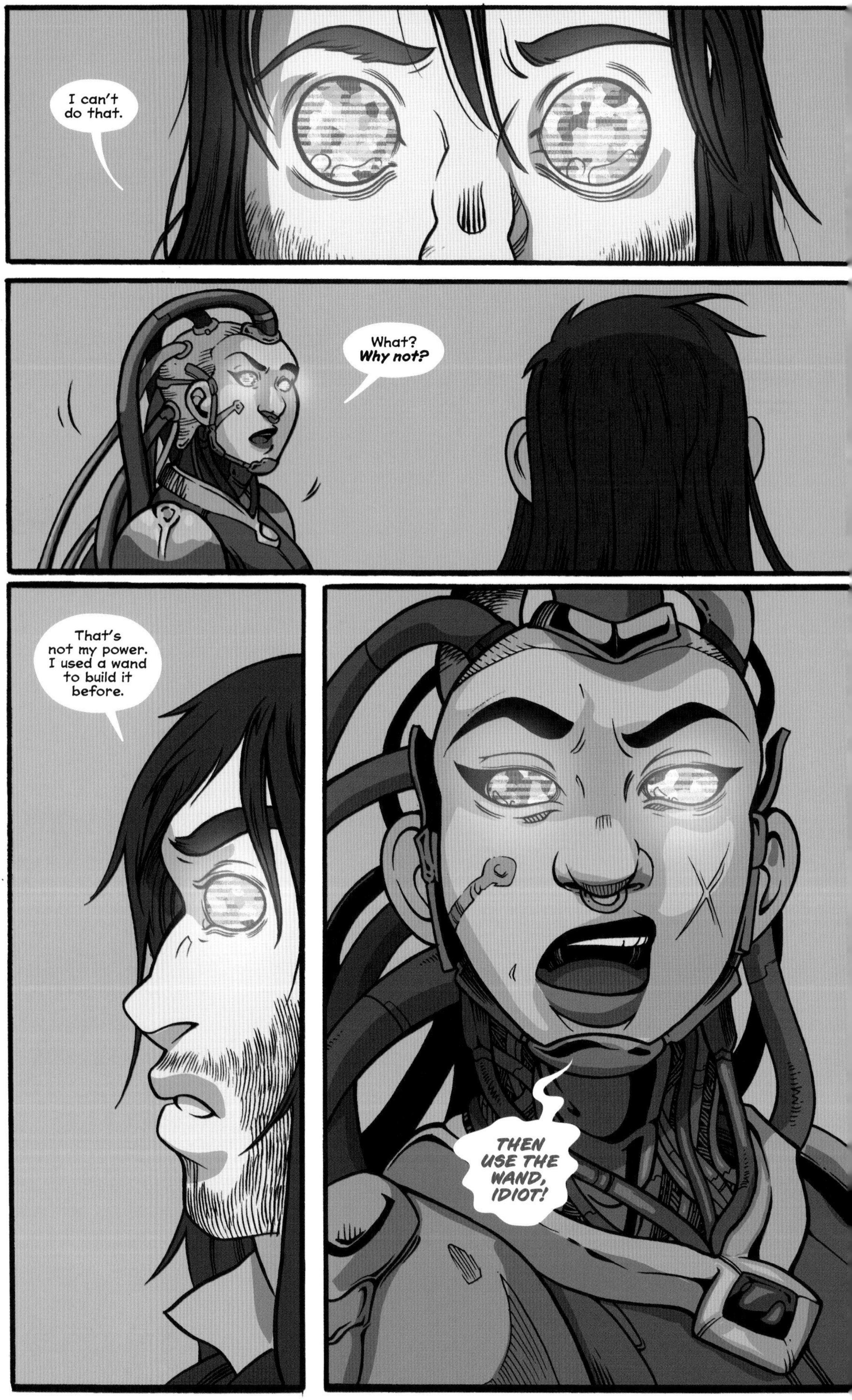
I can't do that.
What? *Why not?*
That's not my power. I used a wand to build it before.
THEN USE THE WAND, IDIOT!

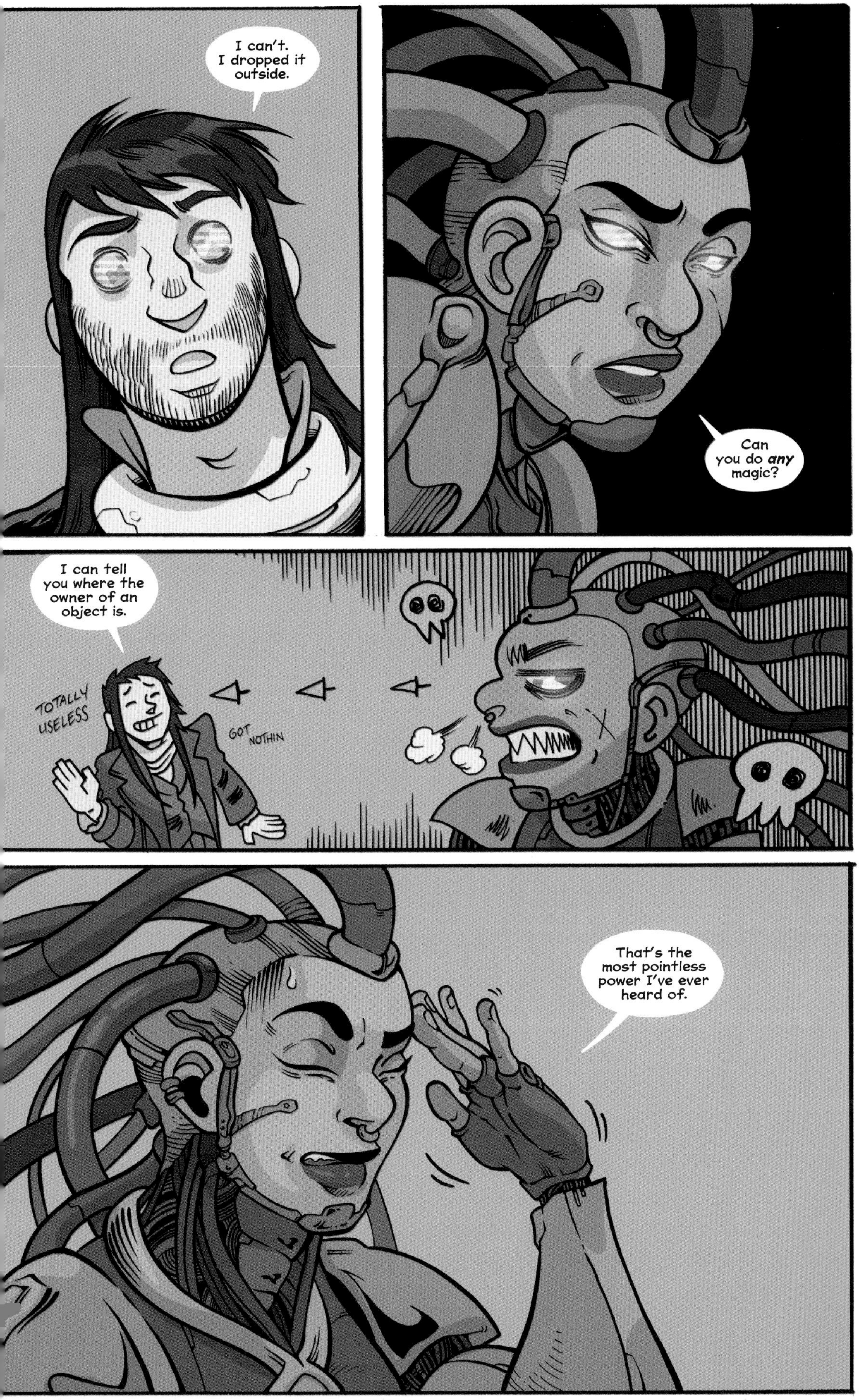
I can't. I dropped it outside.
Can you do *any* magic?
I can tell you where the owner of an object is.
TOTALLY USELESS
GOT NOTHIN
That's the most pointless power I've ever heard of.

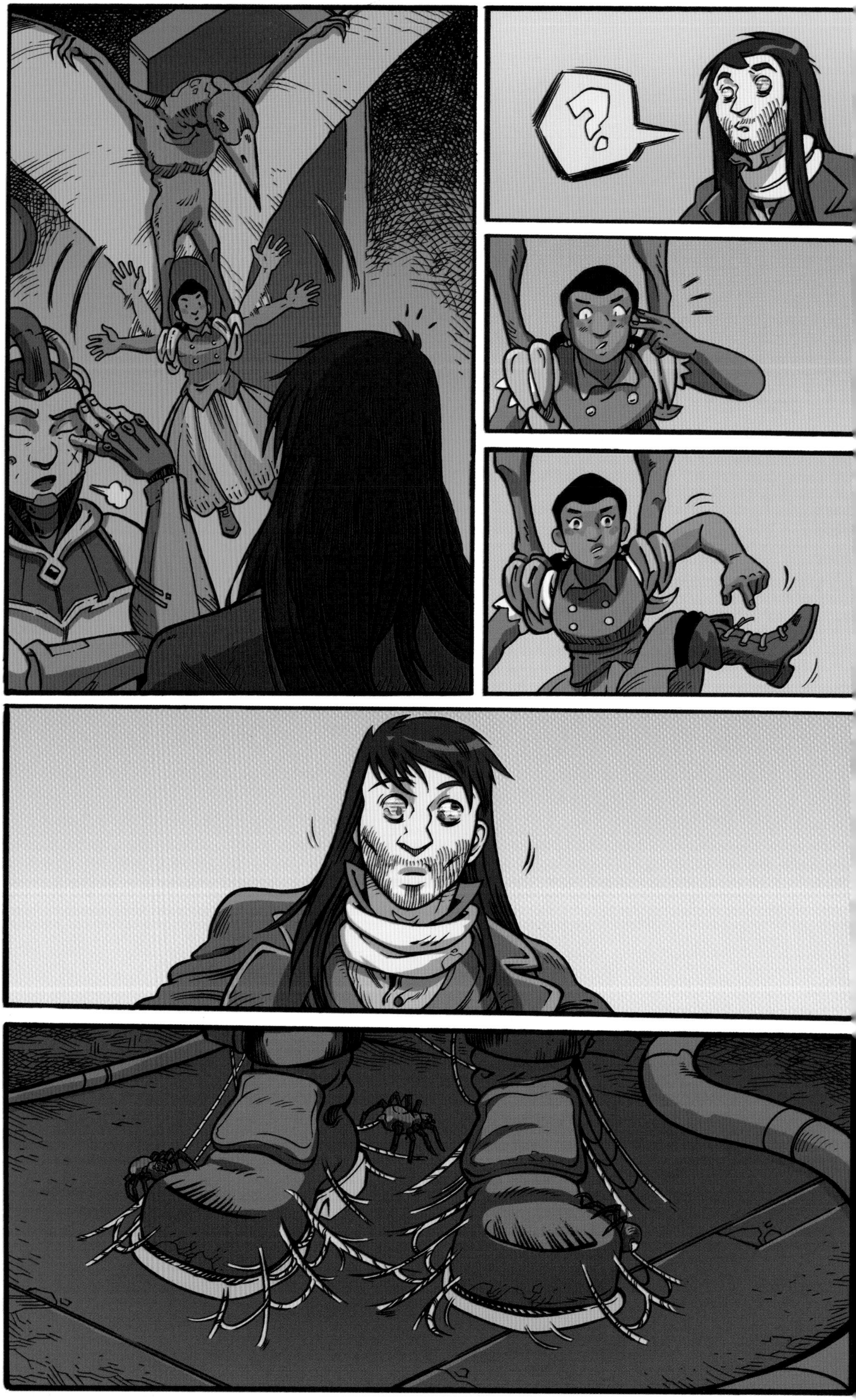
?

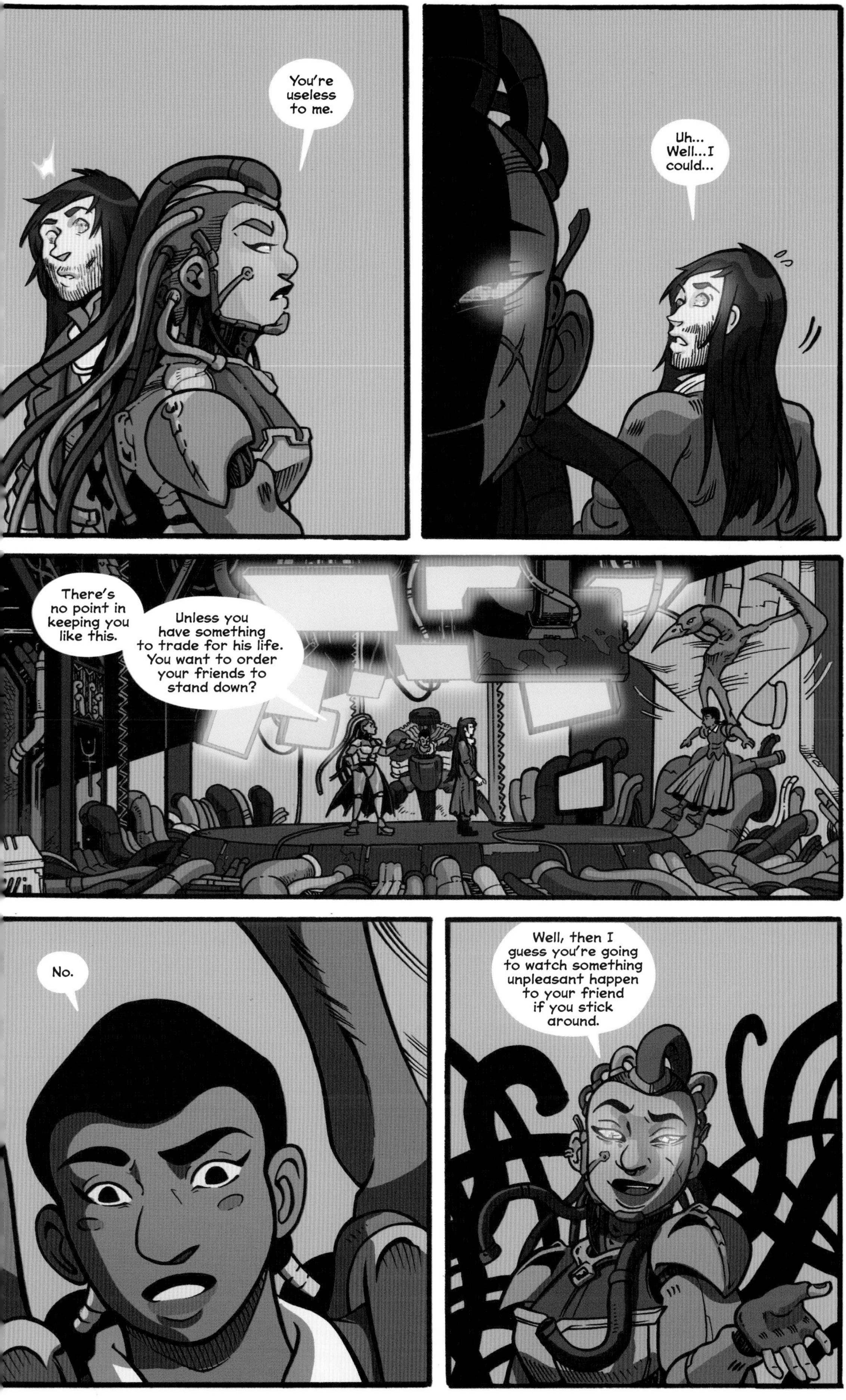
You're useless to me.
Uh... Well...I could...
There's no point in keeping you like this.
Unless you have something to trade for his life. You want to order your friends to stand down?
No.
Well, then I guess you're going to watch something unpleasant happen to your friend if you stick around.

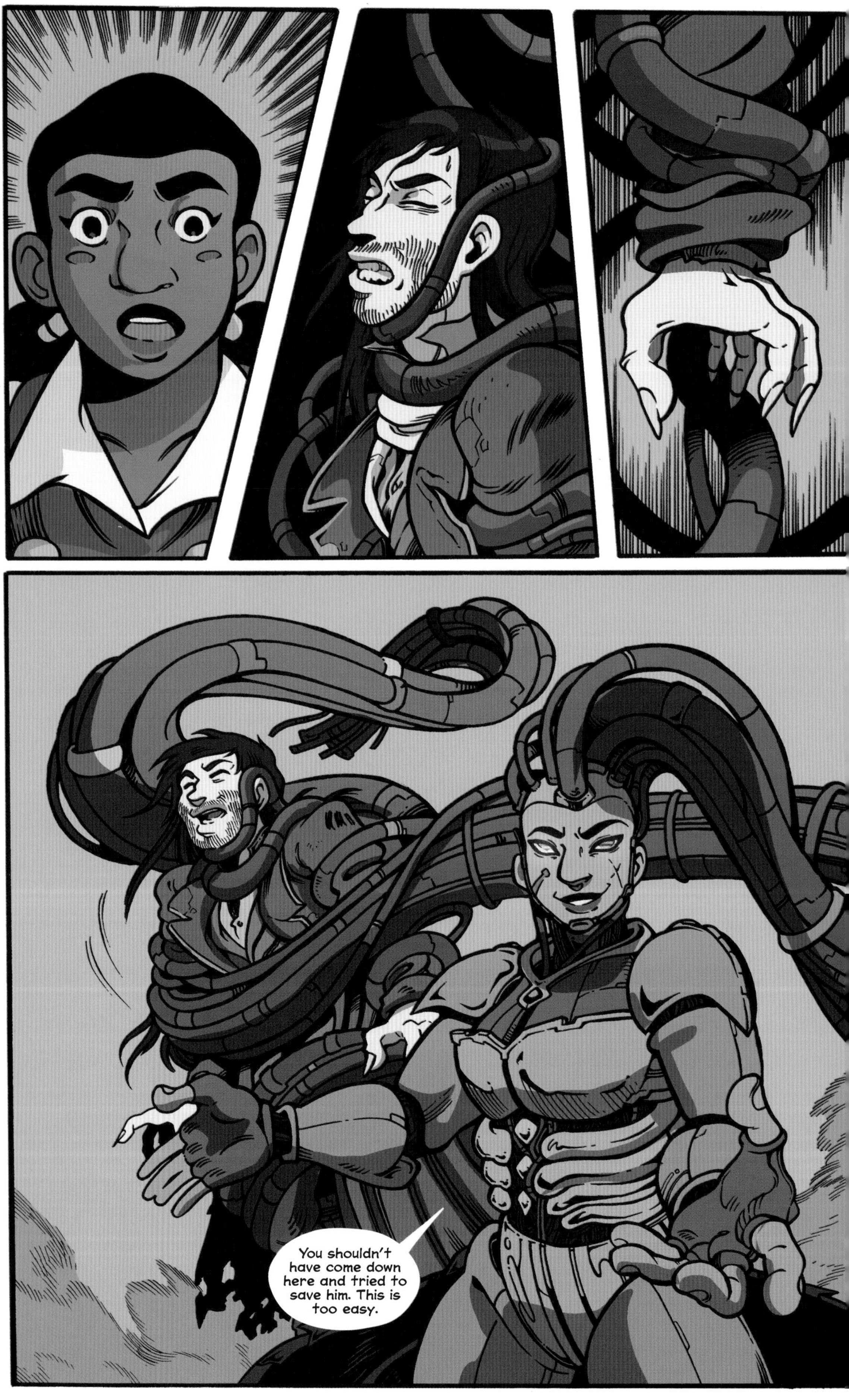
You shouldn't have come down here and tried to save him. This is too easy.

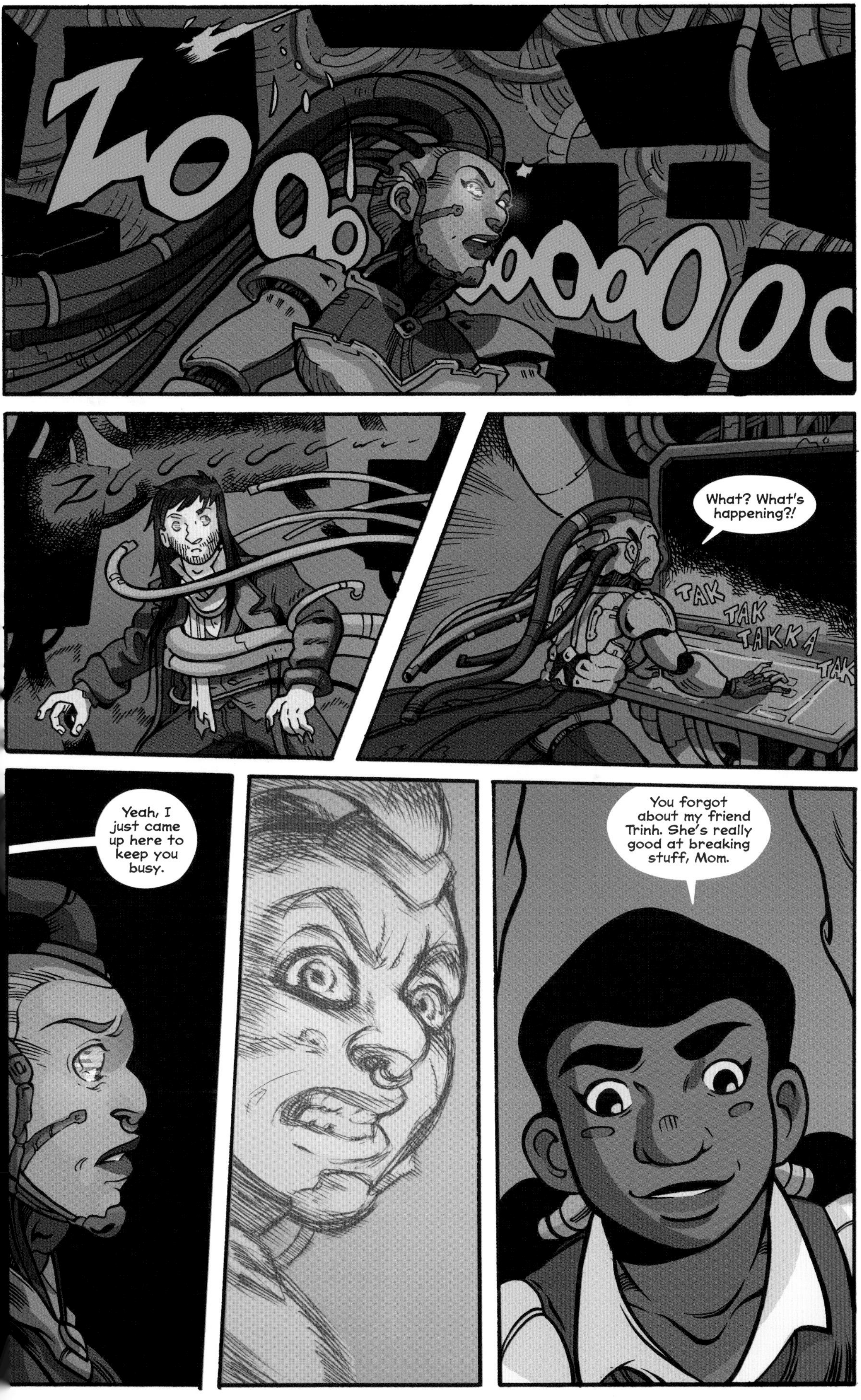
ZOOOOOOOOOOO
What? What's happening?!
TAK TAK TAKKA TAK
Yeah, I just came up here to keep you busy.
You forgot about my friend Trinh. She's really good at breaking stuff, Mom.

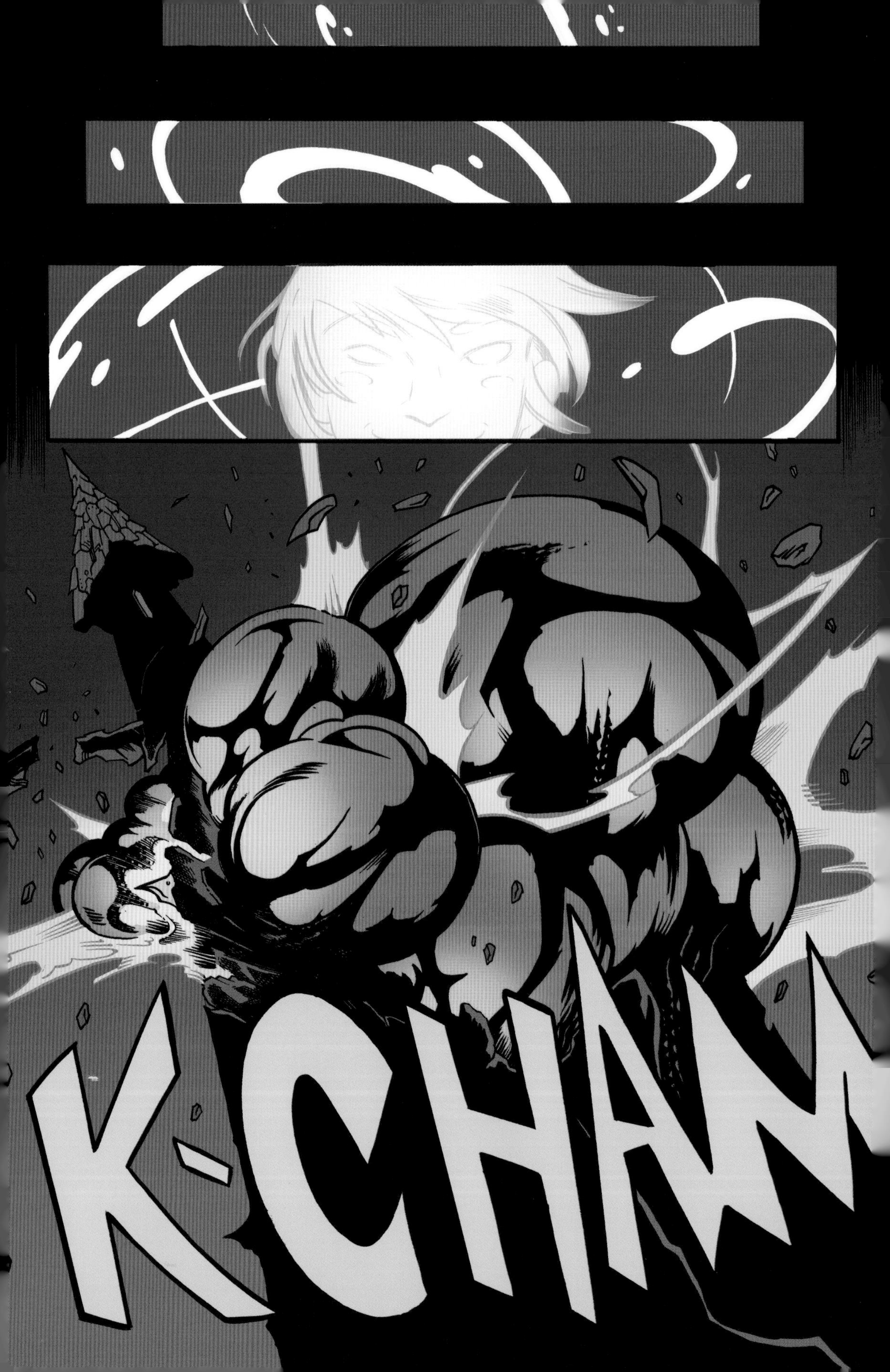
K-CHAM

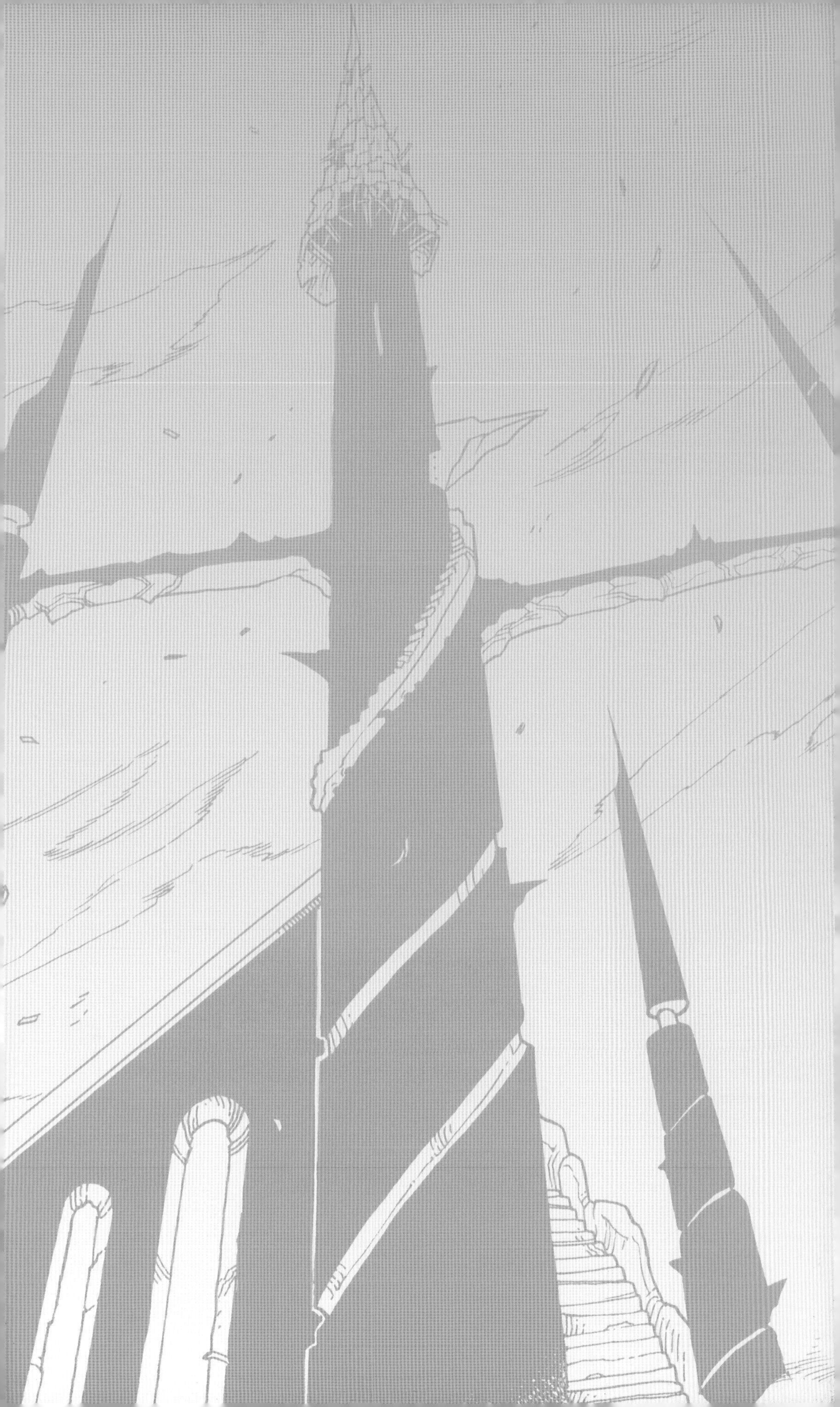

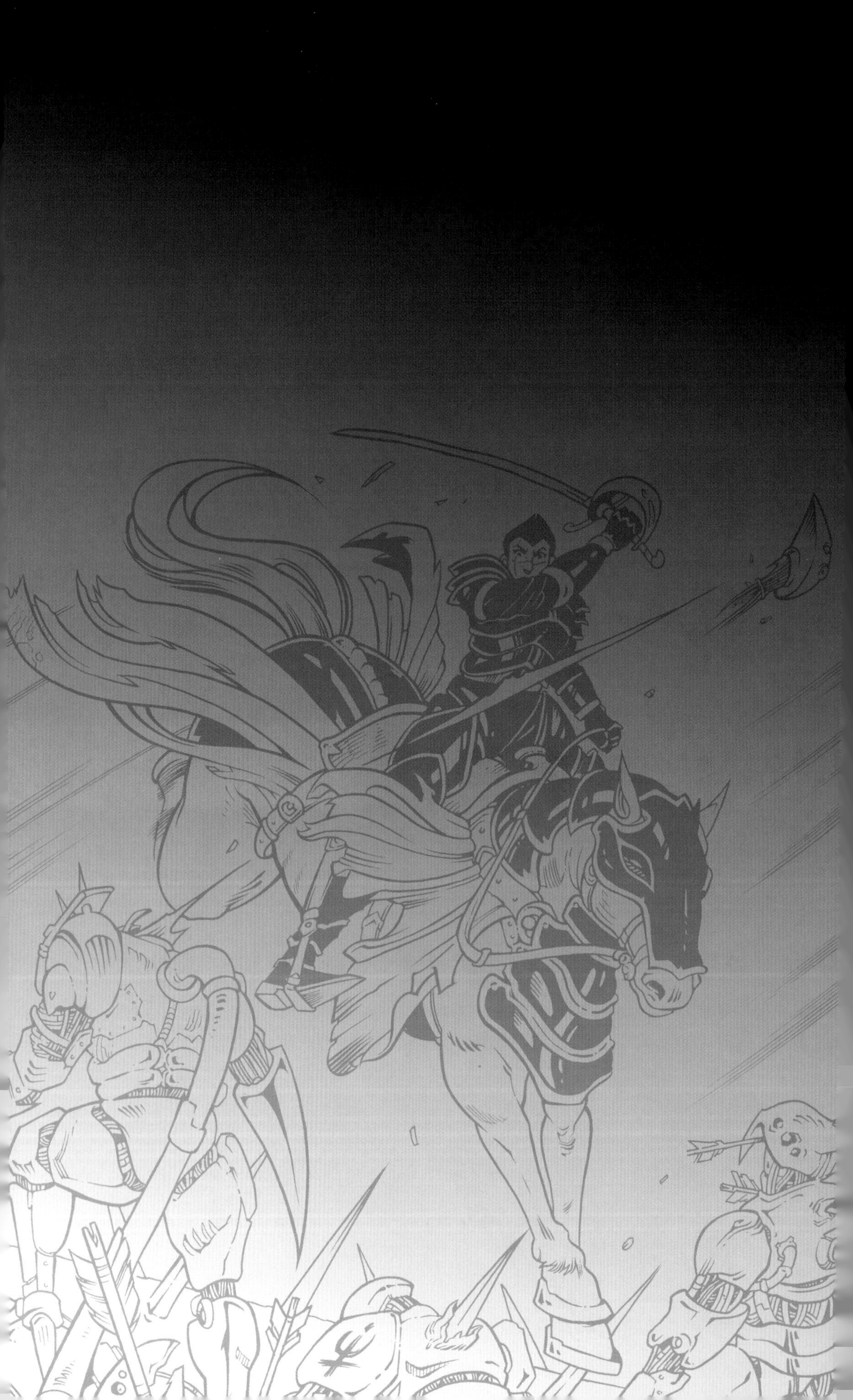

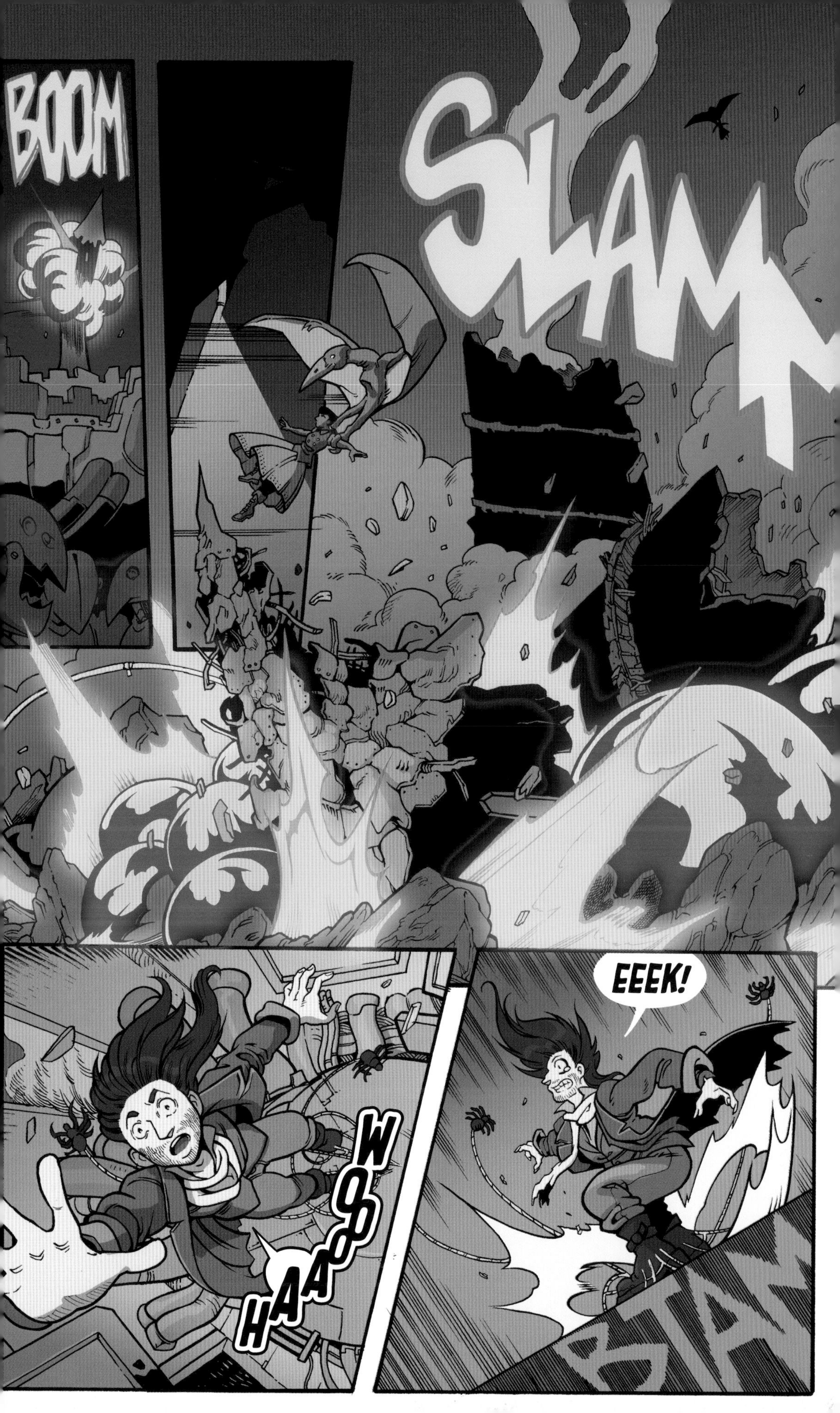
BOOM
SLAM
WHOOOAAAH
EEEK!
BLAM

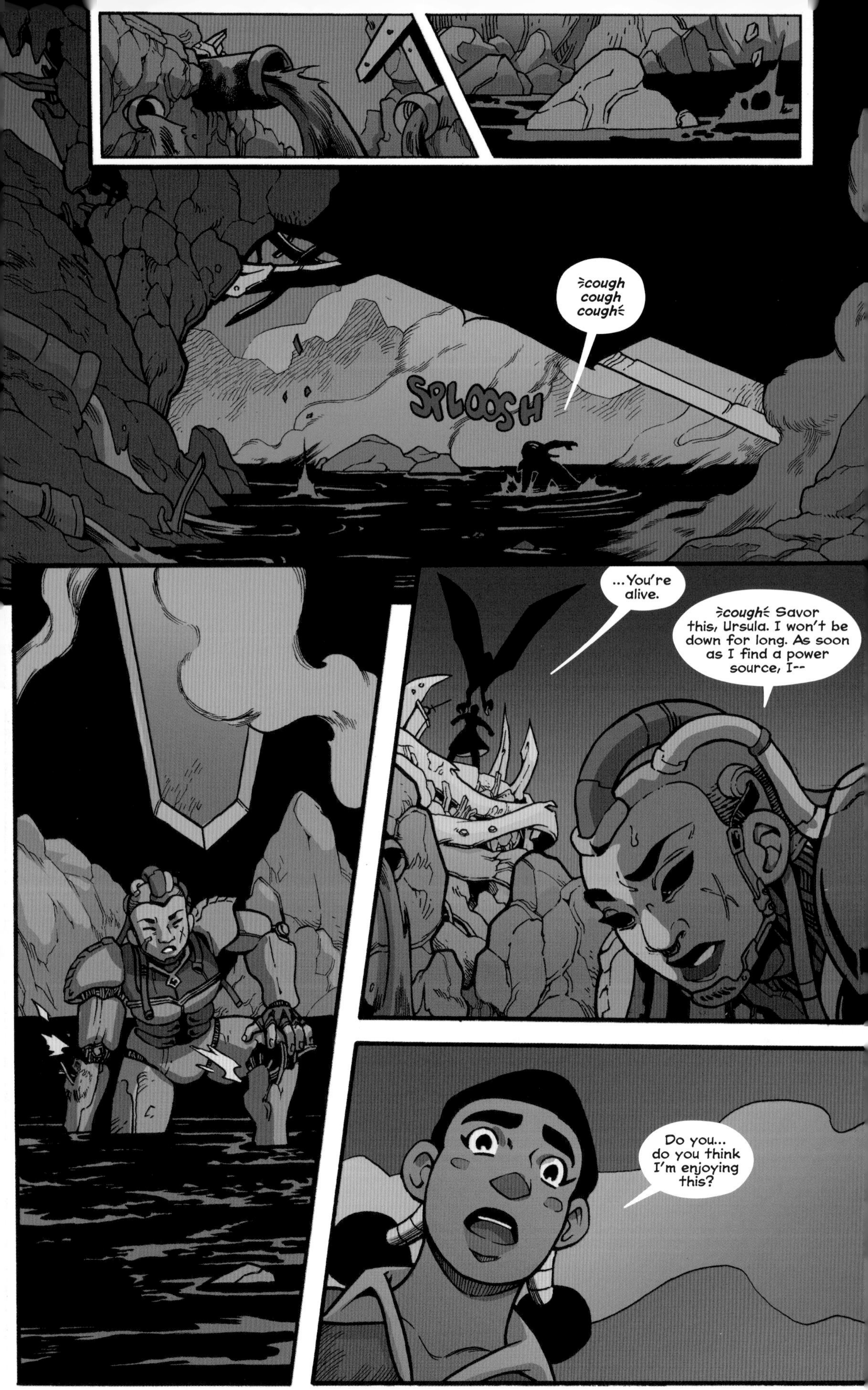
≈cough cough cough≈
SPLOOSH
...You're alive.
≈cough≈ Savor this, Ursula. I won't be down for long. As soon as I find a power source, I--
Do you... do you think I'm enjoying this?

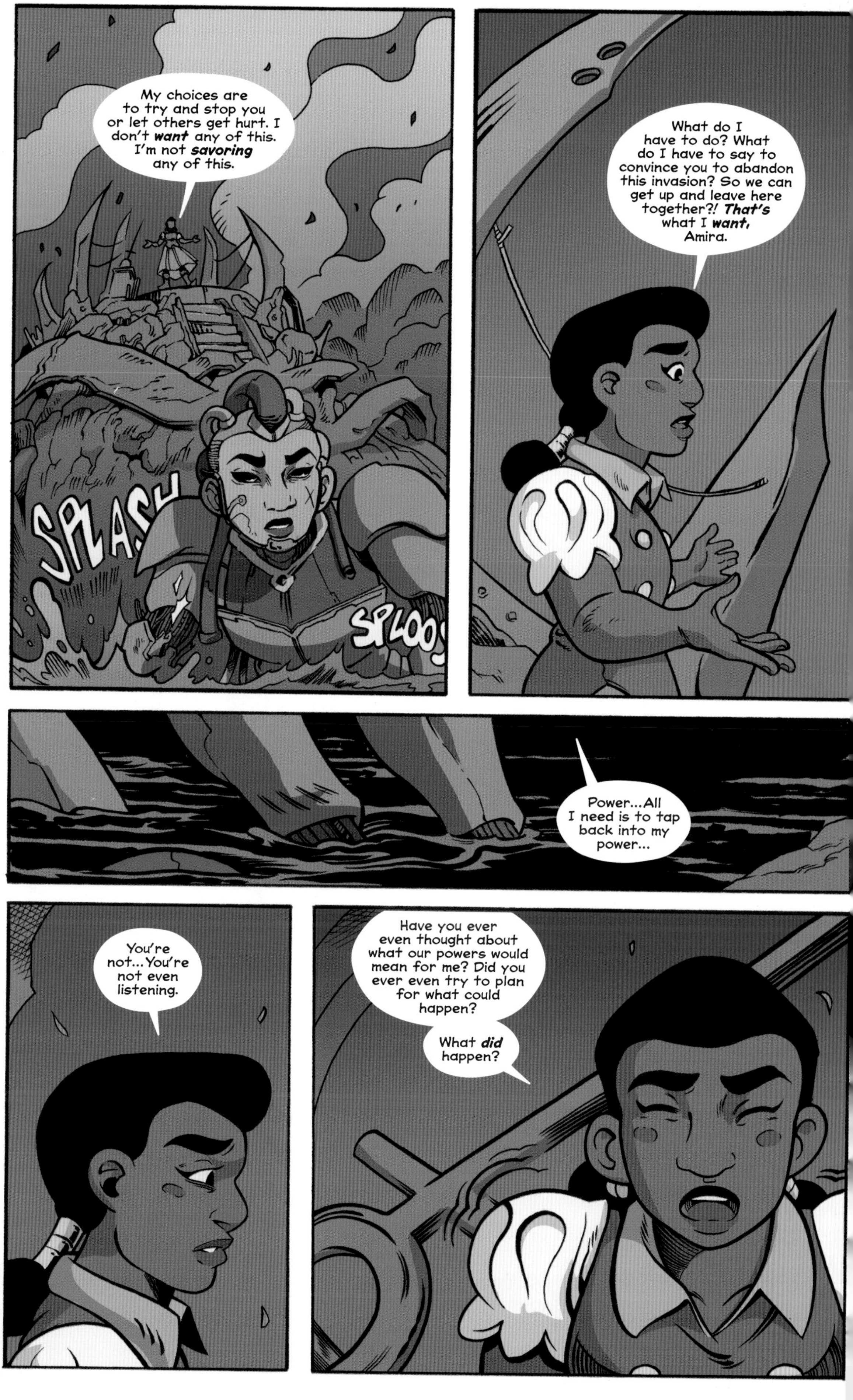
My choices are to try and stop you or let others get hurt. I don't ***want*** any of this. I'm not ***savoring*** any of this.
SPLASH
SPLOO
What do I have to do? What do I have to say to convince you to abandon this invasion? So we can get up and leave here together?! ***That's*** what I ***want,*** Amira.
Power...All I need is to tap back into my power...
You're not...You're not even listening.
Have you ever even thought about what our powers would mean for me? Did you ever even try to plan for what could happen?
What ***did*** happen?

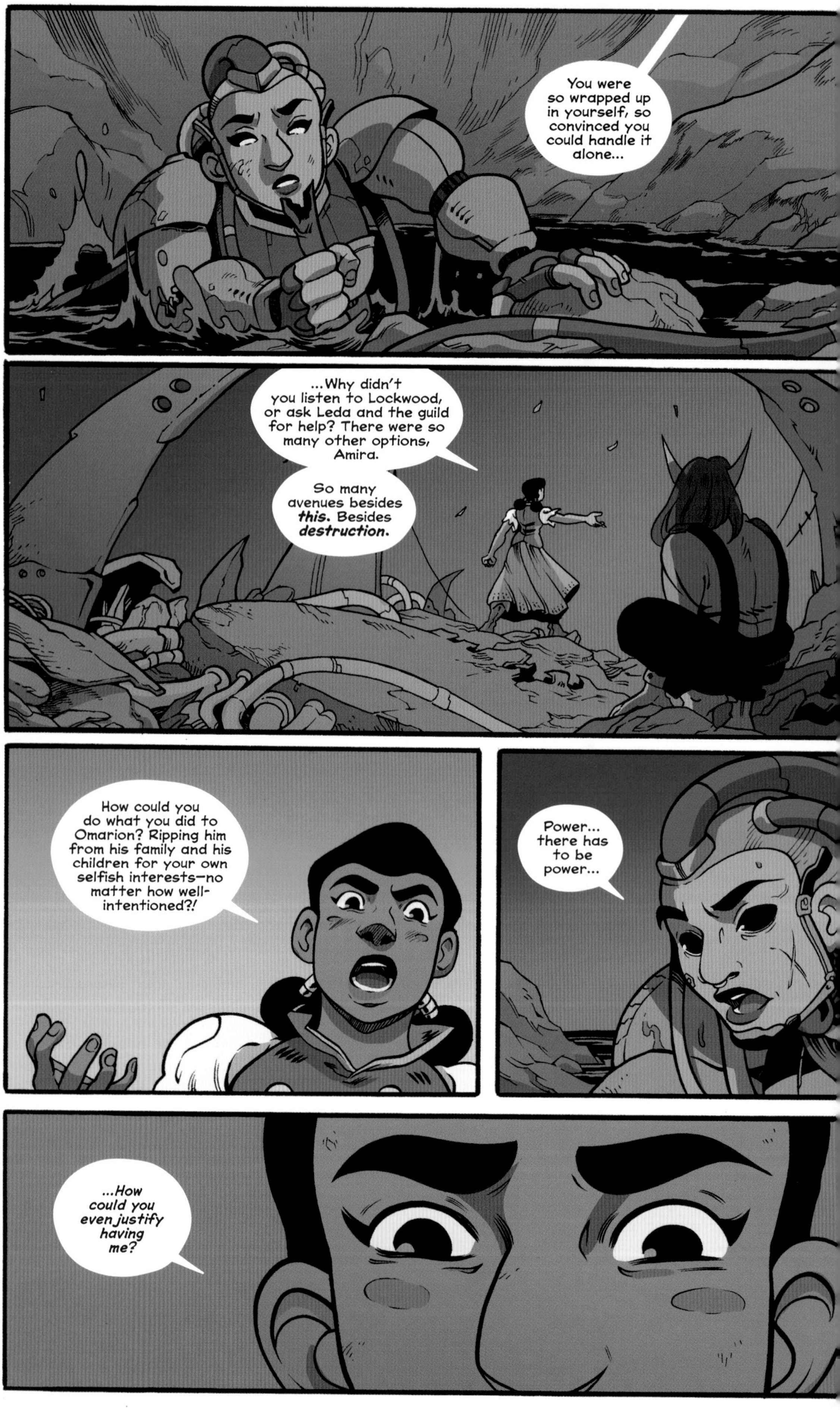
You were so wrapped up in yourself, so convinced you could handle it alone...
...Why didn't you listen to Lockwood, or ask Leda and the guild for help? There were so many other options, Amira.
So many avenues besides **this.** Besides ***destruction.***
How could you do what you did to Omarion? Ripping him from his family and his children for your own selfish interests—no matter how well-intentioned?!
Power... there has to be power...
...How could you even justify having me?

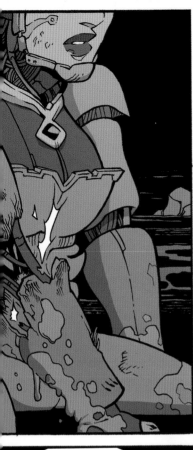

I saw the entire world burn at the hands of the Surrogate, Ursula. Saw my friends turned into machines, or cut down by them.

By the inventions of non-magical humans. Machines made only in response to our magical ways.

SPLASH

Our power-hungry, callous magical ways. We mages looked down on the non-magical people, back then...as I'm sure we do now. Their lives meant less, simply because of the way they were born.

It's easy to understand why they'd create such machines...to level the playing field.

You have to understand Ursula... some things are bigger than you or me. When I destroyed the Surrogate all those years ago? I saw something.

"I saw the aim of the Surrogate. I saw its ultimate goal.

"A simple truth. A hivemind, storing invaluable and incalculable amounts of data...

"A new world laid in wait there, with a new kind of consciousness. Where the life, stories, and experiences of everyone who ever lived were stored and shared, and could be accessed by everyone else.

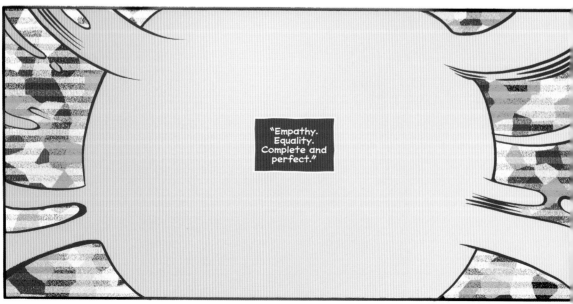

"Empathy. Equality. Complete and perfect."

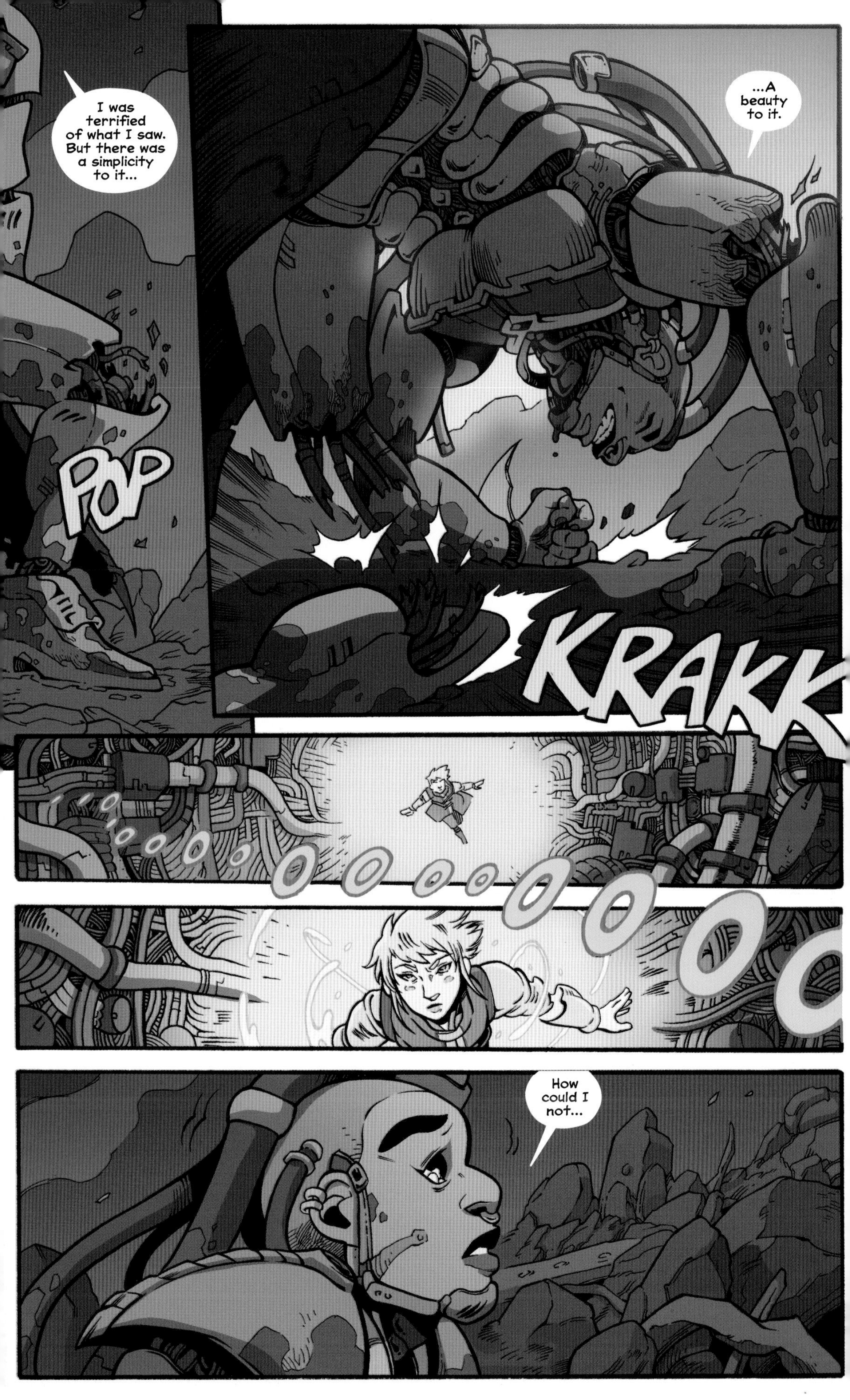
I was terrified of what I saw. But there was a simplicity to it...
POP
...A beauty to it.
KRAKK
How could I not...

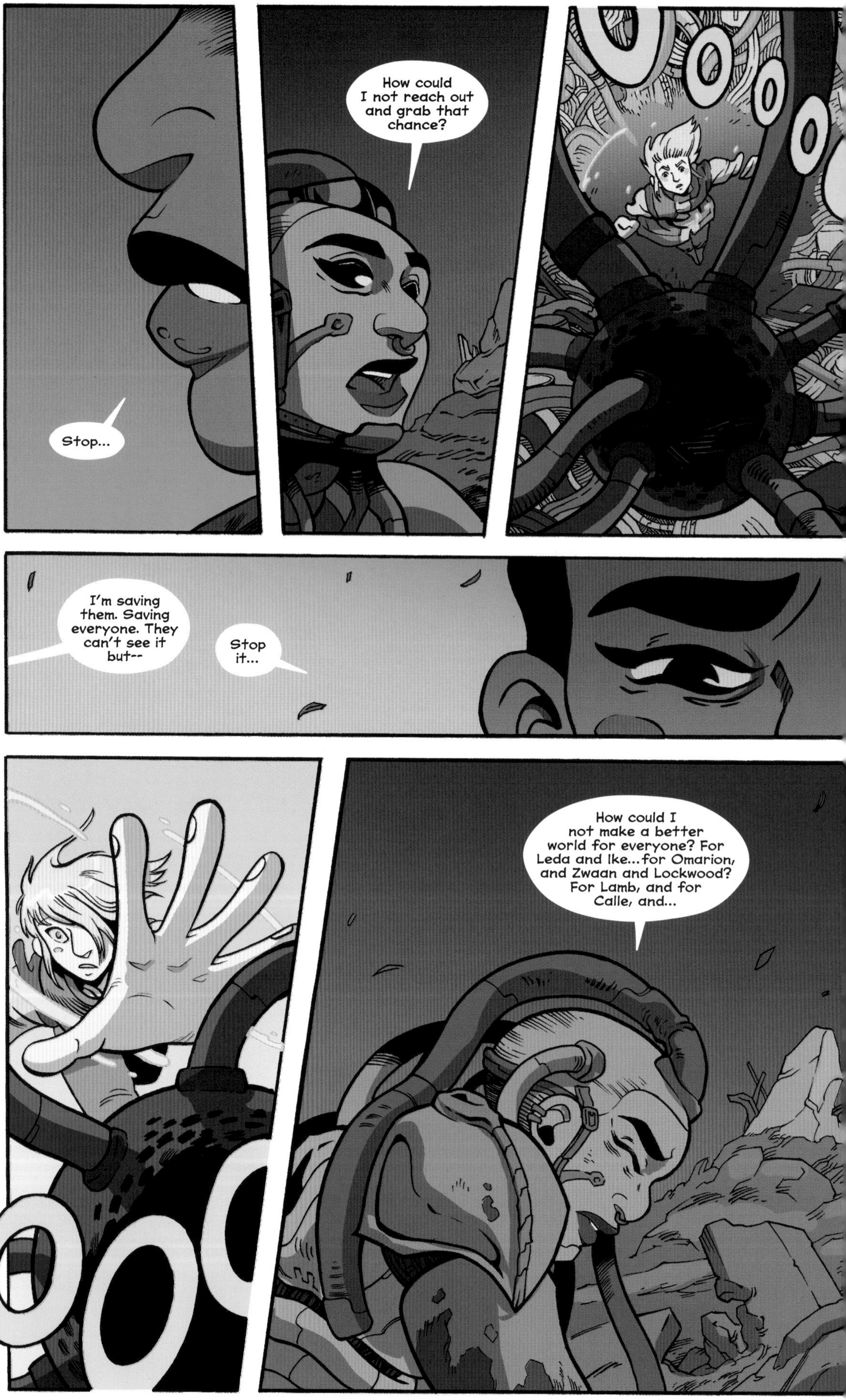
Stop...
How could I not reach out and grab that chance?
I'm saving them. Saving everyone. They can't see it but--
Stop it...
How could I not make a better world for everyone? For Leda and Ike...for Omarion, and Zwaan and Lockwood? For Lamb, and for Calle, and...

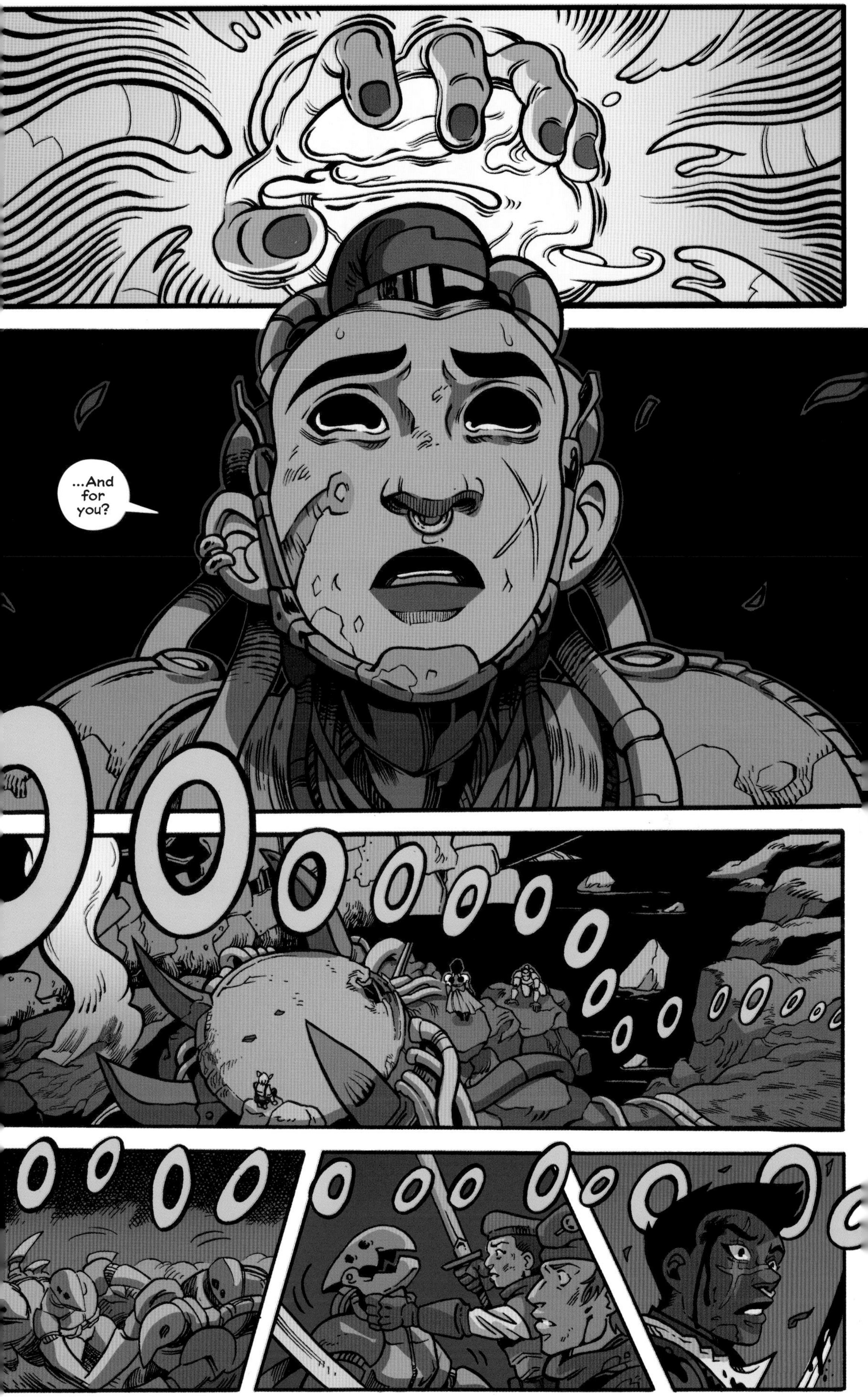
...And for you?

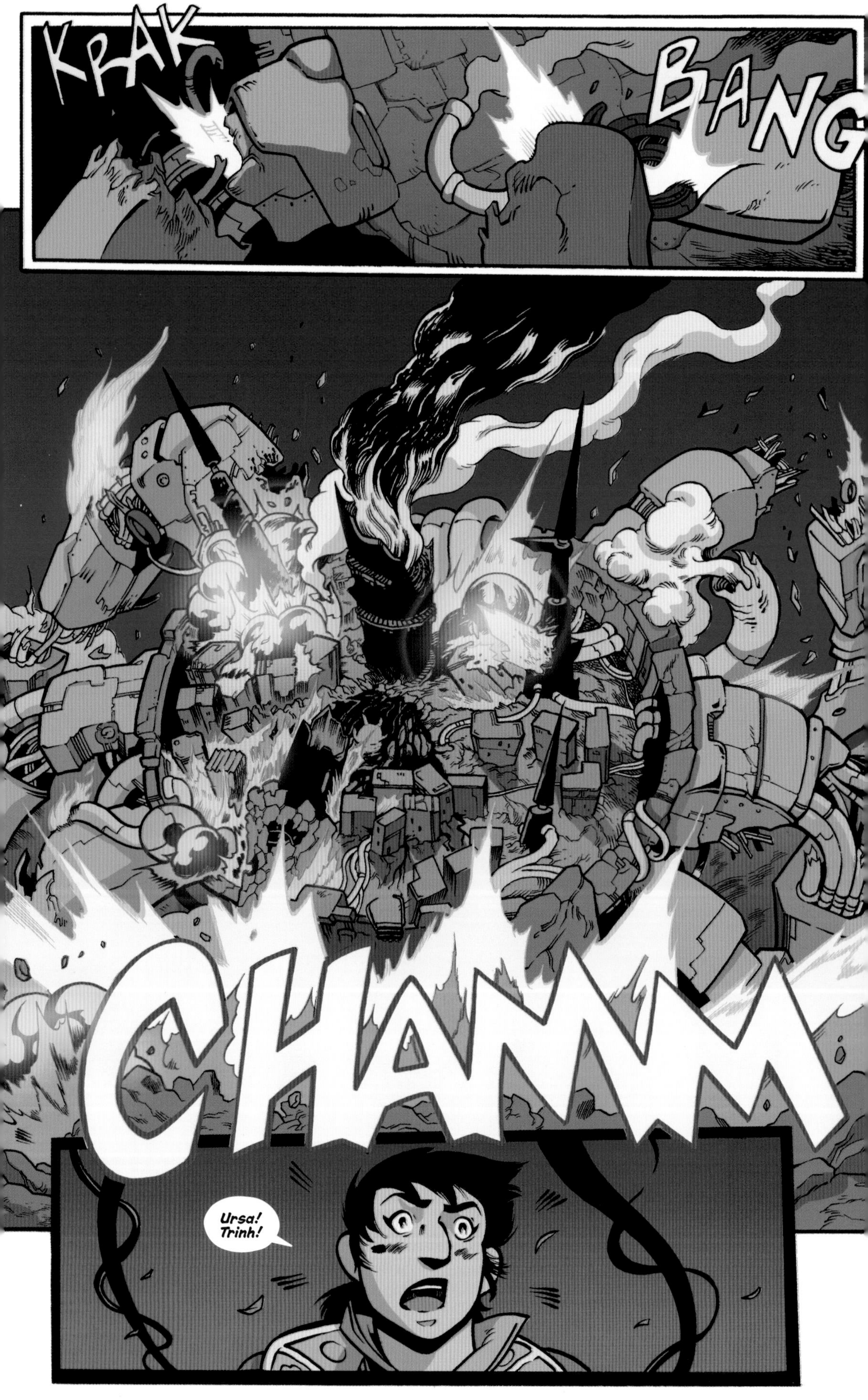
KRAK
BANG
CHAMM
Ursa! Trinh!

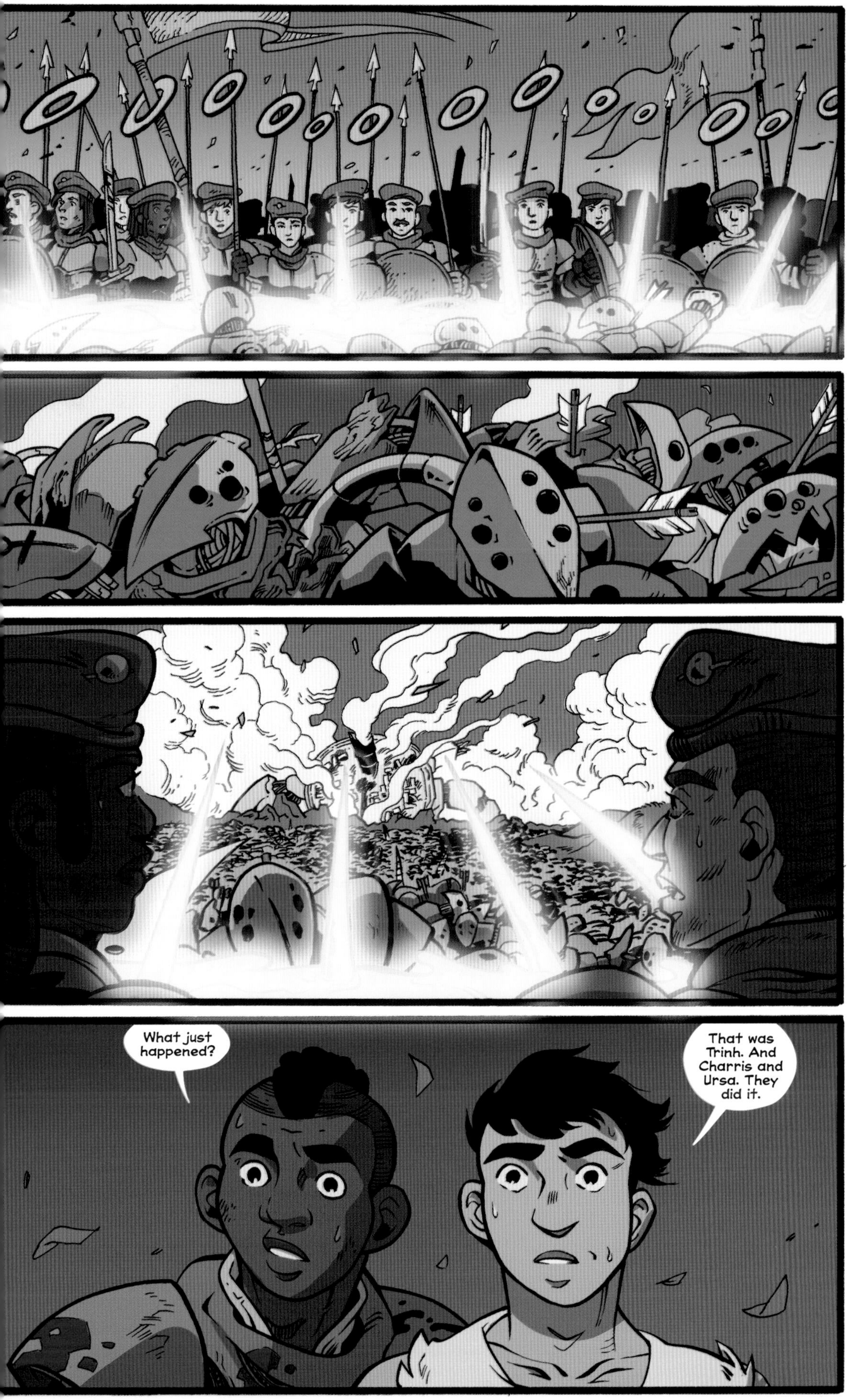
What just happened?
That was Trinh. And Charris and Ursa. They did it.

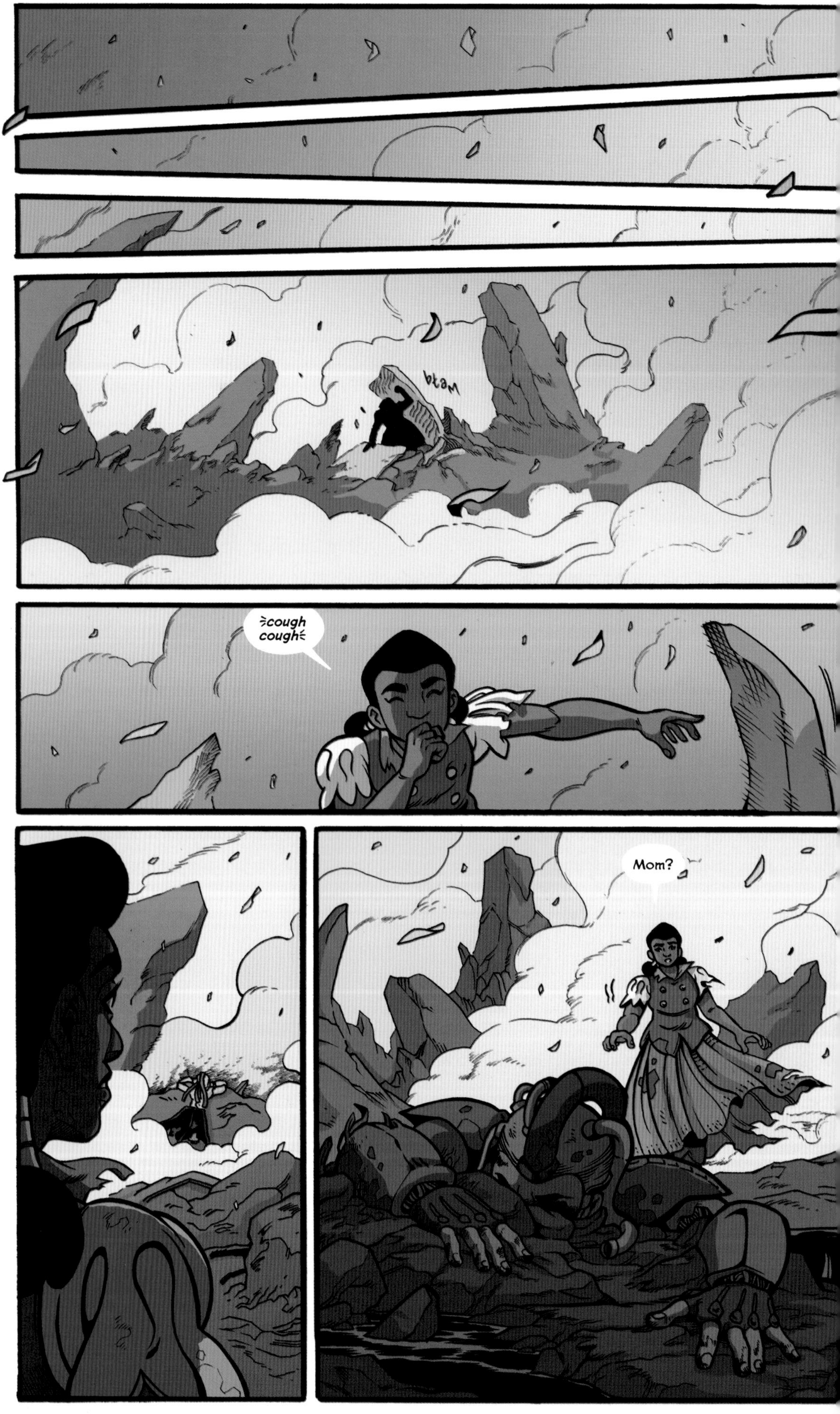
cough cough
Mom?

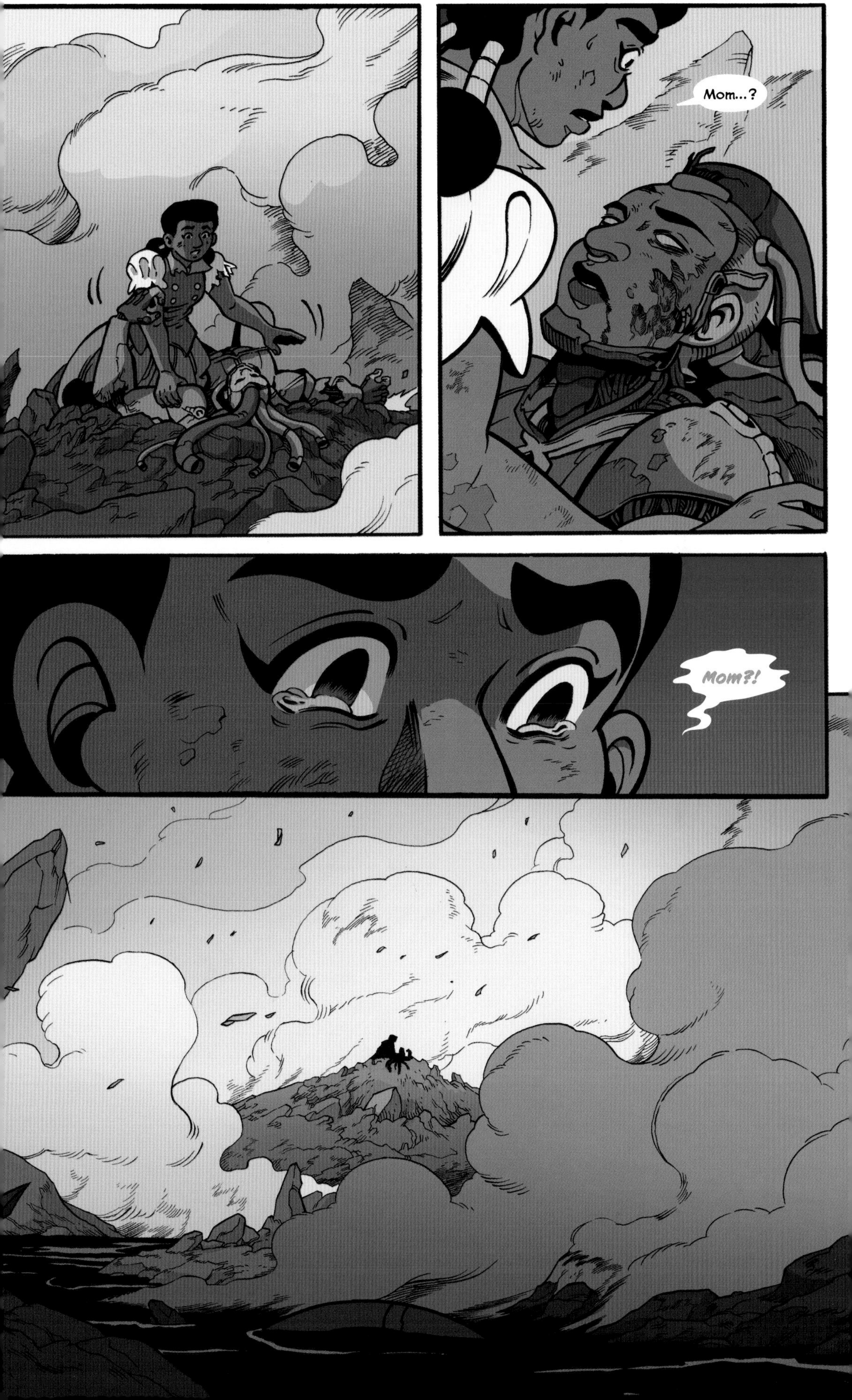
Mom...?
Mom?!

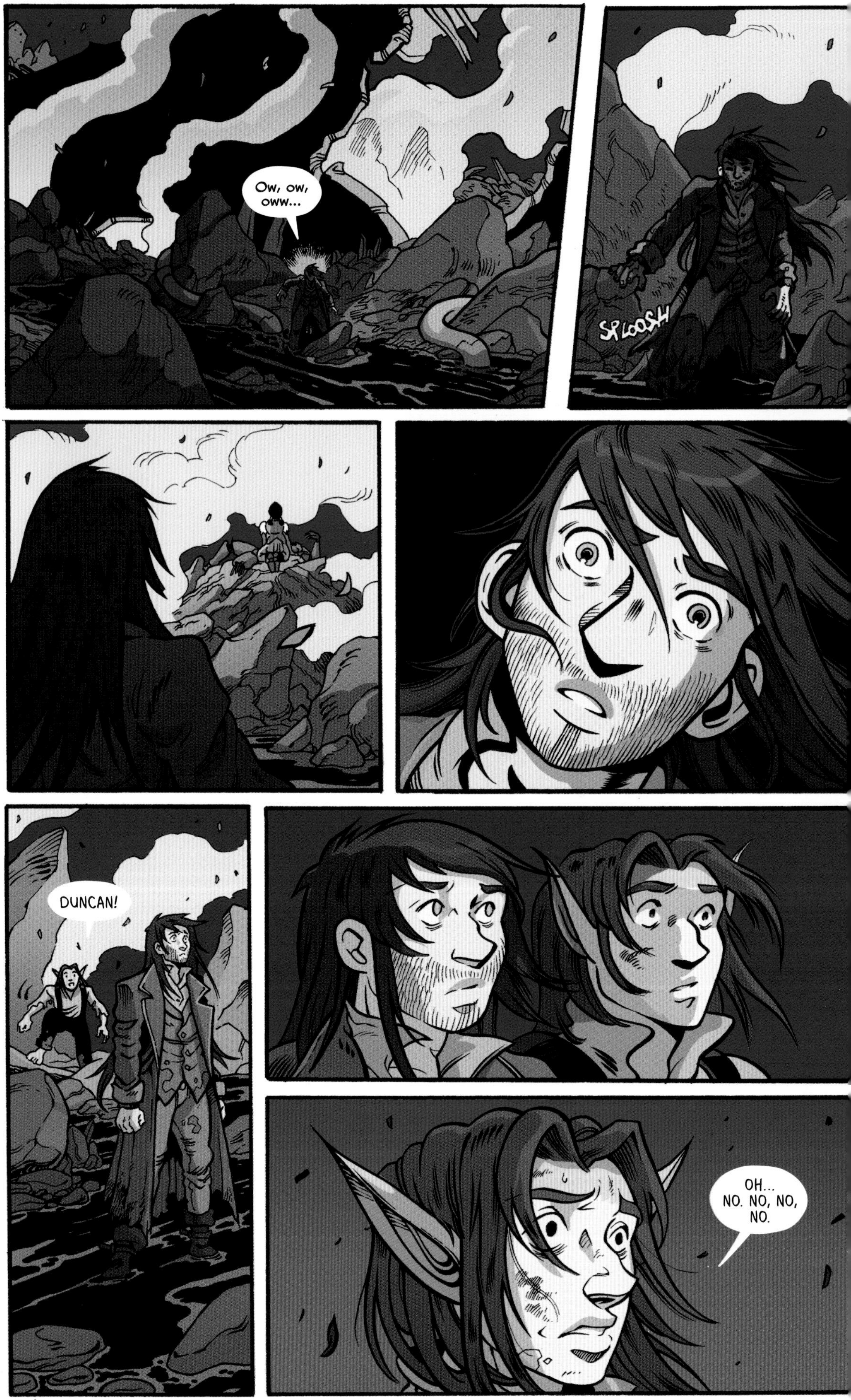
Ow, ow, oww...
SPLOOSH
DUNCAN!
OH... NO. NO, NO, NO.

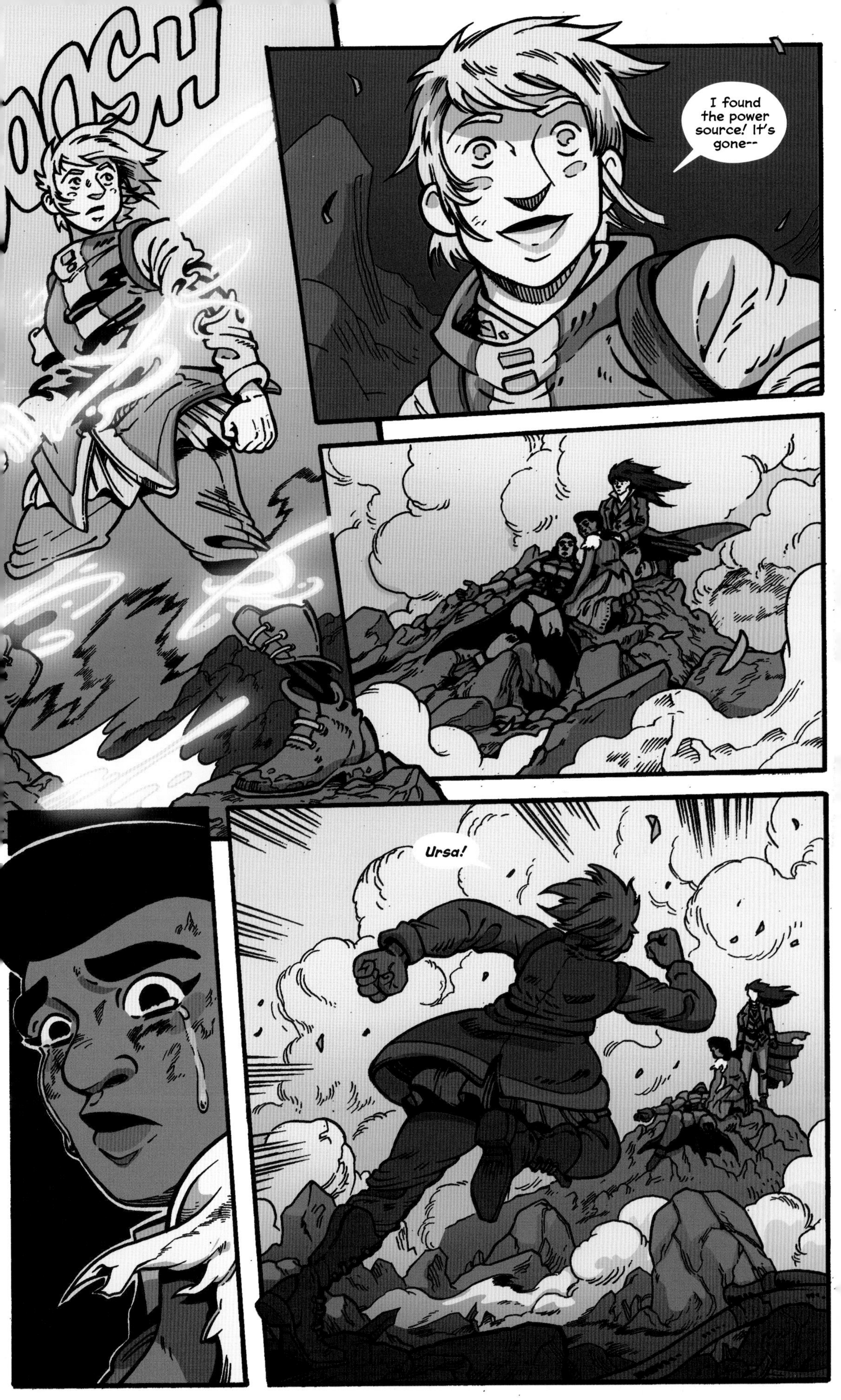
OOSH
I found the power source! It's gone--
Ursa!

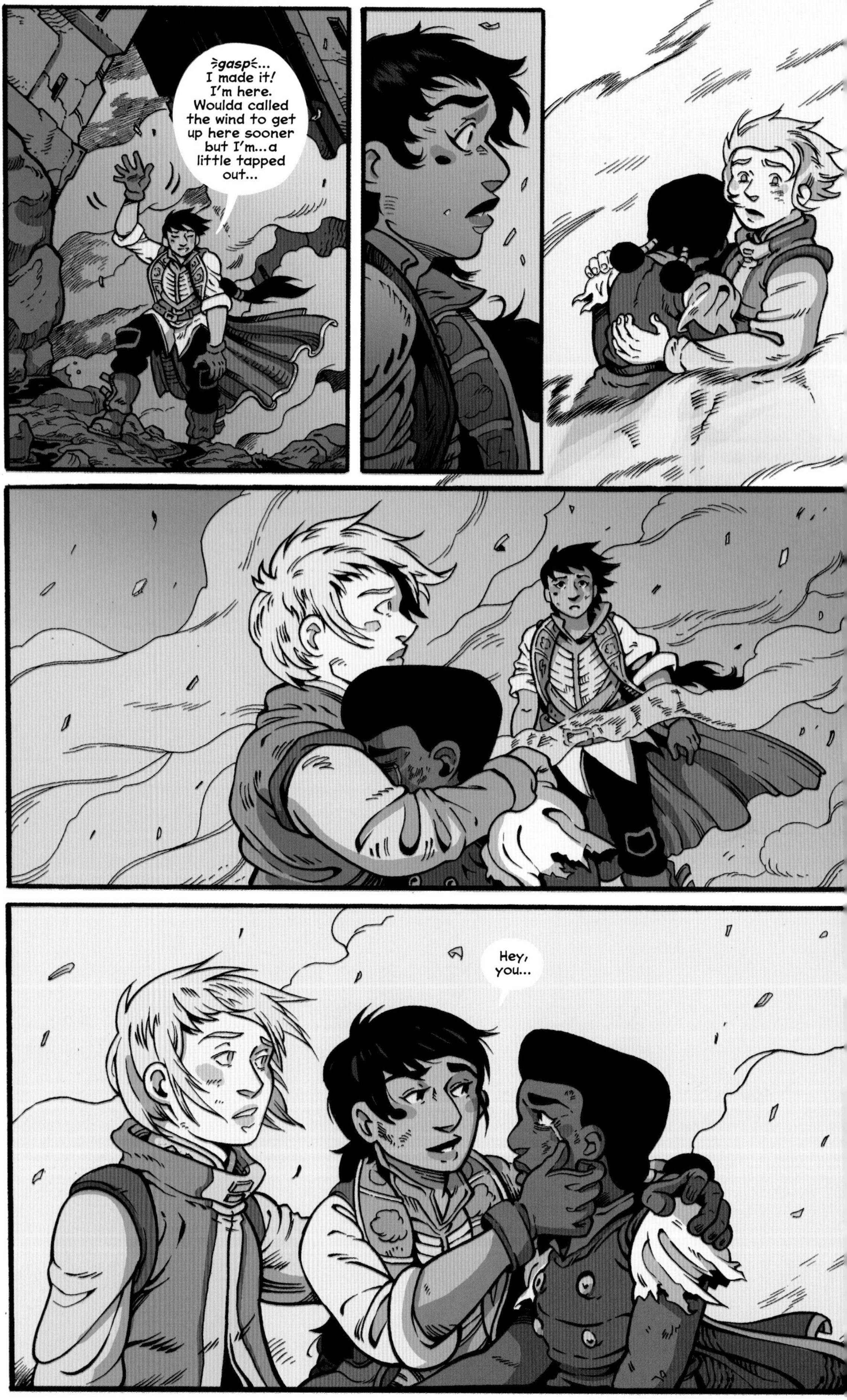

⋟gasp⋞... I made it! I'm here. Woulda called the wind to get up here sooner but I'm...a little tapped out...
Hey, you...

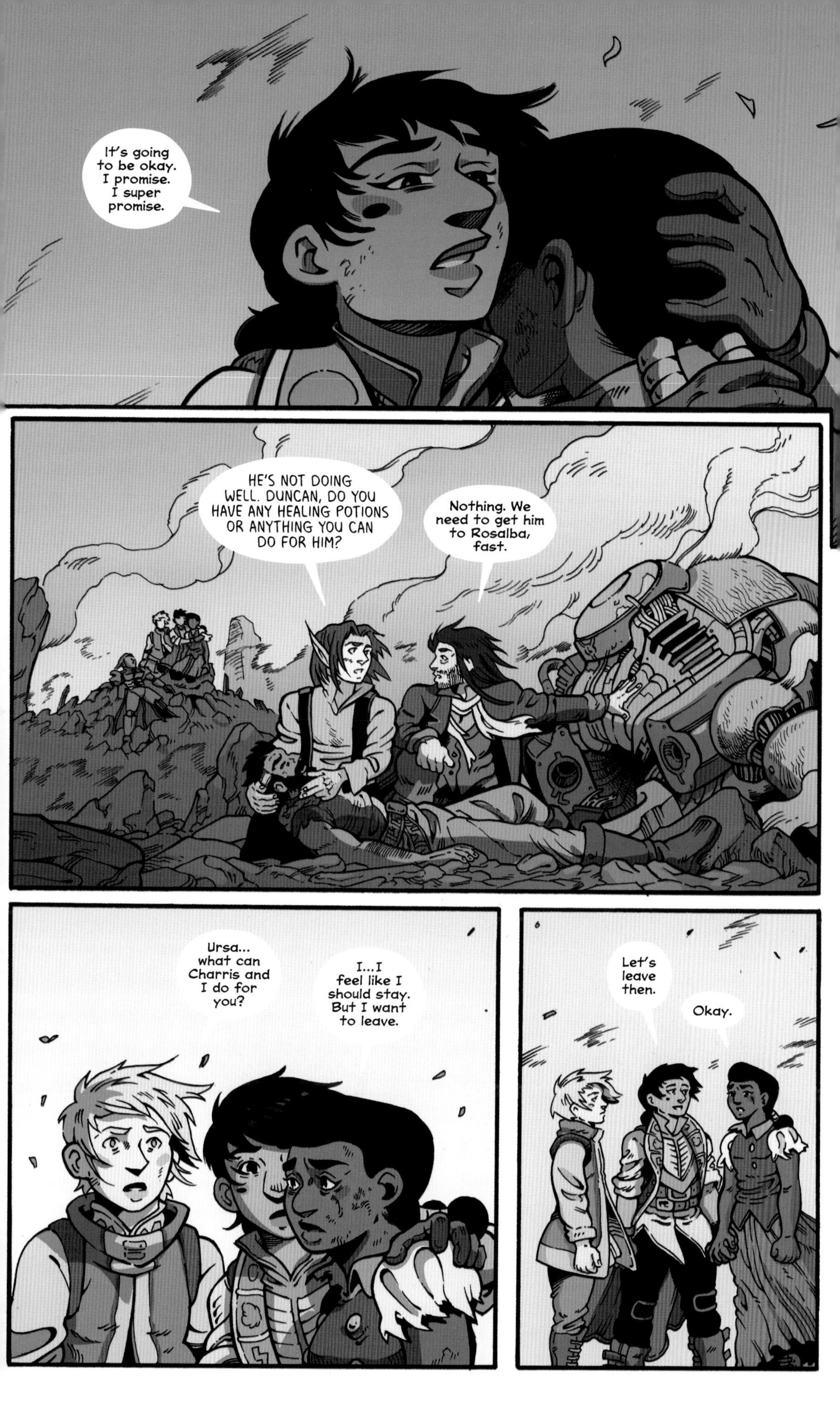
It's going to be okay. I promise. I super promise.
HE'S NOT DOING WELL. DUNCAN, DO YOU HAVE ANY HEALING POTIONS OR ANYTHING YOU CAN DO FOR HIM?
Nothing. We need to get him to Rosalba, fast.
Ursa... what can Charris and I do for you?
I...I feel like I should stay. But I want to leave.
Let's leave then.
Okay.

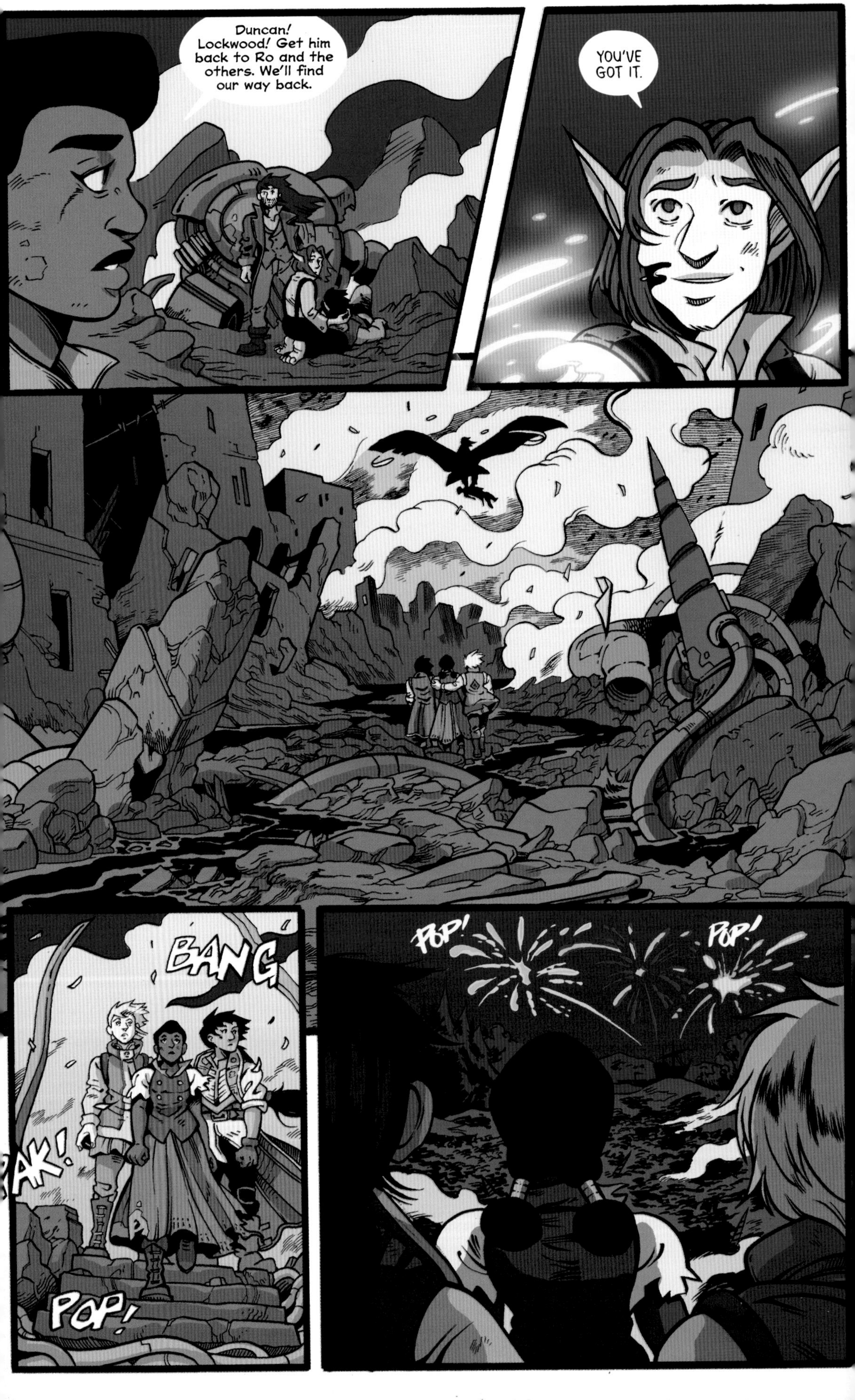
Duncan! Lockwood! Get him back to Ro and the others. We'll find our way back.
YOU'VE GOT IT.
BANG
AK!
POP!
POP!
POP!

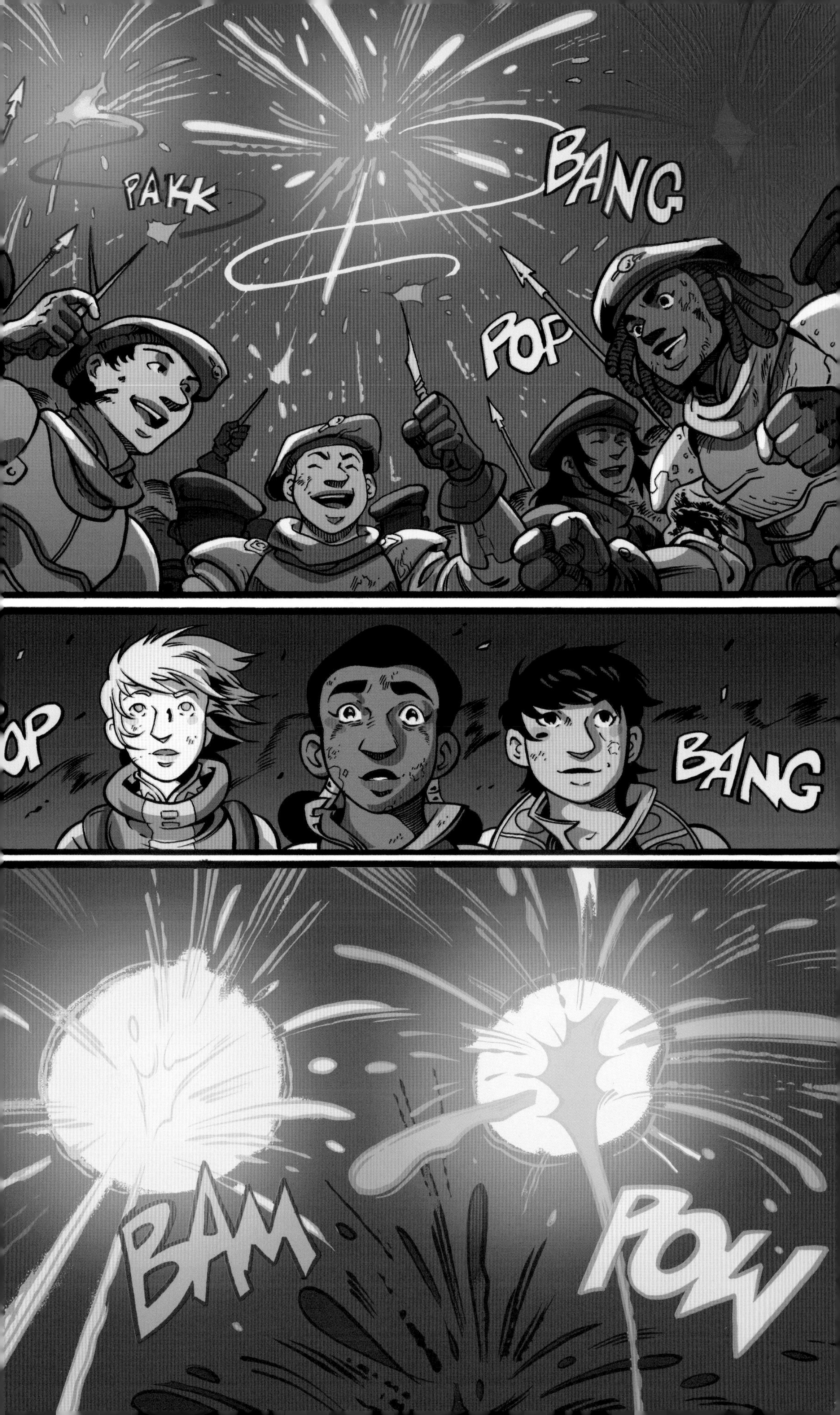
PAKK
BANG
POP
OP
BANG
BAM
POW

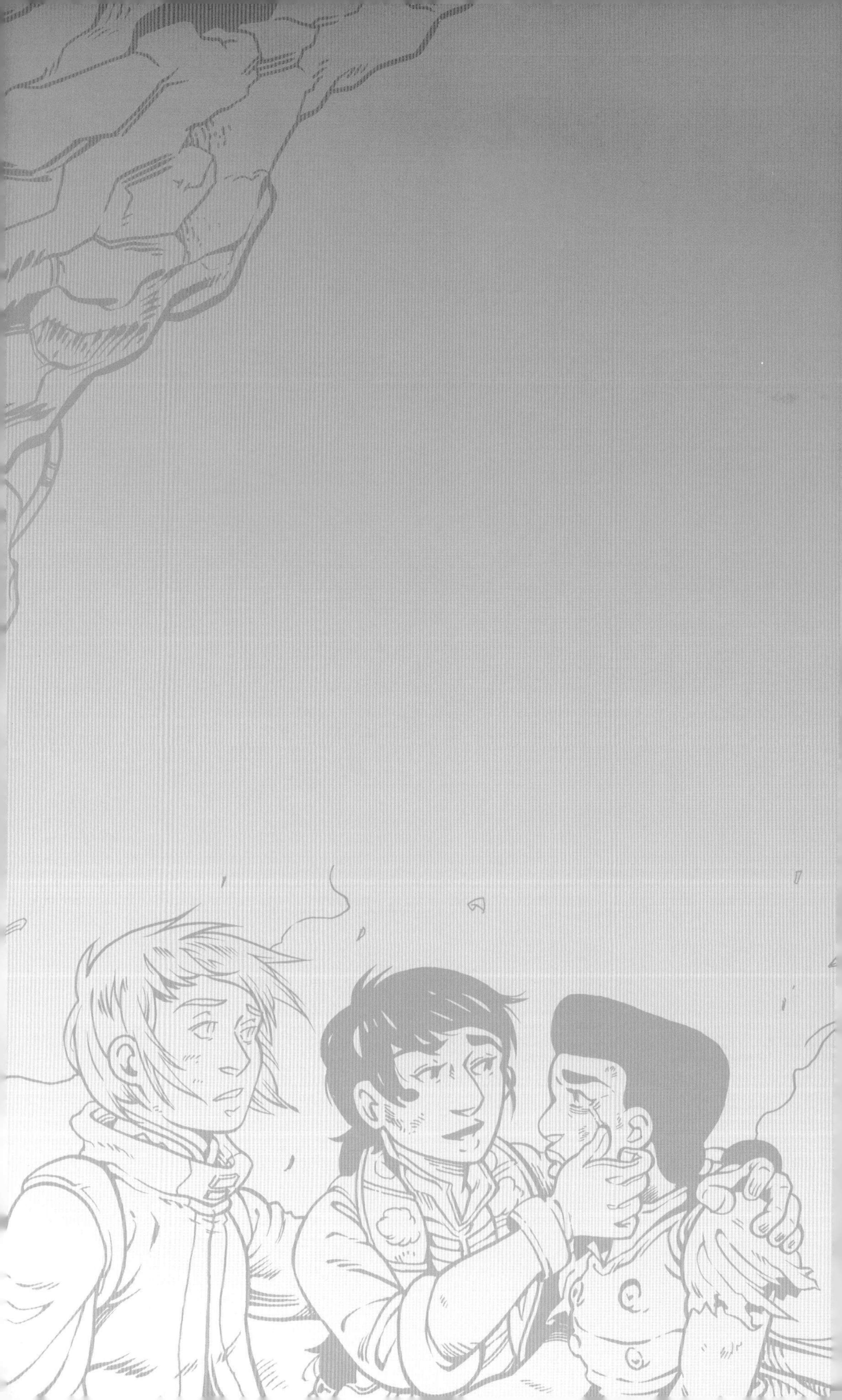

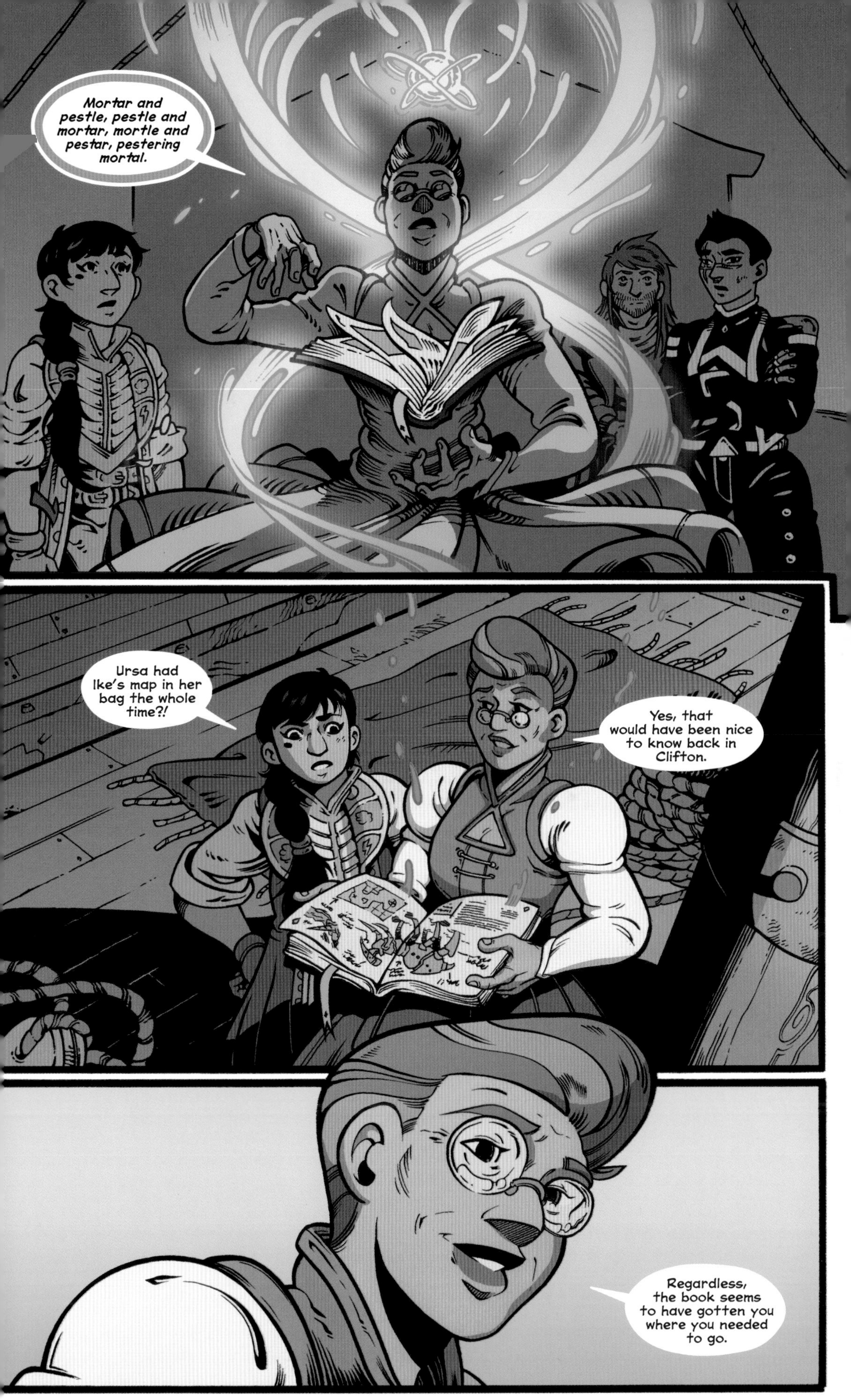
Mortar and pestle, pestle and mortar, mortle and pestar, pestering mortal.
Ursa had Ike's map in her bag the whole time?!
Yes, that would have been nice to know back in Clifton.
Regardless, the book seems to have gotten you where you needed to go.

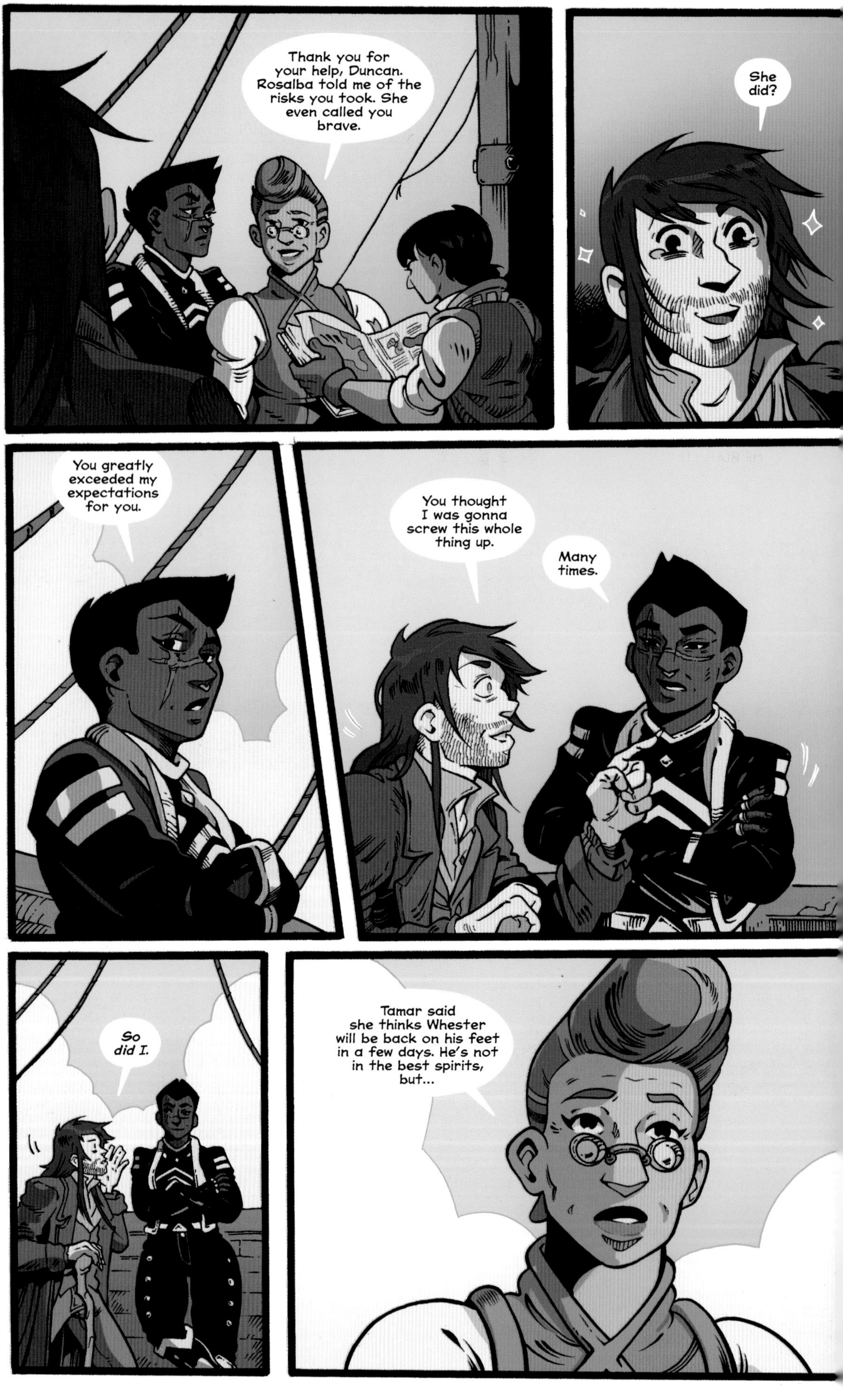
Thank you for your help, Duncan. Rosalba told me of the risks you took. She even called you brave.
She did?
You greatly exceeded my expectations for you.
You thought I was gonna screw this whole thing up.
Many times.
So did I.
Tamar said she thinks Whester will be back on his feet in a few days. He's not in the best spirits, but...

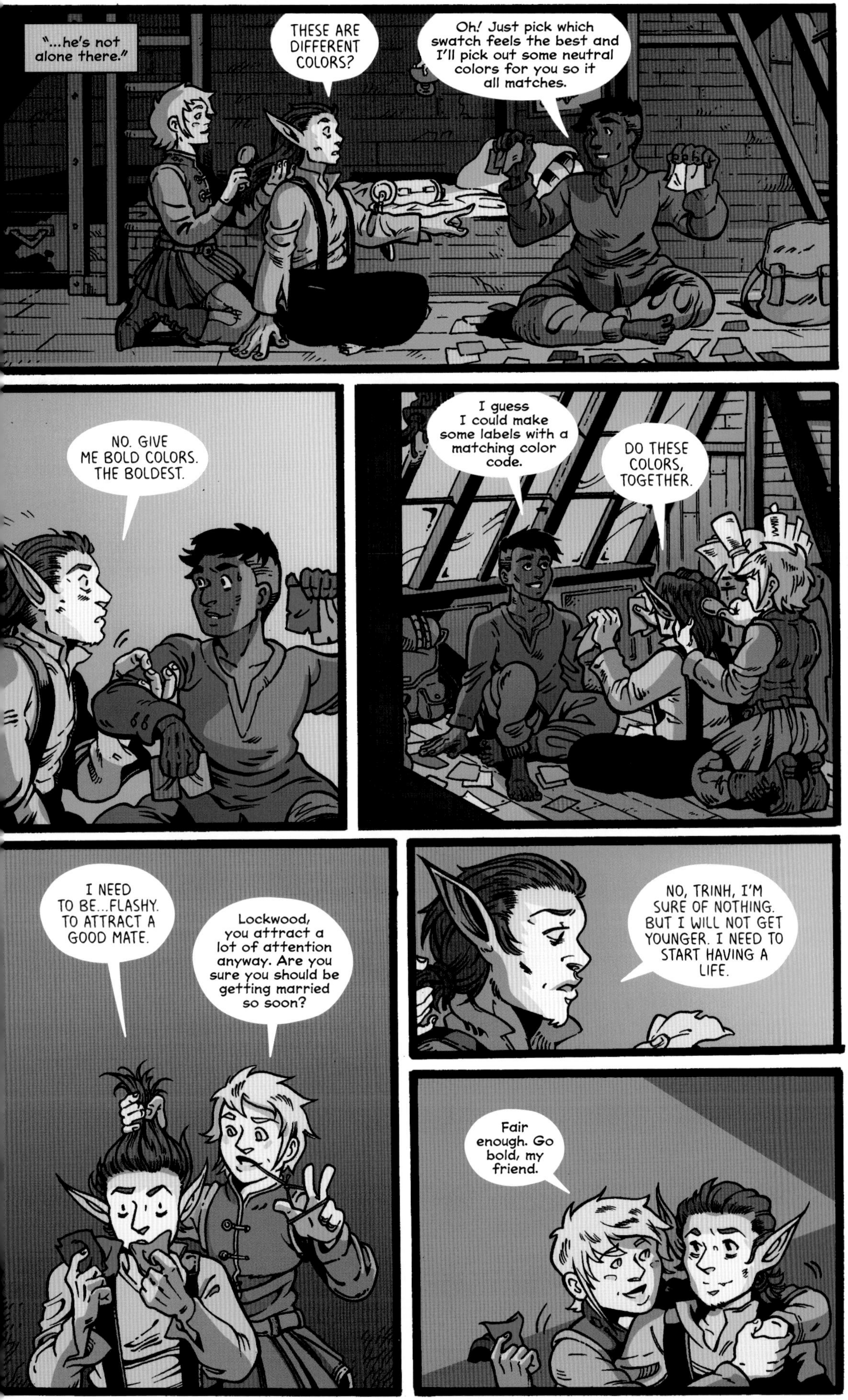
"...he's not alone there."
THESE ARE DIFFERENT COLORS?
Oh! Just pick which swatch feels the best and I'll pick out some neutral colors for you so it all matches.
NO. GIVE ME BOLD COLORS. THE BOLDEST.
I guess I could make some labels with a matching color code.
DO THESE COLORS, TOGETHER.
I NEED TO BE...FLASHY. TO ATTRACT A GOOD MATE.
Lockwood, you attract a lot of attention anyway. Are you sure you should be getting married so soon?
NO, TRINH, I'M SURE OF NOTHING. BUT I WILL NOT GET YOUNGER. I NEED TO START HAVING A LIFE.
Fair enough. Go bold, my friend.

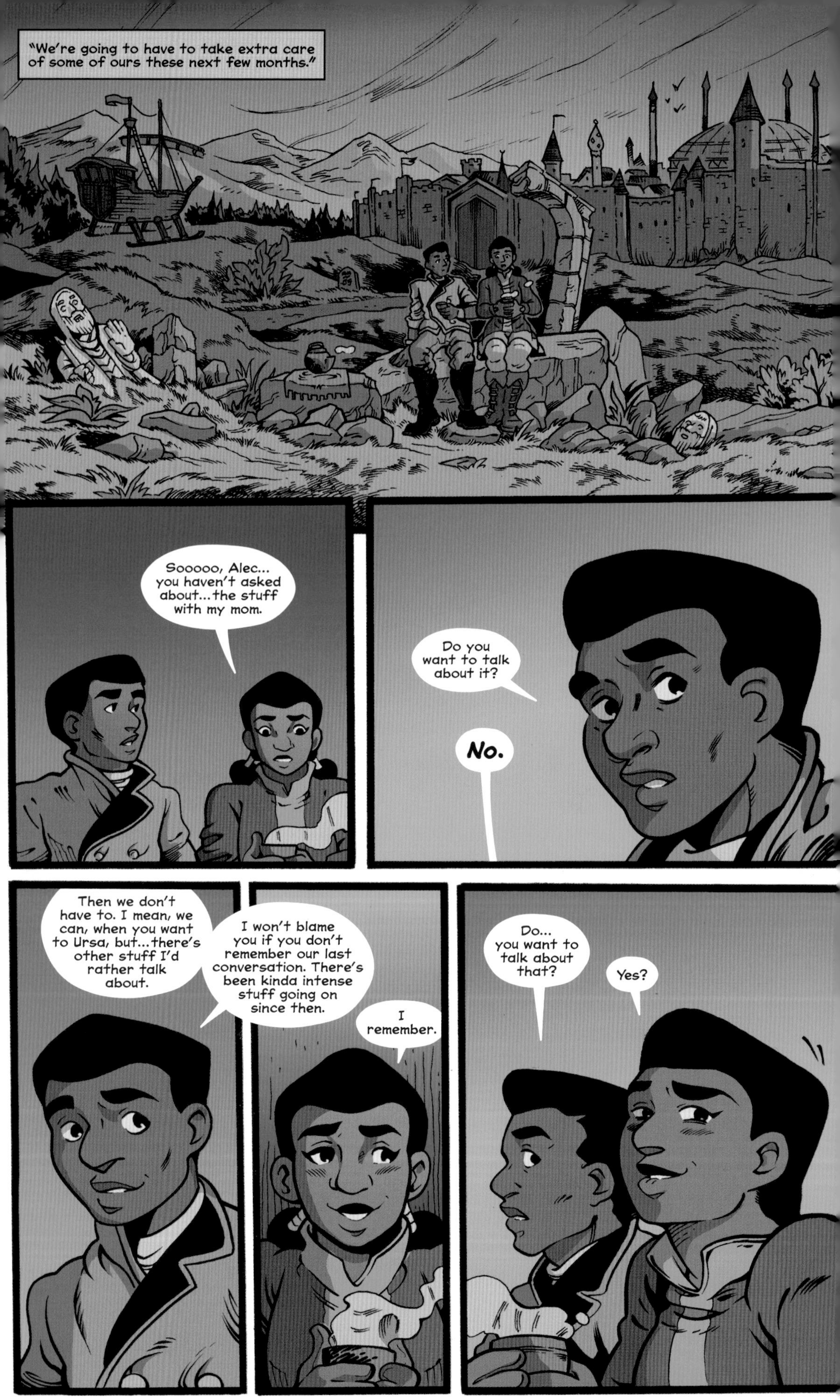
"We're going to have to take extra care of some of ours these next few months."
Sooooo, Alec... you haven't asked about...the stuff with my mom.
Do you want to talk about it?
No.
Then we don't have to. I mean, we can, when you want to Ursa, but...there's other stuff I'd rather talk about.
I won't blame you if you don't remember our last conversation. There's been kinda intense stuff going on since then.
I remember.
Do... you want to talk about that?
Yes?

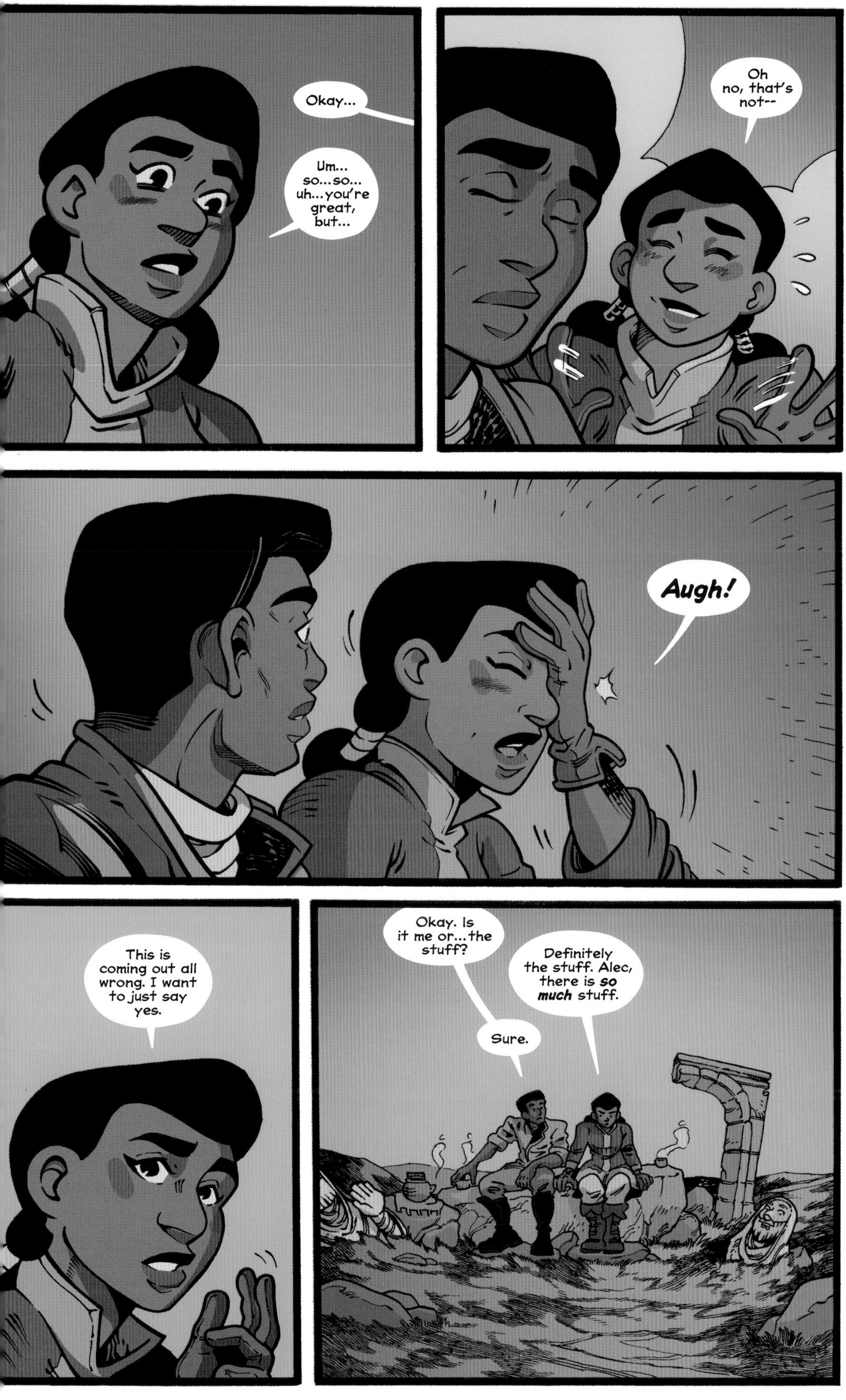
Okay...
Um... so...so... uh...you're great, but...
Oh no, that's not--
Augh!
This is coming out all wrong. I want to just say yes.
Okay. Is it me or...the stuff?
Sure.
Definitely the stuff. Alec, there is so *much* stuff.

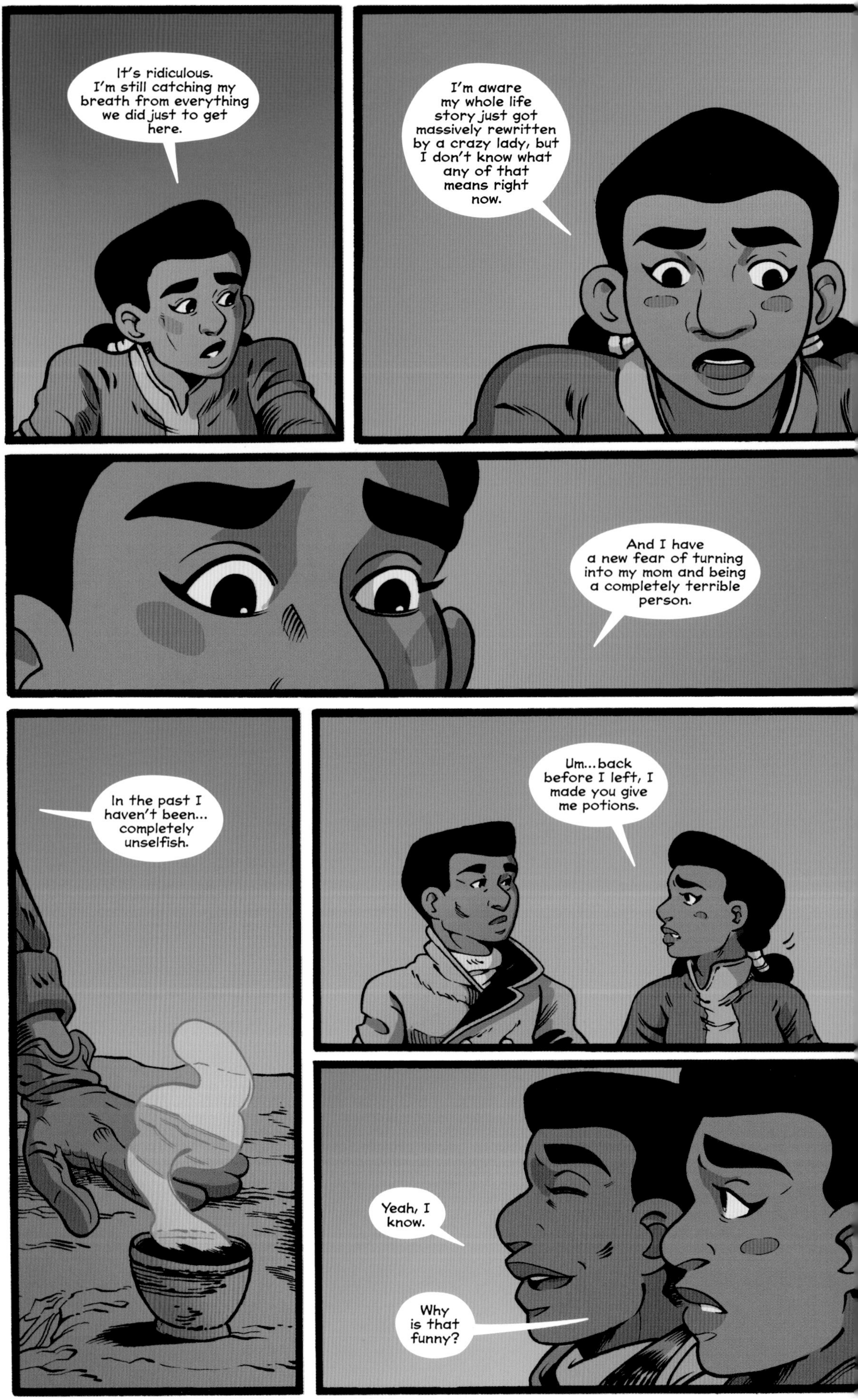
It's ridiculous. I'm still catching my breath from everything we did just to get here.
I'm aware my whole life story just got massively rewritten by a crazy lady, but I don't know what any of that means right now.
And I have a new fear of turning into my mom and being a completely terrible person.
In the past I haven't been... completely unselfish.
Um...back before I left, I made you give me potions.
Yeah, I know.
Why is that funny?

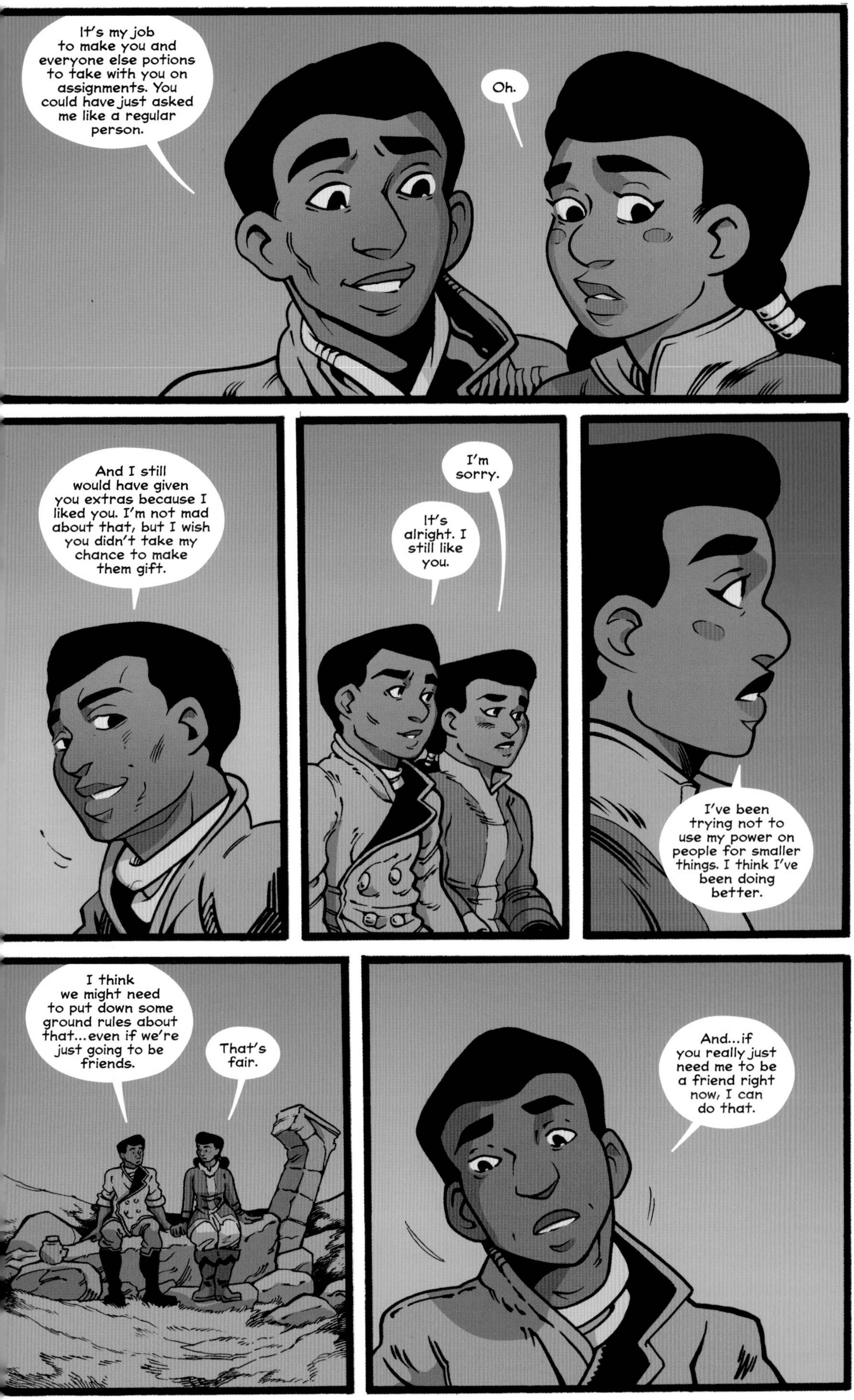

It's my job to make you and everyone else potions to take with you on assignments. You could have just asked me like a regular person.
Oh.
And I still would have given you extras because I liked you. I'm not mad about that, but I wish you didn't take my chance to make them gift.
I'm sorry.
It's alright. I still like you.
I've been trying not to use my power on people for smaller things. I think I've been doing better.
I think we might need to put down some ground rules about that...even if we're just going to be friends.
That's fair.
And...if you really just need me to be a friend right now, I can do that.

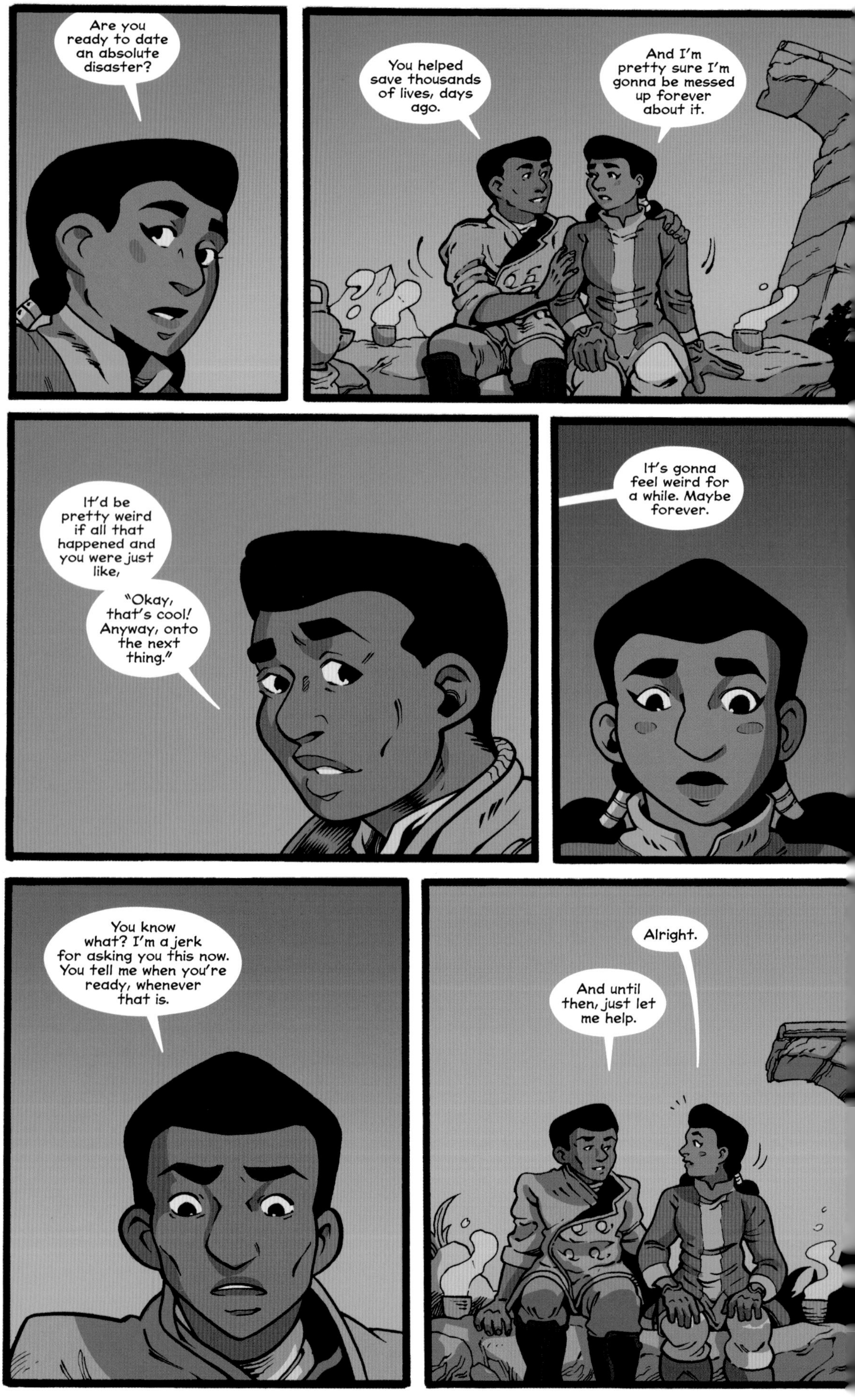

Are you ready to date an absolute disaster?
You helped save thousands of lives, days ago.
And I'm pretty sure I'm gonna be messed up forever about it.
It'd be pretty weird if all that happened and you were just like,
"Okay, that's cool! Anyway, onto the next thing."
It's gonna feel weird for a while. Maybe forever.
You know what? I'm a jerk for asking you this now. You tell me when you're ready, whenever that is.
And until then, just let me help.
Alright.

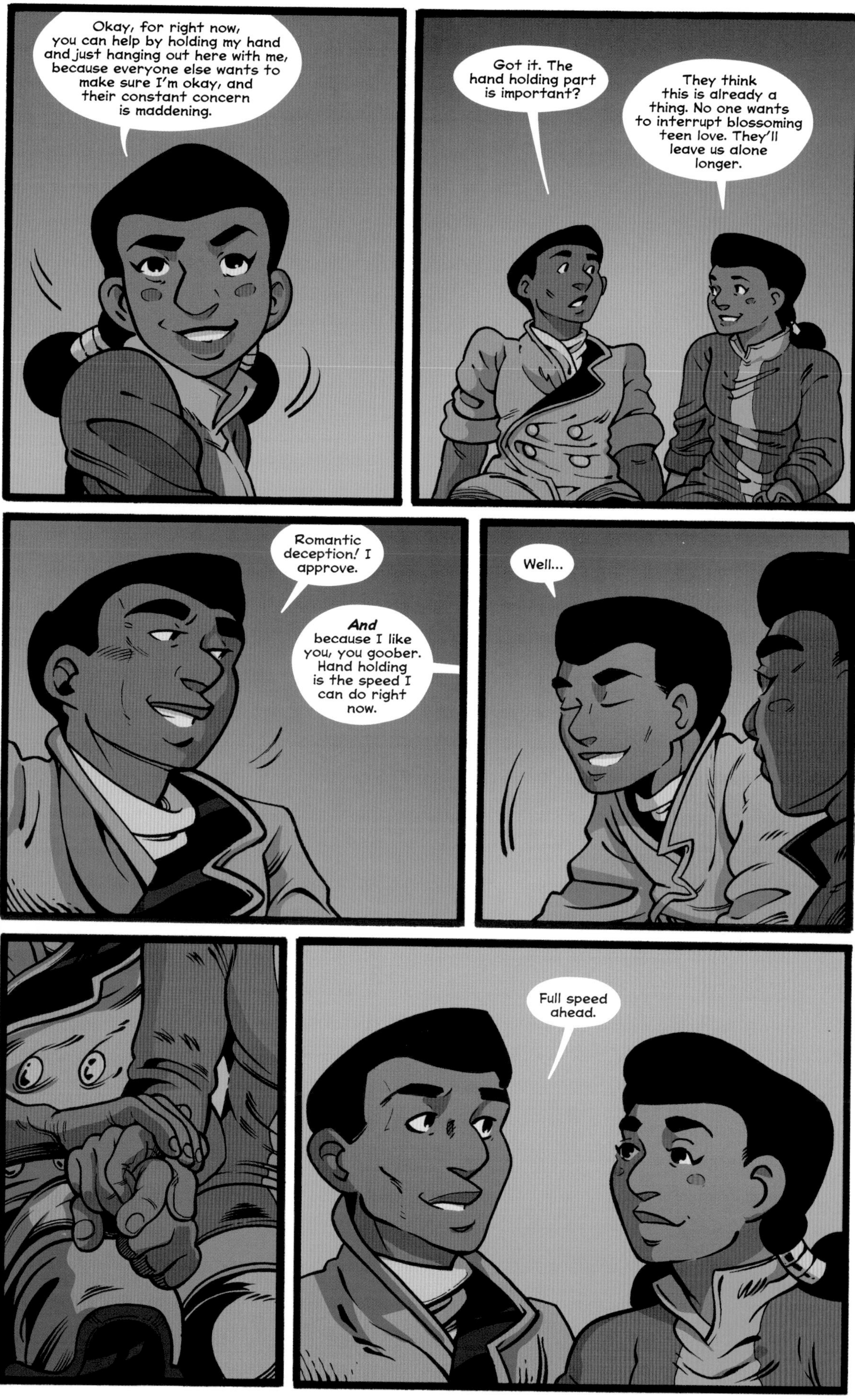

Okay, for right now, you can help by holding my hand and just hanging out here with me, because everyone else wants to make sure I'm okay, and their constant concern is maddening.
Got it. The hand holding part is important?
They think this is already a thing. No one wants to interrupt blossoming teen love. They'll leave us alone longer.
Romantic deception! I approve.
And because I like you, you goober. Hand holding is the speed I can do right now.
Well...
Full speed ahead.

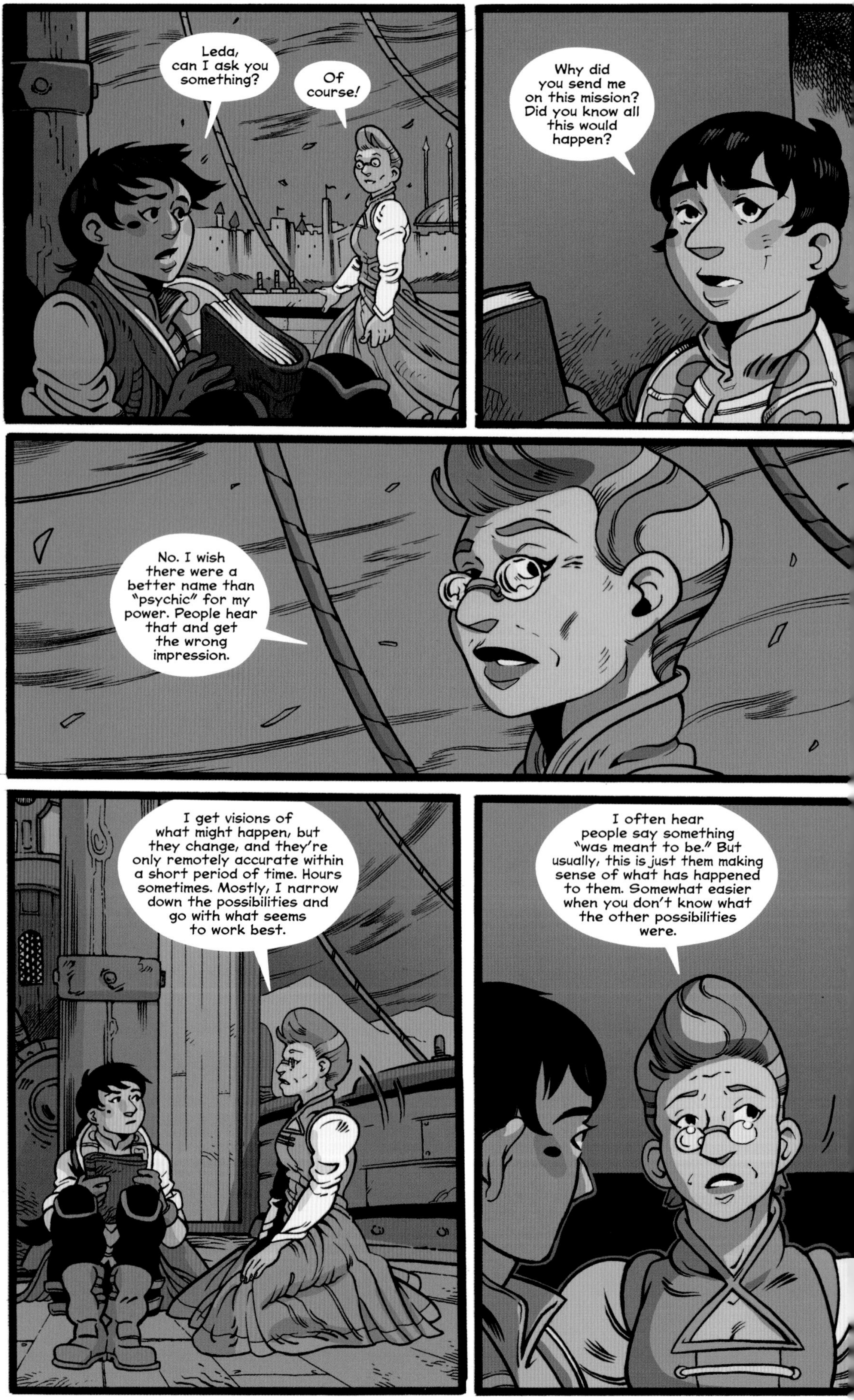
Leda, can I ask you something?
Of course!
Why did you send me on this mission? Did you know all this would happen?
No. I wish there were a better name than "psychic" for my power. People hear that and get the wrong impression.
I get visions of what might happen, but they change, and they're only remotely accurate within a short period of time. Hours sometimes. Mostly, I narrow down the possibilities and go with what seems to work best.
I often hear people say something "was meant to be." But usually, this is just them making sense of what has happened to them. Somewhat easier when you don't know what the other possibilities were.

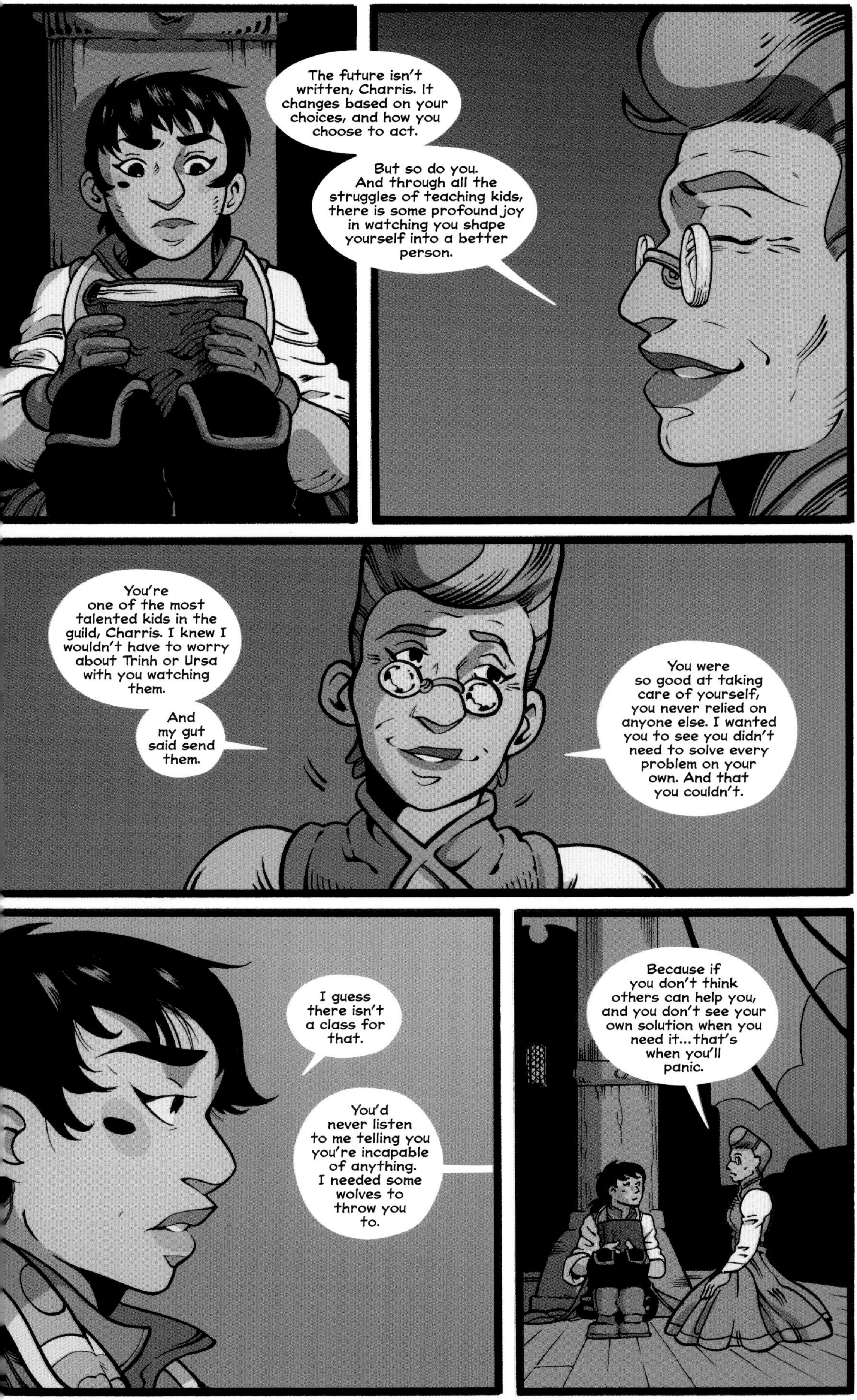
The future isn't written, Charris. It changes based on your choices, and how you choose to act.
But so do you. And through all the struggles of teaching kids, there is some profound joy in watching you shape yourself into a better person.
You're one of the most talented kids in the guild, Charris. I knew I wouldn't have to worry about Trinh or Ursa with you watching them.
And my gut said send them.
You were so good at taking care of yourself, you never relied on anyone else. I wanted you to see you didn't need to solve every problem on your own. And that you couldn't.
I guess there isn't a class for that.
You'd never listen to me telling you you're incapable of anything. I needed some wolves to throw you to.
Because if you don't think others can help you, and you don't see your own solution when you need it...that's when you'll panic.

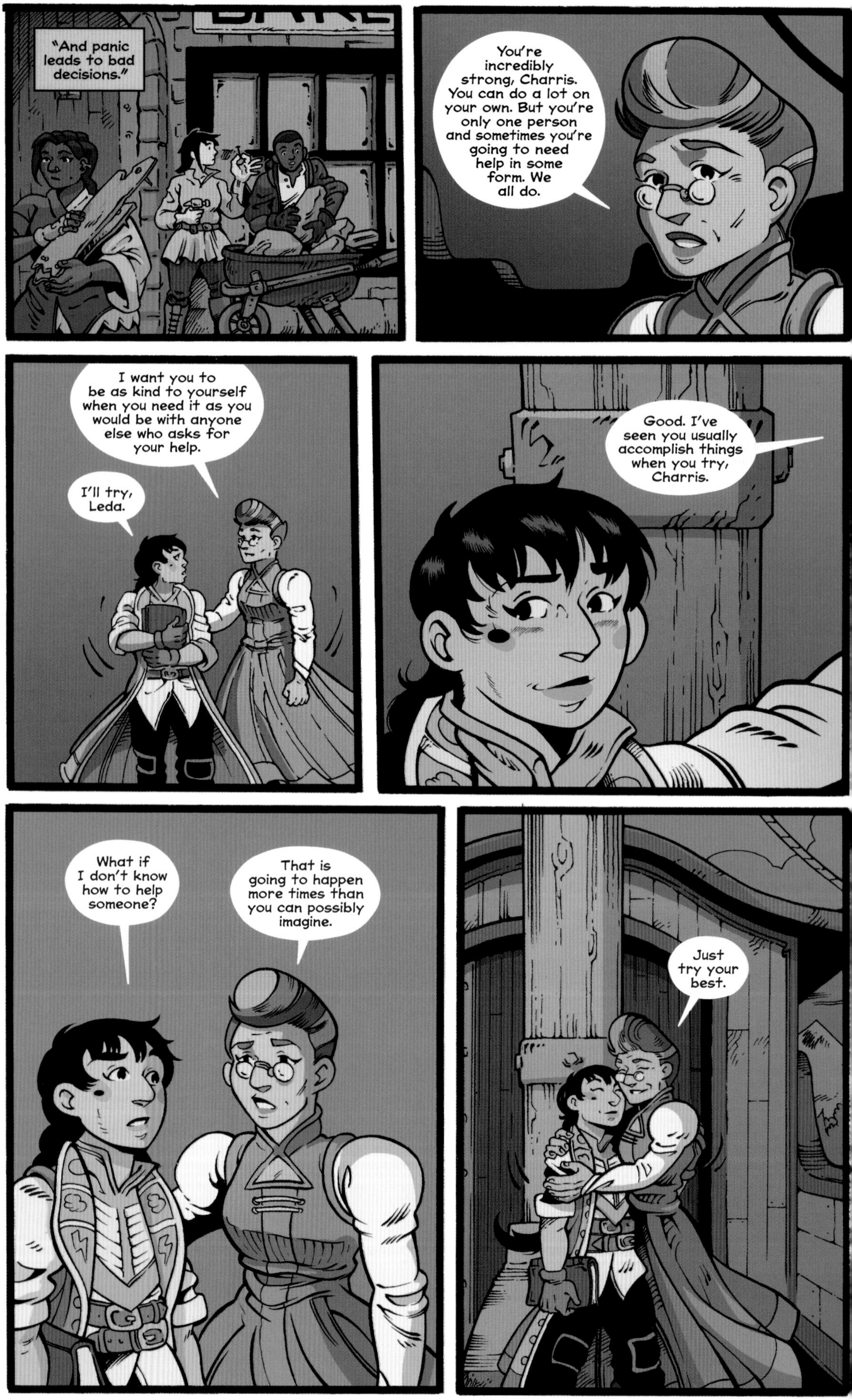
"And panic leads to bad decisions."
You're incredibly strong, Charris. You can do a lot on your own. But you're only one person and sometimes you're going to need help in some form. We all do.
I want you to be as kind to yourself when you need it as you would be with anyone else who asks for your help.
I'll try, Leda.
Good. I've seen you usually accomplish things when you try, Charris.
What if I don't know how to help someone?
That is going to happen more times than you can possibly imagine.
Just try your best.

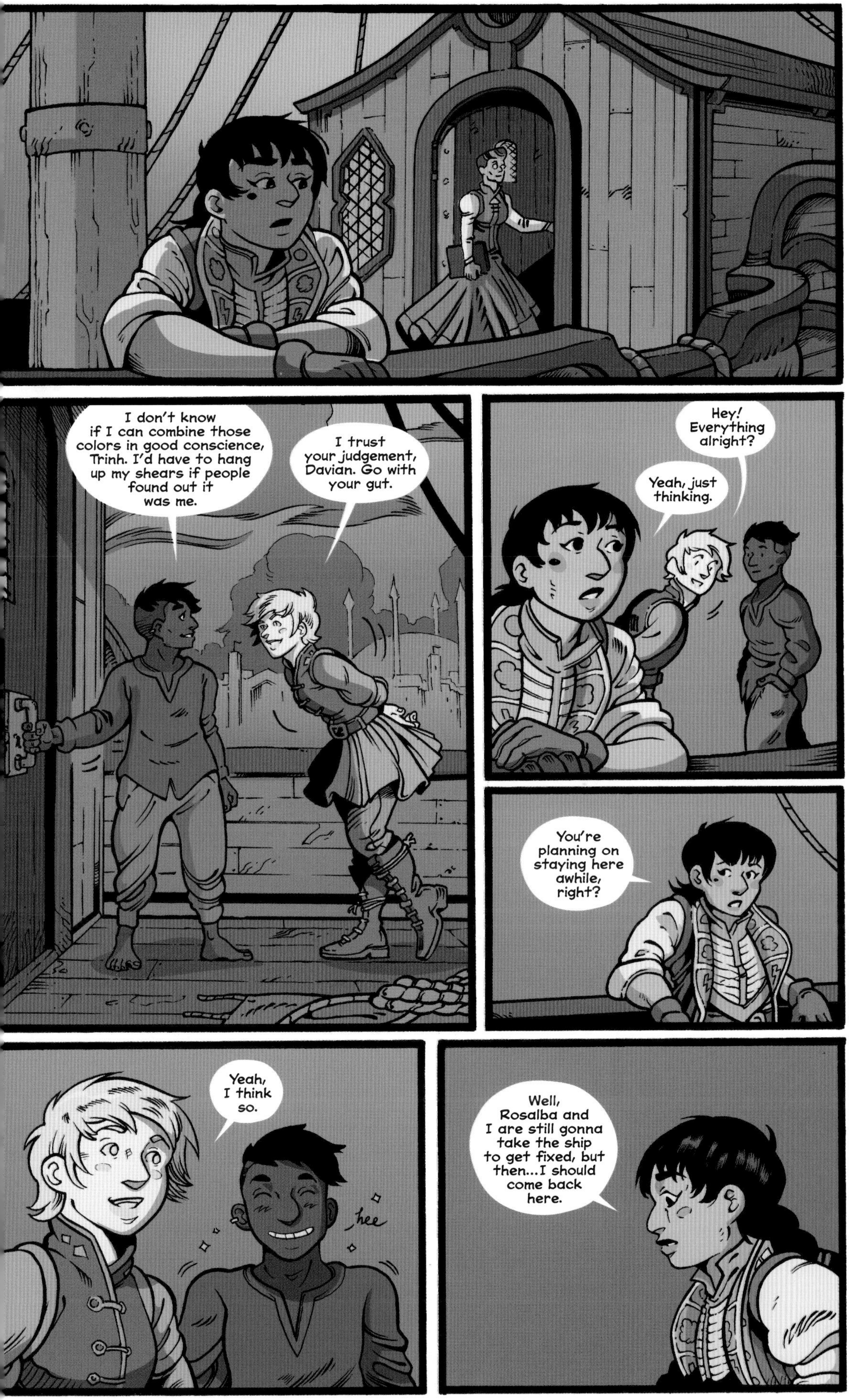
I don't know if I can combine those colors in good conscience, Trinh. I'd have to hang up my shears if people found out it was me.
I trust your judgement, Davian. Go with your gut.
Hey! Everything alright?
Yeah, just thinking.
You're planning on staying here awhile, right?
Yeah, I think so.
hee
Well, Rosalba and I are still gonna take the ship to get fixed, but then...I should come back here.

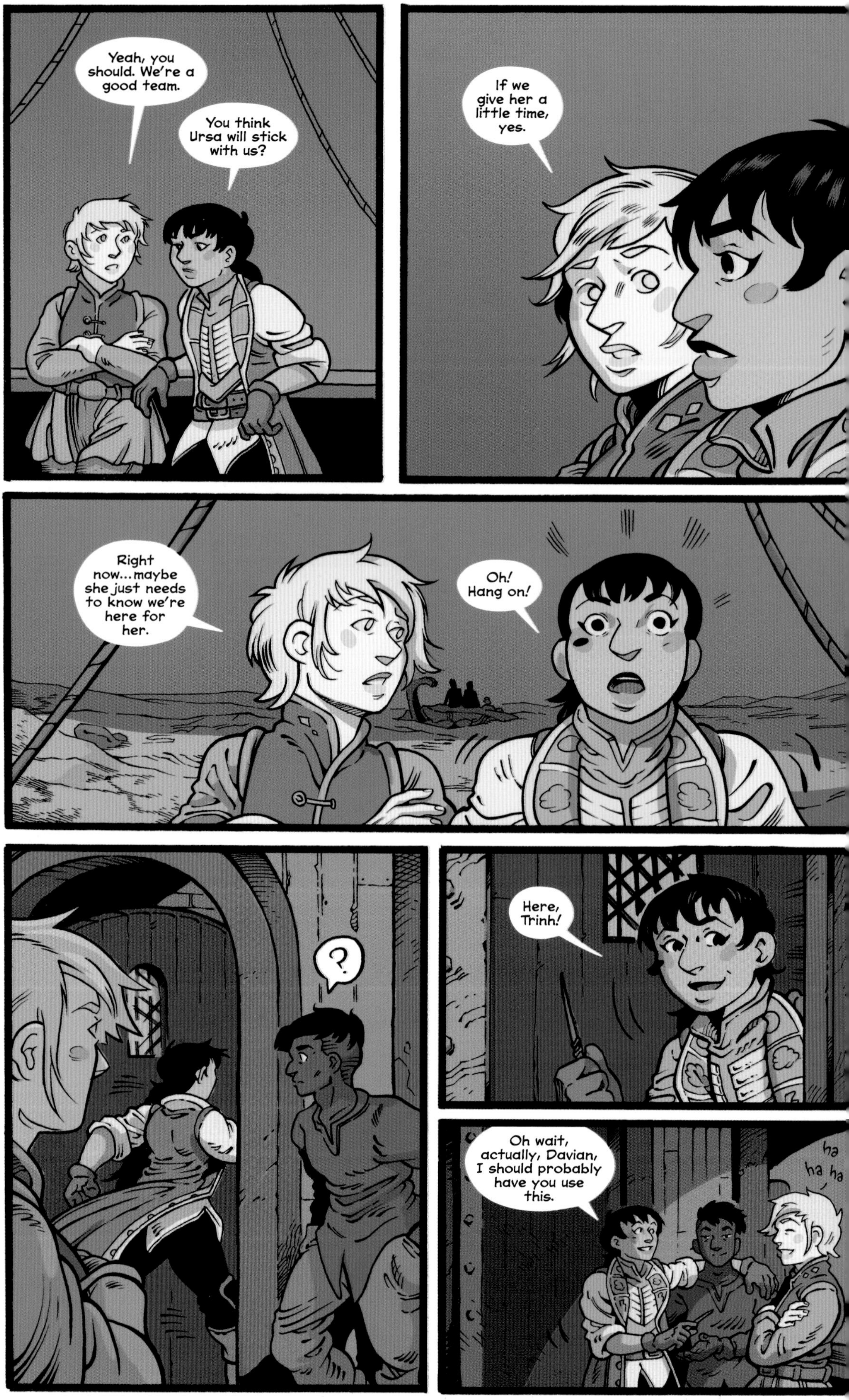
Yeah, you should. We're a good team.
You think Ursa will stick with us?
If we give her a little time, yes.
Right now... maybe she just needs to know we're here for her.
Oh! Hang on!
?
Here, Trinh!
Oh wait, actually, Davian, I should probably have you use this.
ha ha ha

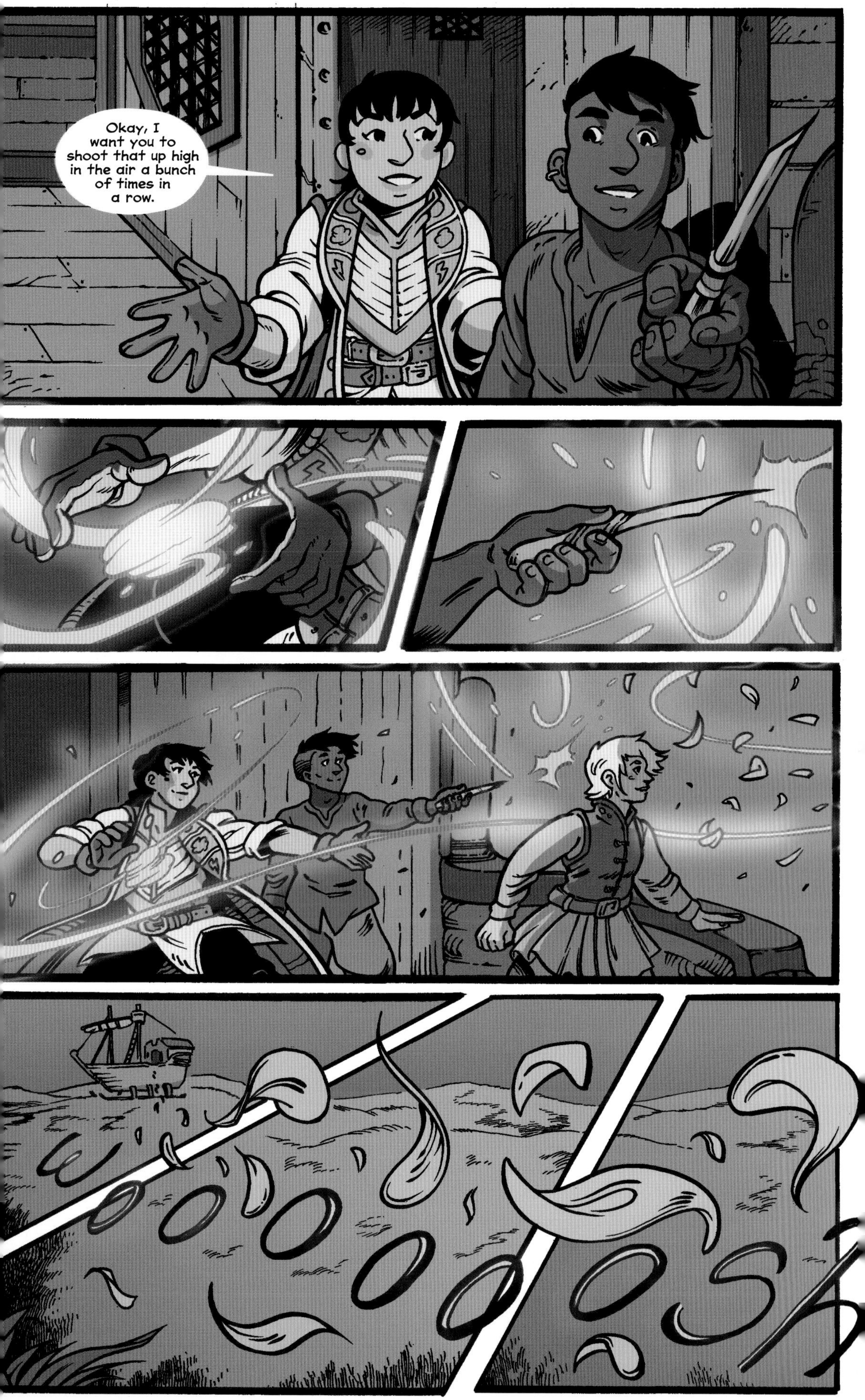
Okay, I want you to shoot that up high in the air a bunch of times in a row.
WOOOOOOOSH

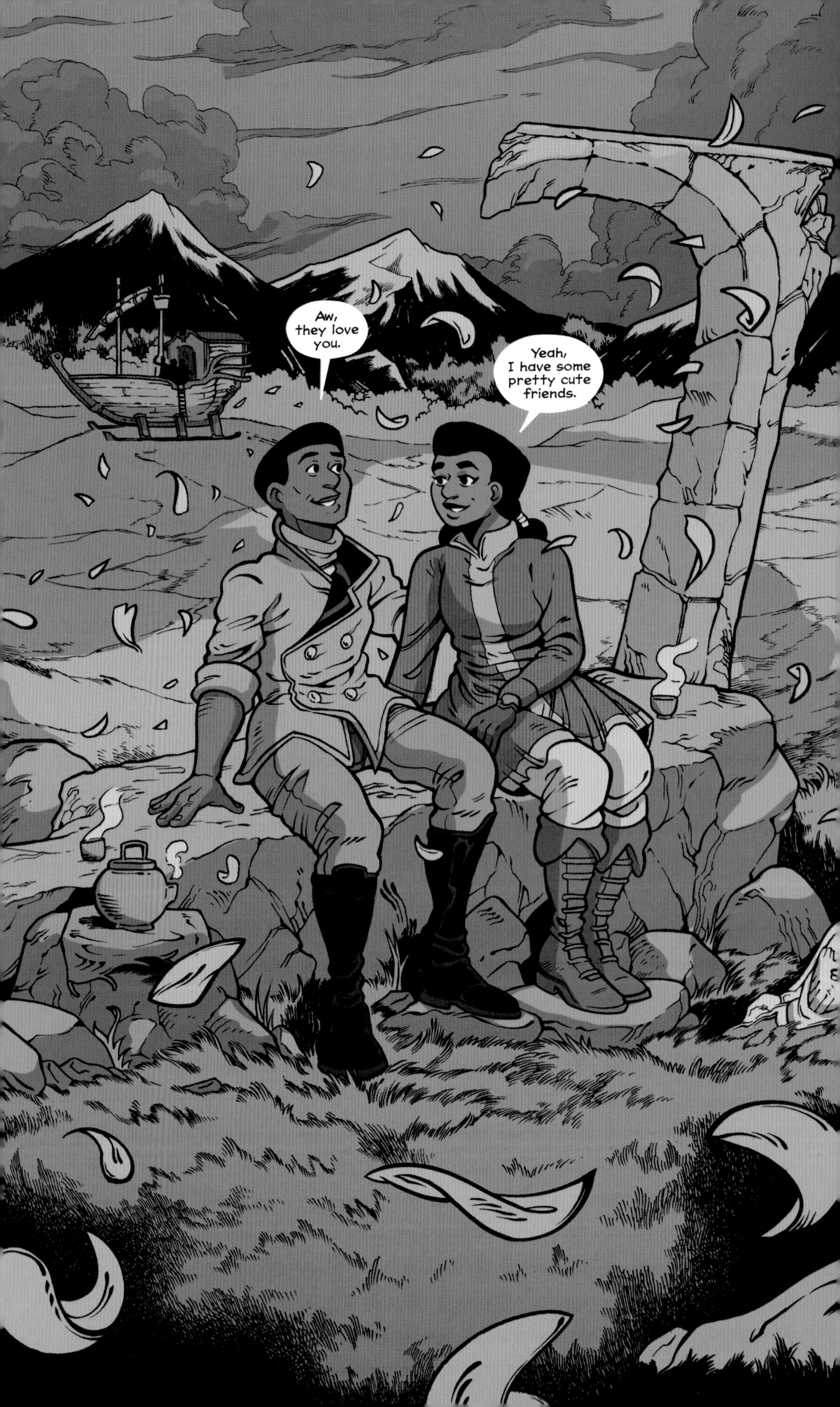
Aw, they love you.
Yeah, I have some pretty cute friends.

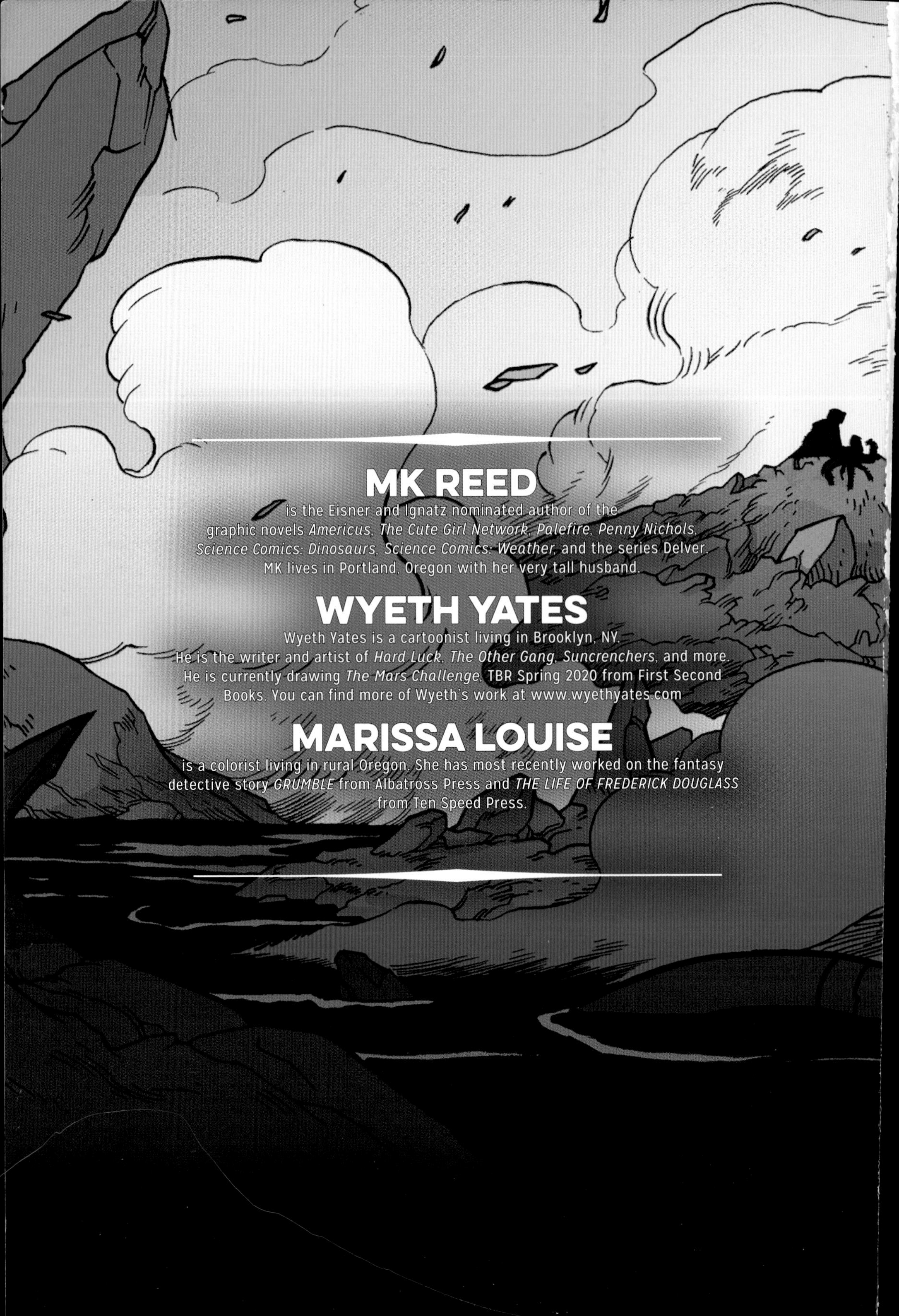

MK REED

is the Eisner and Ignatz nominated author of the graphic novels *Americus*, *The Cute Girl Network*, *Palefire*, *Penny Nichols*, *Science Comics: Dinosaurs*, *Science Comics: Weather*, and the series Delver. MK lives in Portland, Oregon with her very tall husband.

WYETH YATES

Wyeth Yates is a cartoonist living in Brooklyn, NY. He is the writer and artist of *Hard Luck*, *The Other Gang*, *Suncrenchers*, and more. He is currently drawing *The Mars Challenge*, TBR Spring 2020 from First Second Books. You can find more of Wyeth's work at www.wyethyates.com

MARISSA LOUISE

is a colorist living in rural Oregon. She has most recently worked on the fantasy detective story *GRUMBLE* from Albatross Press and *THE LIFE OF FREDERICK DOUGLASS* from Ten Speed Press.